SEA KILLERS
IN
DISGUISE

by the same author
Field Gun Jack versus the Boers
(Leo Cooper, 1998)

SEA KILLERS IN DISGUISE

The story of
the Q-Ships and Decoy Ships
in the First World War

by
TONY BRIDGLAND

Pen & Sword
MARITIME

First published in the Great Britain in 1999
by LEO COOPER
Republished in this format in 2013 by

PEN & SWORD MARITIME
an imprint of
Pen & Sword Books Ltd
47 Church Street
Barnsley
South Yorkshire
S70 2AS

Printed and bound in England by
CPI Group (UK), Croydon, CR0 4YY

Pen & Sword Books Ltd incorporates the Imprints of Pen & Sword Aviation,
Pen & Sword Family History, Pen & Sword Maritime, Pen & Sword Military,
Wharncliffe Local History, Pen & Sword Select, Pen & Sword
Military Classics, Leo Cooper, Remember When, Seaforth
Publishing and Frontline Publishing

For a complete list of Pen & Sword titles please contact
PEN & SWORD BOOKS LIMITED
47 Church Street, Barnsley, South Yorkshire, S70 2AS, England
E-mail: enquiries@pen-and-sword.co.uk
Website: www.pen-and-sword.co.uk

Contents

Acknowledgements

The fascination in the research and writing of an historical book which deals with events teetering on the brink of the span of living memory is that, whilst it is unlikely that the author will find any of the characters in the story themselves still alive, persistent searching can put him in contact with people who remember those characters well. Thus, a picture of the vastly different world of eighty-odd years ago can be drawn from verbal information, and there is no more valuable or colourful source than the spoken word.

Having found such people, the prospective author then hopes to avail himself of their kindness in providing him with the desired information. In this, I have indeed been fortunate, and my sincere thanks are due to Nancy Mark-Wardlaw and her daughters in this country, John and Henry Blackwood in Australia, and Peter Kircheiss in Canada, for their instant willingness to give most generously of their time and assistance and for allowing access to private family papers and photographs, as well as their own personal recollections.

I needed to tap the brains of many other people, too. The staffs of Royal Naval Hospital, Haslar, the Manx National Heritage Museum, Suffolk Records Office, Lowestoft and East Suffolk Maritime Museum, the Public Record Office, the Imperial War Museum, Rye and Hastings Public Libraries were all most helpful, as were Charles and Irma Whiting, Neil Hyslop, Charlie Piggott of Peasmarsh, Peter Gath and Martin Sykes of the Lerwick Coastguard, Derek Barnard of Messrs Boosey & Hawkes, Barbara Boock of the Deutsches Volksliedarchiv in Freiburg, Robin Cookson of the National Archives, Maryland, USA and Jack Weiser of Time-Life Books Inc. of Virginia, USA. Graham Mathews of Coastal Solutions and my colleague Duncan Coleman were both super guides through the desk-top maze. I am most grateful to all of them. I am also grateful for the editorial assistance of Tom Hartman.

I am also much obliged to Messrs Hodder & Stoughton for their kind permission to include certain tracts from Gordon Campbell's book, *My Mystery Ships*.

As regards special permission to use photographic illustrations, my thanks go to Peter Parker and the Committee of the Lowestoft and East Suffolk Maritime Museum, and the Peter Kircheiss Collection, Toronto, Canada. Thanks, too, to both Jon Webb and Peter Harris of the Photographic Department of Boots the Chemists, whose technical know-how was of great value in maximizing the quality of presentation of old, and often battered, photographs. I must also thank ex-Petty Officer Dave Mead, not only for his help with photographs, but for a renewed friendship that was first forged on many runs ashore together over forty years ago!

It is believed that most, if not all, of the photographs, other than those acknowledged above, are no longer subject to copyright. Where any doubt exists, every reasonable effort has been made to trace copyright holders. If, therefore, there has been any unwitting breach of copyright, due apology is given without hesitation, and a suitable acknowledgement will be made in future editions.

Finally, the chore of compiling the index was cheerfully undertaken by Gina-Marie Bridgland in her usual painstaking way. A special 'thank you' to her from her computer-illiterate father.

Tony Bridgland,
Rye, East Sussex,
August 1998.

Introduction

The use of the decoy in warfare is an ancient and cunning art. As a *ruse de guerre* it is as old as the Wooden Horse of Troy. Maybe it is even older. The annals of sea-fighting through the ages are generously scattered with instances of such subterfuge. In 1722 Captain Sir Challoner Ogle was careening his ship, HMS *Swallow*, in a lonely cove on the coast of West Africa. He spied three vessels passing by and recognized them as buccaneers engaged in the slave trade under the command of a notorious freebooter by the name of Bartholomew Roberts. Ogle had been chasing Roberts for months. Putting to sea, he followed the pirates to where they had come to anchor in a bay near Cape Lopez. He disguised his ship as a French merchantman and proceeded to sail innocently across the entrance to the bay, under their very noses. Roberts, unable to resist a valuable prize, sent one of his ships, the *Ranger*, in pursuit. Ogle allowed his pursuer to gain on him, slowly, until he was close at hand. Then he suddenly tacked round, struck his French colours, hoisted the White Ensign and poured a full broadside into the pirate. The *Ranger* was taken. Ogle put a prize crew aboard her, raised the Skull and Crossbones above the French flag on the *Swallow* and they returned to the bay in time to meet Roberts putting to sea in his other two ships, the *Royal Fortune* and the *Little Ranger*. Thinking that the *Ranger* had met with success, Roberts sailed towards her to offer his congratulations. He was met with "the rough welcome of a shotted broadside", and was himself killed in the ensuing battle, after which Ogle carried off all three prizes.

In 1811 a contributor to the *Naval Chronicle* posed a suggestion which he hoped would free the Channel of the troublesome French privateers which were harrying British merchantmen.

"Dear Editor,

The plan which has often engaged my thoughts is that two or three merchant vessels, having as little as possible appearance of ships of war, or armed vessels, each having on board such a number of men as may be considered sufficient, well trained to the use of the musket and rifle, should be kept sailing on such parts of our coast as are most infested by privateers, and that when attacked by the enemy under a conviction of they being private vessels, in their favourite place of boarding, our men (who might easily keep themselves for this period in concealment) might, without difficulty, give them such a lesson . . .

As soon as it was conjectured that the enemy would be able to particularise the vessels in question, they might be either new painted or changed for others with little inconvenience."

It is not known whether Winston Churchill, the First Lord of the Admiralty in 1914, had ever seen or heard of this letter, written over a century before, when he sent a signal to the Commander-in-Chief, Portsmouth, Admiral Sir Hedworth Meux, on 26 November, 1914:

"It is desired to trap the German submarine which sinks vessels by gunfire off Havre. A small or moderate sized steamer should be taken up and fitted very secretly with two twelve-pounder guns in such a way that they can be concealed with deck cargo or in some way in which they will not be suspected. She should be sent when ready to run from Havre to England, and should have an intelligence officer and a few seamen and two picked gunlayers who should all be disguised. If the submarine stops her she should endeavour to sink her by gunfire. The greatest secrecy is necessary to prevent spies becoming acquainted with the arrangements."

Throughout the First World War hundreds of British merchant ships, ranging from cargo liners down to fishing smacks of under fifty tons, were eventually to serve as "Q-ships", as these decoys became known. There was a vast number of these vessels, which operated under tight wartime secrecy and censorship, changing their names and appearances at frequent intervals. On occasions, even officialdom itself was confused by its own cunning. For example, when the Cork Harbour Commissioners sent a bill to the Accountant-General for the pilotage of a ship known as the *Waitono* it was refused, referring the Commissioners to the ship's owners, the Union Steam Ship Co. of New Zealand. The owners also refused to pay, saying that on the day in question the *Waitono* had been on the other side of the world, in the

Pacific. When the matter came to the ears of the Fourth Sea Lord, who happened to know that *Waitono*, as well as *Waitopo*, were aliases of a 4,832 ton Q-ship, HMS *Intaba*, or Q2, he hastened to request the Accountant-General to see that the bill be quickly paid and not to ask questions!

The keeping of diaries by Royal Navy personnel was officially banned after the Battle of Jutland in 1916, after a chest of drawers had been found floating in the North Sea containing the complete diary of an officer. Thus, what is normally a major source of interesting material in such a book as this is denied to us. Such factors combine to make it well-nigh impossible to produce what might be claimed, even most brazenly, to be a definitive history of the subject. Indeed, this book is not intended to be read so much as a work of reference, but more as a good (I hope) historically true 'yarn'. Therefore, I have restricted my detailed work, cautiously, to the more notable ships and their exploits, but at the same time tried to paint an interesting picture of the general background of what was, of necessity, a very murky scene.

The use of disguise and decoy at sea was not only confined to the British side. It was very skilfully employed by the Germans. Submarine warfare was still in its infancy in 1914, and U-boats had but a limited operational range. Therefore, in order to operate far beyond the seas surrounding Europe, Germany could only rely on surface raiders. Some of these were already at sea at the outbreak of war. In due course these were all either forced into internment or sunk by the Royal Navy. This left the German High Seas Fleet effectively besieged in its home ports by the solid blockade set up by the British. To filter through this barrier with surface ships the Kaiser was forced to apply some cunning of his own. It called for ships in disguise.

The story of the decoy ships of both sides is truly remarkable. On the one hand, the British Q-ships were faced by a dangerous enemy who could disappear within seconds if he chose, or indeed could mount an attack without being seen at all. Their aim was to lure that enemy to within point-blank range of their hidden guns. Their disguise needed to be sufficiently convincing to lull a U-boat captain into a sense of false security and they went to some astonishing lengths to achieve this. Their crews needed to demonstrate cast-iron discipline and an enormous amount of cool courage if they were to fulfil their aims, and the number of Victoria Crosses won by Q-ship men is testament to this.

On the other side were the German raiders in disguise. Their need for a perfect fake identity was as great as that of their British counterparts, but theirs was a different game. Most of them were restricted to forays around the coast of Britain, but others managed to break out from the North Sea. Once free of the Royal Navy's stranglehold, they were able to roam the oceans on marathon pilgrimages of destruction. Their prey was easy to kill, but they, the hunters, soon became hunted themselves by packs of Allied cruisers. Living for months on end on nothing but their wits, their superb seamanship, whatever they could loot, and not a little help from Lady Luck, their success was phenomenal.

Those who "sailed in disguise", on both sides, can rightly claim a place among the greatest seamen, and the bravest men, that the world has ever seen.

Maps

ATLANTIC
OCEAN

Shetland
Islands
Lerwick

Orkney Islands
Scapa Flow
Kirkwall
Long Hope
South Ronaldsay
Pentland Firth

Outer Hebrides

Stornoway

Moray Forth

Peterhead

Aberdeen
Girdle Ness

SCOTLAND

NORTH SEA

Lough Swilly

Tory I.

Buncrana

Glasgow
Firth of Forth
Edinburgh

Belfast

Newcastle

Mull of
Galloway
Isle of
Man

York
Hull

IRISH SEA

Amlwch

Liverpool

Grimsby

IRELAND

Dublin

Isle of
Anglesey

The Wirral

Jim Howe Bank
Smith's Knoll

Galway Bay

Barmouth

Dyffryn

ENGLAND

Walsall

Cromer
Great Yarmouth
Lound
Lowestoft

WALES

Birmingham

The Leman

Queenstown
(Cobh)

Strumble
Head

Milford Haven

Swansea

Newport

Harwich

The Outer
Gabbard

Beerhaven

Haulbowline
Dockyard
(at Queenstown)

Cardiff
Avonmouth
Bristol

LONDON
Sheerness

Bantry Bay

Old Head of Kinsale
Fastnet Rock

Lundy I.

Southampton

Dover
Rye

Weymouth
Portsmouth

Straits of Dover

Falmouth

Plymouth

Isle of
Wight

Beachy Head

Scillies

Bishop Rock

Cawsand
Bay

Dartmouth
Start Point

Lizard Point

Plymouth Sound

Alderney

Swanage

English Channel

Cherbourg

Dieppe

Le Havre

Guernsey

WESTERN
APPROACHES

Jersey

FRANCE

Nautical miles
0   50   100   150

Chapter 1

1914–15
U-Boat versus Q-Boat
The Duel Begins

In the course of the latter part of the nineteenth century it had become apparent that France, which had been Britain's natural enemy, it seemed, since time began, was less likely than Germany to pose a serious future threat, despite the strong family ties between the Royal Families of the two countries. The German Kaiser, Wilhelm II, Queen Victoria's vain grandson, loved to pay visits to his adored Grandmama. His favourite uncle, Bertie, the future King Edward VII, would suffer his presence with good grace, although privately he said that 'Willy' was "the most brilliant failure the world has ever seen". Constantly aware of his English blood, although in truth he possessed very little of it, 'Willy' had a passion for all things English, and a particular admiration for the Royal Navy. He yearned to own one just like it. That, in essence, was one of the root causes of the eventual conflict.

With the canny old Admiral, von Tirpitz, as his guide and mentor, the Kaiser set about building his Navy. In June, 1904, he managed to persuade his Uncle Bertie to come over to Kiel to inspect his fine Fleet. 'Willy' could be remarkably feckless, as his words in one after-dinner speech demonstrated. "When, as a little boy," he said, "I was allowed to visit Portsmouth and Plymouth hand in hand with kind aunts and friendly admirals, I admired the proud English ships in those two superb harbours. Then there awoke in me the wish to build ships of my own like these someday, and when I was grown-up to possess as fine a Navy as the English."

When, at last, Armageddon was reached in 1914, the British had few doubts about the ability of the Royal Navy to protect their merchant ships. They were, of course, fully aware of the strength of the Navy that Willy had built, but felt that such heavy ships as he possessed could be elbowed aside from the shipping lanes by sheer weight of numbers. Individual German cruisers would cause some early problems but these would soon be mopped up. That prophecy was to prove absolutely accurate. By the end of 1914 the threat posed by the big German surface raiders was erased when the last of them, the ill-fated *Königsberg*, was bottled up at its camouflaged moorings in the swamps of the Rufiji Delta on the coast of East Africa. The sea-lanes, it seemed, were safe for British shipping.

In the course of 1915, however, it became a different story. The Germans had been busy building their stocks of a new weapon – the U-boat – and now they introduced it into the conflict in increasing numbers. With all its traditional myopia, the British Admiralty had considered such novelties as little more than playthings. The Royal Navy did possess a considerable number of these toys, but they were far too flimsy, too vulnerable and lightly armed to be used to attack merchant ships on the surface, their Lordships argued. A submarine had no accommodation for the crews of any merchant ships that it sank, and the whole world knew that International Law prohibited leaving men adrift in open boats. By the end of that year they were eating their words. In the course of it U-boats had sunk 748,000 tons of British shipping.

Only 'Jacky' Fisher, with his usual prescience, had foreseen the danger from submarines. He had long been warning the Government that merchant shipping could be destroyed by torpedoes from submerged submarines. But the Prime Minister had refused even to consider that a civilized nation would embark on such a barbarous practice.

Indeed, the German Government itself had initial misgivings about the use of its U-boats. The admirals, with the exception of Tirpitz, were eager to press ahead, but Chancellor Theobald von Bethmann-Hollweg opposed the suggestion, fearing that it would create strong ill-feeling towards Germany. This fear was justified. Already, a dozen or so Allied merchantmen had been sunk by German submarines, several without warning, but the worst instance of all had been by the *U-20*, on

1 February, when her captain, Droescher, had torpedoed the hospital ship *Asturias* off Havre, despite her bright lights and prominent red crosses. Nevertheless, Bethmann-Hollweg, a fifty-nine-year-old scholarly pacifist, eventually relented under the pressure from the *Admiralstab*. Only days after the *U-20*'s action, they persuaded him that Britain was breaking International Law herself by her methods of blockade, and that any neutral ship carrying cargo to or from Britain was aiding and abetting her in this cowardly crime. That was sufficient to cause a chilling announcement to be made:

> "Germany hereby declares all the waters surrounding Great Britain and Ireland, including the entire English Channel, an area of war, and will therein act against the shipping of the enemy. For this purpose, beginning February 18, 1915, she will endeavour to destroy every enemy merchant ship that is found in this area of war, even if it is not always possible to avert the peril which threatens persons and cargoes. Neutrals are therefore warned against further entrusting crews and passengers and wares to such ships. Their attention is also called to the fact that it is advisable for their ships to avoid entering this area, for, although the German naval forces have instructions to avoid violence to neutral ships, in so far as they are recognisable, in view of the mis-use of neutral flags ordered by the British Government, and the contingencies of naval warfare, their becoming victims of attack directed against enemy ships cannot always be avoided."

The Germans had let their U-boats off the leash. They had released the Submarine Menace. At the outset of the U-boat campaign, the Royal Navy was at a complete loss as to how to deal with it. In fact, with a perversity which has typified the thinking of many of Britain's military and naval chiefs throughout history, the Admiralty committee which was set up to study anti-submarine warfare had been actually disbanded in 1914! As had happened in the Boer War, fifteen years before, when a baffled Britain had faced another innovative enemy, many members of the public came up with "helpful" ideas. One suggested that seagulls could be trained to alight on its periscope to betray the submarine's presence. Another said that seals could be trained to bark when they heard a U-boat's engines. Even the Royal Navy's own answer, in the early stages, was absurd. They equipped picket boats with a canvas bag and a hammer. The bag was to slip over a U-boat's periscope and the hammer was to smash it!

The depth-charge had only just been invented, and British designs were still in primitive form. As such, it had little success until later in the war, when German designs were copied. Slightly more effective was the explosive sweep, towed between two ships. A long line of drifters, joined by nets with indicator buoys, sometimes loaded with explosive charges, could seal off a narrow strait. In fact, one such line in the narrow part of the English Channel successfully deterred the larger U-boats from using it much after April, 1915, although surprisingly many of the smaller Germans submarines did break out successfully via that route.

On 18 February, 1915, Germany could boast of only twenty U-boats, and of these a mere four were ready for action. The *U-30* was already at sea, having worked her way round the north of Scotland. She sank two steamers in the Irish Sea and had a narrow escape when she became entangled in the nets of a fishing boat, but got home safely. The *U-8* took the far more perilous route through the Straits of Dover. Hunting off Beachy Head, she sank five steamers before returning to Zeebrugge. By the end of the month, the soon-to-be-notorious *U-20* and the *U-27* had accounted for six more in the Bristol Channel and off the Isle of Man.

The Germans suffered a setback in early March with the loss of the *U-8*. On her second sortie she had the misfortune to be spotted by some British destroyers. They towed their explosive sweeps over the area and that of HMS *Gurkha* caught the submarine, which shot to the surface almost vertically, stern first, to be met with a deluge of shell-fire.

The commander of the *U-28*, Forstner, displayed a ruthlessness which was ominous. On 27 March he sank three ships off the Scillies, including a passenger liner, the *Aguila*, the survivors from which alleged that he fired on them as they took to the lifeboats. The next day he stopped another liner, the Elder-Dempster Line's *Falaba*, of 4,800 tons. She was a legitimate target, because she was carrying thirteen tons of explosives to West Africa, but Forstner was both impatient and callous. He put a torpedo into the liner before all her passengers and crew had got into the lifeboats and 104 people drowned out of a total of 242.

From the beginning of the campaign until the end of April, 150 U-boat attacks were recorded, which resulted in eighty-eight ships being sunk and many more damaged. In return, the British had destroyed five U-boats, but the Germans had commissioned twenty-five more. Throughout May, June and July the massacre intensified. In the

Western Approaches alone, where sea-routes from the Americas, Africa, the Mediterranean, India, the Far East and Australia all converged, nearly fifty ships were sunk, including the *Lusitania*. Even fishing smacks, suppliers of valuable foodstuffs to a hungry population, now came under attack. In June alone fifty-eight of them were sunk in the North Sea and Bristol Channel. 'Jacky' Fisher's anxiety grew. "It is starvation we have to fear," he said, "not invasion."

The Admiralty ordered more anti-submarine craft and decided upon the use of various kinds of decoy vessel, on the principle that the newer U-boats, with their 19-knot surface speed, may be more easily lured to their destruction than chased and caught. The earliest success of the decoy system came in the North Sea, where U-boats were attacking the fishing fleets. A group of trawlers, sitting fishing like a flock of sheep grazing peacefully in a maritime meadow, would suddenly find shells bursting among them. By the simple ploy of surreptitiously arming one or two of them, such attacks could be repelled, or even avenged.

The captain of *U-14*, Hammerle, found out how successful this simple idea could be on 5 June, 1915, when he opened fire on such a group off Peterhead. The U-boat was instantly set upon by the 168-ton armed steam trawler *Oceanic ex-Oceanic II*, with its single 12-pounder, and others rushed to assist. Hammerle tried to dive, but such was the confusion aboard the submarine, surrounded as she was by a pack of spitting 'sheep', that a mistake was made with the flooding of her tanks, and her bows remained above water. She was rammed by HMS *Hawke* and sunk. Twenty-seven men were picked up, but her captain paid with his life.

Two fishing smacks, requisitioned by the Admiralty and working out of Lowestoft, had brushes with U-boats within days of each other. On only her fourth day in the service of the Royal Navy, the 61 ton *G & E*, which also sailed under the aliases of *Bird, Extirpator, Foam Crest, I'll Try* and *Nelson*, managed to hit the *UB-6* with her little 6-pounder on 11 August, but it escaped. Four days later the *Inverlyon* LT687, also armed only with a 6-pounder, attacked an unidentified U-boat off Smith's Knoll on the Norfolk coast. The submarine was thought to have sunk, but, as was so often the case, the very nature of such an engagement made it impossible to confirm the 'kill'. Had the sub. dived to escape, or had she dived to die? The question may never be answered, although Robert Grant, in his *U-boats Destroyed*, seems to have been able to identify the submarine as the *UB-4*. According to him, she was shelled at the point blank range of thirty yards. The *Inverlyon*'s Royal Navy gunner put six shells into her, two of which exploded in the conning-tower, and she went down with her hatch open.

Another early idea was for a trawler and British submarine to hunt as a pair. The trawler would tow the submerged boat and was connected to her by telephone cable. As soon as the trawler was attacked, she would inform the sub, which would slip the tow and set off to stalk the U-boat. On 23 June this method met with success. The 247-ton Aberdeen steam trawler *Taraniki* A445, alias *Laureate* SN257, under the command of Lieutenant-Commander H.D. Edwards, was working with the submarine C-24 when she sighted the *U-40* about fifty miles off Girdle Ness, and informed her invisible escort. The trawler's crew tumbled into their lifeboat in a great show of 'panic', but, unbeknown to them, the C-24 had become entangled in her own tow and telephone cables. She could not slip as planned, she could not surface and she had lost her trim. The U-boat's crew were pre-occupied with watching the antics of the trawler's 'panicking' men. It was costly entertainment. They did not notice the periscope of the C-24 a short distance away. Her captain, Lieutenant F.H. Taylor, had managed, somehow, to extricate her from the cables, regain her trim and work her into a firing position. Only three of the *U-40*'s men, including her captain, Furbringer, survived the single torpedo Taylor fired.

A month later, on 20 July, the 222-ton Ostend trawler *Princess Marie Jose*, O38, alias *Princess Louise*, now serving with the Royal Navy under Lieutenant Cantlie, was towing the submarine C-27 (Lieutenant Claude C. Dobson). The trawler met the German *U-23* and held its attention for long enough for the future Rear-Admiral Dobson, VC, DSO, to slip his tow and torpedo the U-boat. A handful of decoy ships seem to have spent the entire war on this type of work, although it had little success after the sinkings of the *U-40* and the *U-23*.

By July, 1915, the Admiralty realized that more co-ordination of effort was essential. For obvious reasons, the heaviest loss of merchant ships was occurring in the Western Approaches. Based on Queenstown (Cobh), Ireland, Admiral Sir Lewis Bayly was given control of a 25,000 square mile area from the Hebrides in the north to Ushant off the point of Brittany in the south.

The fifty-eight-year-old Bayly, tall, gruff, grey and teetotal, had over forty years in the Royal Navy behind him. The new appointment breathed fresh life into a career which had appeared to be on the wane. Only the previous December he had been relieved of command of the Channel Fleet, a prestigious position, following the loss of the battle-ship *Formidable*, which had been torpedoed during exercises. His sea-going days were over, but, nonetheless, he was grateful for an opportunity to redeem himself and threw all his energy into his new job.

Bayly's attitude to any task was simple. Get it done with the minimum of fuss. He even deplored such frippery as "dressing" for dinner, and boring after-dinner speeches, when there were so many other things to be getting on with. In Queenstown he set up his austere operations room in the basement of his unpretentious cottage home, using the billiards table as an operations board, with a meagre staff of three officers and his niece for a housekeeper.

Although he was eventually to have around 450 ships under his command, Bayly was never to have enough of them to cover such a wide and busy area. He was constantly calling for more destroyers, just as Nelson had done for frigates. As for decoy ships, as they were known at first, his opening 'stock' was three ex-colliers. They were the 3,200 ton *Loderer*, commanded by Commander Gordon Campbell, who was to become the most famous of the Q-ship aces; the 2,917-ton *Zylpha*, under Lieutenant-Commander McLeod, whose First Lieutenant, Harold Auten, was later on to win the V.C. in his own Q-ship, and the 1,016 ton *Vala* (Lieutenant-Commander Mellin). These were soon joined by what was to be the "fightingest" Q-ship of all, *Penshurst*, a 1,191 ton freighter, commanded by Commander F.H. Grenfell.

Chapter 2

Mark-Wardlaw
Shows the Way

If they needed any encouragement at all, which was unlikely, the new flotilla of decoy ships had been given a 'show' of what could be achieved by one of their colleagues in the north only a fortnight before. Bayly's opposite number in the north of Scotland, Admiral Sir Stanley Colville, had assembled another small group of decoy ships, in great secrecy, based at Longhope, a bleak little inlet off Scapa Flow. One of Colville's ships was a tiny 373-ton collier, *Prince Charles*, armed with two hidden 6-pounders, two 3-pounder Hotchkisses and rifles. Her peacetime crew of nine, plus her master, F.N. Maxwell, and Chief Engineer Anderson, all volunteered to sail with her into action, and were accepted by the Navy. In command was Lieutenant William Mark-Wardlaw, a popular twenty-eight-year-old, who was usually to be seen accompanied, sometimes even to sea, by a faithful spaniel friend called Rover. Mark-Wardlaw hailed from a family with a long naval tradition. His great-grandfather, after whom he was named, had sailed with Nelson, and both he and his younger brother were one day to become Admirals themselves. Lieutenant J.G. Spencer, R.N.R. and the following naval ratings made up the rest of HMS *Prince Charles*'s crew:

Petty Officer Aubrey Tagg, ON 1673367, and Leading Seaman Green, both ex HMS *Cyclops*.
Able Seamen Garside and Cooney, ex-HMS *Royal Arthur*.
Able Seaman William Kensit, ON 201510, and Able Seaman Cook, both ex-HMS *Crescent*.

Leading Seaman Graham and Able Seamen Harris and Wilson, all ex-HMS *Leander*.

Stoker Petty Officer Callaghan, parent ship unknown.

One stoker RN. Name unknown.

On 20 July, 1915, Mark-Wardlaw received sailing orders:-

SECRET – *NOT TO FALL INTO THE HANDS OF THE ENEMY.*

No.009. Memorandum to Lieutenant W.P. Mark-Wardlaw, R.N. You are to proceed on a cruise as follows:-

From Scapa to

(a) Lat 59.0N Long 0.0 (b) Lat 60.15N Long 1.20E
(c) Lat 61.15N Long 0.5W (d) Lat 61.10N Long 2.40W
(e) Lat 58.50N Long 7.0W

and then to Stornoway to complete with coal and provisions, and report arrival for further orders before proceeding . . .

The object of the cruise is to use the *Prince Charles* as a decoy so that an enemy submarine should attack her with gunfire. It is not considered probable that in view of her small size a torpedo would be wasted on her . . .

Speed during voyage should be eight and a half to nine knots . . .

I wish to impress on you to strictly observe the role of decoy. If an enemy submarine is sighted make every effort to escape; if she closes and fires, immediately stop your engines and with the ship's company (except the guns crews who should most carefully be kept out of sight behind the bulwarks alongside their gun and one engineer at the engines) commence to abandon ship. It is very important if you can do so to try and place your ship so that the enemy approaches you from the beam . . .

Allow the submarine to come as close as possible and then open fire by order or whistle hoisting your colours (red ensign) . . .

If by luck you should succeed in sinking a submarine, on no account are you to allow the information to leak out of your ship; the strictest precautions are to be taken on arrival in a harbour or meeting a ship at sea that none of the officers or men give away the information.

S.C. COLVILLE – ADMIRAL.

Mark-Wardlaw sailed the next day, east from Scapa Flow and then north, intending to loop anti-clockwise around the Shetlands and back to the south-west to head towards the Outer Hebrides where U-boat activity had been reported. For three days he saw few ships, certainly none to cause any alarm. By 6.20 on the evening of the 24th *Prince*

Charles was about ten miles off North Rona Island. A three-masted steamer came into sight. She was black, with a red funnel, and had two large Danish flags painted on her sides. It was the coaster *Louise*. She appeared to have stopped. As *Prince Charles* drew nearer, Mark-Wardlaw could see that there was a submarine lying close to her. He kept on course, apparently minding his own business, as a collier would do, but ready for action, with guns' crews closed up behind their screens, and the merchant seamen ready to lower the boats. He noted that there was another small craft standing off to the west. What was going on here?

The submarine captain, having seen the arrival of *Prince Charles*, left the side of the coaster and roared towards the collier, firing a shell at her as he came. This turn of events left no doubt that they had found a U-boat. Mark-Wardlaw turned his bows into the heavy sea that was running in from the Atlantic, stopped his engines, blew three blasts on his whistle and ordered the boats to be lowered. The German fired again. This time he almost had the range and only missed by a few yards. About 600 yards off, the U-boat stopped, but continued firing. At the same time, it made the fatal mistake of turning broadside on to its victim.

Now was the critical time for Mark-Wardlaw to make his decision. Was he likely to be able to entice the U-boat any nearer? If he missed this chance of firing at a wide target, would he get another one? Should he risk his ship and his men's lives by maintaining the pretence of being a harmless collier? Or should he drop the screens and open fire, possibly to miss and scare the U-boat into diving and escape? It was the heart-stopping moment at which every Q-ship captain held in his hands the fate of all concerned. He hesitated only for an instant.

The two port-side guns of *Prince Charles* cracked out. The shells both missed the submarine, but they were close enough to send her gun's crew scurrying for the shelter of the conning-tower. The little collier fired a second broadside, and this time hit the U-boat square-on, aft. She attempted to dive, but, being damaged, only succeeded in turning a full circle to present the opposite broadside to the *Prince Charles* which was now only 300 yards from her. The Q-ship's gunlayers, Petty Officer Tagg and Able Seaman Kensit, were excellent shots and at such a range they could hardly miss the target. They blasted the U-boat, which was the *U-36*, with a hail of fire, and soon it was steadily sinking by the stern. As the crew came tumbling out of the conning-tower to jump into the sea, it pointed its bows to the sky and within seconds had disappeared.

The *U-36* had left Heligoland on 19 July and had sunk eight trawlers and a steamer before meeting the *Prince Charles*. Mark-Wardlaw searched for survivors and rescued the U-boat's commander, Kapitän-Leutnant Graeff, with Leutnants Loewenstein and Mueller, Engineers Arndt and Bressler, Coxswain Standt, Petty Officers Neutzel, Gerhard, Koehler and Gaede, Wireless Operators Luderer and Gane, *Heizers* (stokers) Miche, Wolcek and Retschke, and Seaman Schaeler. Three Germans had been killed by shell-fire and eighteen others drowned.

But the drama did not quite end there. Mark-Wardlaw, mild-mannered and courteous as ever, had locked Graeff in his own cabin while he attended to other matters. He was back on the bridge when a frightening thought occurred to him. His revolver! He had left it under his pillow! He flew to his cabin, trying to exude an air of calm matter-of-factness as he unlocked the door. Reaching under the pillow, a relieved Mark-Wardlaw found that Graeff had not discovered the weapon. He quickly pocketed it, locked the German in again and returned to his bridge, not a little embarrassed and angry with himself. It was an incident which he would be required to recount over after-dinner coffee for the amusement of his companions for many years to come.

The small boat, which had been nearby throughout the action, turned out to contain the crew of the 33-ton fish-carrier *Anglia*, SN251, which had been sunk by gunfire four hours before, about 25 miles away. *Prince Charles* picked them up and proceeded into Widewall Harbour on South Ronaldsay, followed by the *Louise*. Mark-Wardlaw was suspicious that she may, in fact, have been a German supply ship in disguise, and that he had stumbled on a rendezvous between her and the U-boat, but his fears were unfounded. Her relieved captain assured Mark-Wardlaw that he could depend on him not to report the sinking of the U-boat on his return to Denmark. However, it seems that the story of the British secret weapon was leaked, possibly by the Danish ship's crew gossiping in shoreside taverns. And so, right from the very beginning, the 'mystery ships' were less of a mystery than they would have liked to be. Mark-Wardlaw was awarded the DSC (later upgraded to a DSO) and two of his crew the DSM for the sinking of the *U-36*. In accordance with what was to become usual practice, the sum of £1,000 was awarded to be shared among the crew.

Chapter 3

The Art of Decoy
and Disguise

Mark-Wardlaw's success was the first confirmed case of a German submarine being sunk by an unaided decoy, which augured well for the future success of such operations. But first there was much thinking and planning to be done before the launch of the decoy ship campaign in earnest, none more than by Gordon Campbell, captain of HMS *Loderer*.

A twenty-nine-year-old former pupil of Dulwich College Preparatory School, and the thirteenth child of an Army colonel, Campbell had been in the Navy since he was fourteen, when he joined HMS *Britannia* at Dartmouth. When war broke out, he was a Lieutenant-Commander in command of an ancient Devonport destroyer, HMS *Bittern*. By September, 1915, the somewhat taciturn Campbell, roman-nosed and short of stature, had become bored with his war so far, plodding in and out of Plymouth Sound on escort work in the Channel. He applied for various appointments which he thought might produce some real action, say one of the Harwich destroyers. The Admiralty sent for him and, after a strange interview at which he volunteered for 'special service', he found himself back in Devonport awaiting the delivery of a Cardiff collier named the *Loderer*. By now he knew that he was to serve under the command of Admiral Sir Lewis Bayly, based on Queenstown, and what exactly the Admiralty had meant when they spoke of 'special service'.

By any standards, let alone Navy standards, the *Loderer* was filthy. Campbell ripped out all her lice-ridden bunks, fumigated her thoroughly and gave her accommodation areas a good coat of paint before he would allow any of his men to live on board. She was to carry three 12-pounder guns, one 18-hundredweight and two 12-hundred-weight, and a Maxim gun. Where to mount them? How to disguise them? Campbell, with Lieutenant Beswick, RNR, his reliable First Lieutenant, or Mr Mate, as he would now be known, and some hand-picked craftsmen from Devonport Dockyard all pooled their ideas. The 'heavy' 12-pounder was concealed under a false steering engine housing right aft. To add reality to this, a pipe was fed to it from the real steering engine, amidships, so that a wisp of steam would always be seen hanging over the stern of the *Loderer*, as if there were a donkey engine inside, rather than a gun. The hinged sides of the housing, and also the ensign staff, were all designed to fall down under their own weight as soon as a central 'slip' was knocked off. This ensured that the gun would not be fired until the ensign staff had fallen, and would avoid accu-sations of abuse of a neutral flag. The other two 12-pounders were mounted amidships, port and starboard, on the main deck, hidden behind hinged gunwales which would fall out-board when the pins were drawn from the bolts securing them. The Maxim was housed in a 'hen-coop', again with hinged sides, on the boat-deck abaft the funnel, along with some rifles.

A few months later Campbell was able to purloin two more 12-pounders and two 6-pounders whilst *Loderer* was at Haulbowline, the Queenstown Dockyard. He never revealed how he did this, saying mysteriously, "Even history does not relate how I got them." He built false extensions to a pair of cabins, just forward of the funnel, with dummy scuttles which could be used by lookouts, to house the 12-pounders. The two smaller guns were placed one on each wing of the bridge, behind light screens which could be quickly pushed aside. When compared to other decoy ships, the *Loderer* now fairly bristled with armament, boasting five 12-pounders, two 6-pounders, the Maxim and numerous rifles.

It appears that the 'powers that be' considered that an ideal ship's company for decoy work would be drawn from the Navy's 'hard men' – ex-inmates of the detention quarters, habitual brawlers, leave-breakers and rebels against authority in general. Whether this was because it was felt that such characters would do a better job, or whether it was because they were the most expendable, is a matter for conjecture, but Campbell, as well as other mystery ship captains in the early stages of the war, found that the Depot was drafting this type of seaman for Special Service Duties in disproportionate numbers. These men were exactly the wrong choice and to send them to sea in company with a merchant crew which itself was unaccustomed to naval discipline only served to heighten the problem. In truth, decoy ships' crews needed to possess a very strong sense of discipline. Not parade ground, gunnery school type discipline, but a special self-discipline which is born of a commitment to the success of the operation. To keep perfectly still and quiet, sometimes for hours on end in order to preserve the ship's sham identity, all the while under shell and torpedo fire, and possibly wounded to boot, without attempting to defend oneself until the order was given, did require considerable dedication and control. A decoy ship's gun-layers would perhaps be given the opportunity to fire only one shell at a U-boat before she dived. Their skill was crucial.

There were many volunteers for decoy work from the Regular Service who were not committed in the desired fashion. They had heard that Admiral Bayly had obtained half rates of 'hard-laying' pay for the crews of decoy ships. This was extra pay for living under extraordinarily harsh conditions, and also in recognition of a special danger faced by Q-ship crews. If they were captured by the Germans after being in action while dressed in civilian clothes they were liable to be shot as *francs-tireurs*. The money only amounted to a few extra pence per day, but it resulted in a stream of volunteers – many, unfortunately, with the wrong attitude, who were very quickly 'found out' when they went into action. On balance, though, the *esprit de corps* which quickly developed among decoy-ship men, as the initial teething problems were gradually ironed out and suitable personnel were selected, made for a highly disciplined and very efficient arm of the Service.

A decoy ship's crew numbered far more men than would have been carried in the ordinary way, because, in addition to her own sailors, the men who 'drove' her, there were the Navy guns' crews and miscellaneous 'hands', plus their officers, who would all remain onboard after the ship had, apparently, been abandoned. Not only did they all have to be accommodated, but it was necessary to keep the 'extras' out of sight of watching periscopes. The only sensible approach was to assume that there was a U-boat spying on them every minute of the day. As a merchantman, the *Loderer* would have had a complement of about twenty-five men and half a dozen officers. In her new role as a man o'war, she had fifty-six men and eleven officers. Campbell cleared her upper cargo space for use as the seamens' mess-deck, and the foc'sle, which would normally have accommodated the entire 'lower deck', housed the engine-room men. He cut a trap door beneath the bridge through which access to it could be made, which would avoid too many officers being seen on the ladders outside. It would have defeated the object of the exercise to have guns' crews seen scurrying about and disappearing into 'deck-houses' as soon as 'action stations' was ordered. Therefore, all the gun and lookout positions were entered by a system of trap-doors and concealed alleyways, the main one of which travelled the entire length of the ship through the coal in her hold!

In 1915 not every merchant ship was yet fitted with wireless, although of course *Loderer* would have it as a necessity. For the sake of not 'spoiling the ship for a ha'porth of tar' Campbell thought it best to disguise his aerial. He was fortunate to have among his officers a Mr Andrews, who had worked at Marconi's and who gave invaluable advice on this highly technical matter. The aerial was fitted between the two masts, alongside the usual stays, with the feeder coming down like a pair of extra signal halyards to the wireless office, which was concealed in a space under the chart-room. This clever design almost resulted in the electrocution of a pilot, who went innocently to bend his pilot flag to one of these false 'halyards' when a message was being passed and was only just stopped in time by an anxious Campbell.

HMS *Loderer* herself was now ready for action, but a lot more thought was necessary before she was pitted against the U-boats. For example, say she was seen steering west, and then eastwards on the same track the following day, or, even worse, was seen to be turning round during daylight hours, this would clearly be suspicious behaviour for a 'tramp' steamer. Therefore, standard Q-ship practice was to change course only during hours of darkness. Even then, the question of identity was a worry. A German captain's well-practised professional eye would quickly realize that the steamer he could now see in his periscope proceeding east at a leisurely pace was the same one that he had spied the previous day going west.

The answer lay in a variety of subtle temporary items of disguise, which could be applied or removed during the hours of darkness, so that when the dawn broke it would be an entirely different ship that appeared on the horizon. Slight changes in the placing of the ship's boats, or to her rigging, the wearing of a different 'neutral' flag, a wooden dummy funnel or some false ventilators, a lick of paint to put a coloured band round a previously plain funnel, or canvas screens stretched along the sides of a well-deck to give a 'flush-deck' line, were all typical of the tricks employed by Q-ship captains to alter a ship's identity in a very short space of time. There was a rumour that one Q-ship captain turned a wooden dummy funnel into a lookout position by cutting a slot in it, near the top, and stationing a man inside it. It was claimed that the man had a length of wire tied to his finger which was pulled sharply at intervals throughout the watch to prevent him from going to sleep!

As the number of encounters with British decoys grew throughout the coming months, so the U-boat commanders became more cautious in approaching any merchant ship, which in turn called for more and more ingenuity. Immense pains were taken to continue the deception. HM Trawler No. 628, otherwise known as the *Oyama* CF 23, was owned by Neale & West, a well-known Cardiff company which had several of its vessels serving with the Navy. For such a small craft, 257 tons, she carried an enormous amount of hidden fire-power, with one 12-pounder, four 6-pounders, one 3-pounder, two Maxims and depth charges. In what was one of the most ingenious disguises invented, she went to sea posing as a crashed Zeppelin! It appears that the Germans were not fooled by this, because there is no record of her meeting with any success, and she was withdrawn from service after three months. All the same, it is a great pity that no photographs or drawings seem to have survived of the contraption, which was apparently constructed of material stretched over a huge framework of gas-piping.

Uniforms, of course, were out, and the Admiralty sanctioned a small allowance for some plain clothes to be purchased. Harold Auten recalled that the task of acquiring this clothing for the crew of HMS *Zylpha* fell to him. In a seedy shop in a Portsmouth back-street he negotiated a £60 deal for eighty second-hand suits, two for each man, one fairly new for going ashore and a shabbier one for work, which left the old dealer beaming with delight. The next day there was a measuring-up session on board *Zylpha* which was conducted with as much solemn ceremony as if it had been in a Savile Row tailors and delivery was taken of a huge bundle of smelly togs. In their new attire, the erstwhile spick and span sailors appeared as ruffians. One large stoker sported a parson's frock coat and a bowler hat, which Auten thought was overdoing things a little, but the man seemed quite satisfied with his new 'shore-going' rig.

On one occasion, when lying in harbour, incognito, alongside several real merchant ships, Campbell was both horrified and amused to see one of his sailors swinging high up on the funnel, applying a generous coat of red lead paint to it, dressed in a tail-coat!

Beswick, Campbell's First Lieutenant, had an old reefer jacket with a patch on the back, to go with his equally shabby trousers. He had the misfortune not to enjoy a very amicable relationship with the ship's dog, which resulted in yet another patch being required to the seat of the trousers. Campbell himself, posing as the Master, managed to make a suitable piece of headgear out of an old peaked cap, with a bit of gold lace wound round it.

Even uniform underclothes were barred. It would have given the game away for a line full of laundry strung across the deck of a 'tramp' to consist of Navy issue white flannel 'fronts'.

Going ashore in plain clothes presented some problems for Campbell's crew. They were often 'white feathered' in pubs and in the streets. This had become a common practice, usually by women who assumed any young man in civilian clothes to be a coward who had not volunteered for active service, and involved the aggressive thrusting of a white feather into the face of the unfortunate man. More to the point, the *Loderer*'s crew said, the local girls would not 'walk out' with them. Campbell sympathized, and managed to wangle for each of them the button-hole badge which said "On War Service" as was worn by the "dockyard mateys".

All kinds of other small but vital details emerged as the pantomime performance became more and more polished. Royal Navy parlance would be replaced by that of the Merchant Service, a difficult thing to do after years of calling the wardroom the wardroom and not the saloon. The stokers became firemen. The Captain was the Master. And so on. Men off-duty would be encouraged to lounge around the upper deck, smoking and spitting to their hearts' content, and the apron-clad cooks would whistle happily as they casually tipped buckets of slops over the side, all things which would have enraged the Master-at-Arms of a gleaming cruiser.

One decoy ship, the little Grimsby smack *Linnet*, GY999, had her disguise penetrated in an instant. Luckily, it was by a friendly skipper from Hull, who spotted that, although she had her gear about, it was plain that she had not been fishing, because there was no flock of squawking seagulls hovering over her. This was a good tip for the future. It was best to have a few dead fish strewn around the deck to attract the gulls if you were pretending to be a fishing boat.

When under attack by shellfire, Harold Auten devised a plan to give the impression that his ship was on fire by setting light to a tubful of dried seaweed on deck, which, of course, gave the submarine's gunners a totally false reading of the range by making them think that their firing had been far more accurate than was the case.

But of all the 'acts' in the pantomime, the one which needed the most 'rehearsal' to make it realistic was that of the 'panic party'. The natural thing for a merchant ship's crew to do if their ship were attacked by a submarine would be to take to the boats and here was a great opportunity to put on a convincing show and entice the U-boat still nearer. Leaving the Navy gunners in their hidden positions on board, absolutely still and not making a sound, the 'panic crew' would 'abandon ship' with a marvellous display of confusion.

At the given order, pandemonium broke out as men scrambled out from the stokeholds, the galley and the fo'c'sle, and ran in terror along the upper deck, all shouting and tripping over each other as they struggled into the lifeboats. When the boats were lowered this was done with feigned clumsiness, so that one came down 'end up' into the sea, most un-Navylike, and the oarsmen would be hopeless, 'catching crabs' like mad as they frantically pulled away from the sides of the 'doomed' ship. Campbell's men, warming to the act, introduced a few variations into their routine. After the lifeboat had gone a few yards, a sooty-faced stoker would appear at the rail, yelling for help. It would appear that he had been in the 'heads' or had not heard the alarm, and the boat would have to return to fetch him. A final touch of realism, a *pièce de résistance* if ever there was one, was provided by the last man into the lifeboat, who would clamber into it clutching a large cage in which was perched a magnificent stuffed parrot.

To all outward appearances, this would leave the ship deserted, but in truth the guns would all be manned, and down in the silent engine-room everybody would be ready and waiting for orders down the voice-pipe from the Captain, who would still be on the bridge with the Quartermaster. In Campbell's case this entailed lying prone on his belly and peering through a small slit in the bridge screen. Lastly, there would be a signalman ready to break out the White Ensign when the neutral flag collapsed on its staff over the stern and the sides of the false steering-engine house and the other bogus fittings fell down to expose the muzzles of the guns.

One evening, when *Loderer* was about to sail, a naval officer came on board and handed Campbell a sealed envelope, not to be opened until after he had sailed. There had been rumours that German agents had obtained information about her while she had been fitting out. The envelope bore orders that HMS *Loderer* had ceased to exist. Thenceforth, she was to assume the name HMS *Farnborough*.

Under intense American diplomatic pressure, the Kaiser called a 'cease-fire' in his U-boat onslaught in the middle of September, 1915, at least in northern waters. For the coming winter *Farnborough* was to trudge into the Atlantic to about 18 degrees west and back again in a fruitless search for action. Her fellow decoys did much the same, not only those under Bayly's command, but also those in the North Sea, all around Scotland, and in the Channel.

But one event had taken place in the August of that year which cannot be allowed to pass without recording it.

Chapter 4

The *Baralong*:
Germany is outraged.

When Kapitänleutnant Walther Schweiger, commander of the *U-20*, torpedoed and sank the liner *Lusitania* on 7 May, 1915, thirteen miles off the Old Head of Kinsale, it sparked an outrage that festered for years. Indeed, it is one of the most remembered episodes of the war.

Germany claimed that it was legal to have sunk the liner, because she was not only flying a false flag, the Stars and Stripes, but was armed and carrying munitions. She was even listed in *Jane's Fighting Ships*. Therefore, any passengers were travelling at their own risk. 124 Americans had lost their lives in the sinking, which pushed an enraged but indecisive USA a little nearer to declaring war on Germany. For obvious reasons, the British were seethingly angry. 1,195 innocent people had met their deaths, whatever the legal position.

The Q-ship, HMS *Baralong*, was cruising off the Channel Islands when she heard the distress signals go out from the liner. She tore flat out, as fast as her sweating stokers could urge her, towards the coast of southern Ireland, but it was too late. Later, *Baralong*'s captain and crew walked past the long lines of dead bodies laid out on the Queenstown jetty. It was a sight which affected many of them deeply for the rest of their lives.

The bulldog-faced captain of the *Baralong*, thirty-one-year-old Lieutenant-Commander Godfrey Herbert, was somewhat of a maverick. He paid scant heed to the red tape of the Navy and had made a name for himself by his unconventional methods. His roistering style, love of horse-play and practical jokes, but ruthless disposition when the occasion demanded it and steely nerves when faced with danger, were probably major reasons why he found himself in command of a Q-ship. His earlier career had been spent in submarines, then in their infancy. He had received much public praise for his cool bravery in saving the experimental boat *A-4*, when it dived ninety feet out of control off Portsmouth in 1905. However, such moments of glory had been interspersed with episodes of disaster. In the early days of the war, in the submarine *D-5*, he had missed a sitting target, the cruiser *Rostock*, off the Danish coast, when he had fudged his torpedo attack. Three months later he had hit a British mine off Yarmouth, which had resulted in the loss of the *D-5* and the deaths of nineteen sailors. For all that, their Lordships had never forgotten his saving of the *A-4*. It seemed he would be forgiven almost anything. Before he sailed from Queenstown in the *Baralong* he had been summoned by one of the senior officers of the Admiralty's Special Service branch, to be told, "This *Lusitania* business is shocking. Unofficially, we are telling you . . . take no prisoners from U-boats."

The *Baralong* was not Herbert's first decoy-ship command. Early in 1915 he had been given HMS *Antwerp*, the former Great Eastern Railways steamer *Vienna*, whose name had been changed to something a little less Germanic. His first, and so far only, encounter with a U-boat had been when he came across the *U-29* off the Scillies just after she had pulled off a major *coup* which rocked British morale; the sinking of the three cruisers *Aboukir*, *Hogue* and *Cressy*. The German submarine had slipped away from him, only to be snapped in two like a baby carrot when she was rammed and sunk by the battle-cruiser HMS *Dreadnought* when trying to make her way back to Germany via the Pentland Firth. Herbert had been scornful of the *Antwerp's* slowness and clumsy handling, blaming it for preventing him from opening his 'score'. In his usual forthright fashion, he reported his feelings to the Admiralty, and a few days later was summoned to Whitehall by 'Jacky' Fisher himself. Clearly, he must have put on a good performance, because he was given a more or less free hand to select a more suitable ship. He had seen just the thing in Portland. Strong and handy, she was listed as Mercantile Fleet Auxiliary No. 5. She was to become famous, and infamous, as HMS *Baralong*.

Baralong was an ex-Ellerman Line, 4,000-ton 'three island' tramp with capacity in her bunkers for 3,000 tons of coal, built by Armstrong & Whitworth in 1901. She had been known to make twelve knots on a good day. In March, 1915, Herbert took her to Pembroke Dock to carry out her conversion. The *Antwerp*'s two 12-pounders and another similar gun were mounted aft, on *Baralong*'s poop deck. One was disguised as a sheep-pen and the other two hidden by dummy life-belt lockers. The new Q-ship had four capacious holds. Allowing the two which were amidships for coal, Herbert obtained thousands of empty casks which he stowed in No. 1 hold for'ard and No. 4 hold aft. If she were hit by a torpedo, these would help to keep her afloat.

Herbert had been impressed with the young Sub-Lieutenant Gordon Steele, who had been his First Lieutenant in the *Antwerp*, and arranged for the twenty-two-year-old to be transferred to his new command. A brilliant student at the Merchant Navy training school *Worcester*, and winner of a P & O Scholarship, Steele came from an old sea-faring family, his father having had charge of the merchant training ship *Cornwall*, and his grandfather a officer in the Royal Marines. At the outbreak of war he had been serving as Third Officer in the *Caledonia* and was soon mobilized with the Royal Naval Reserve. Other ex-*Antwerp* crew to join Herbert were Chief Petty Officer Dickinson, who had accompanied Scott's expedition to the Antarctic, and Royal Marine Corporal Fred Collins. The original master of the *Baralong*, when she was simply "Mercantile Fleet Auxiliary No. 5", Lieutenant Swinney, joined the RNR and stayed on board as navigator to make up the complement of officers. The lower deck ship's company numbered sixty-six. Of these, only nineteen were Royal Navy regulars, nine were Merchant Navy men, and the rest were all Royal Naval Reservists or Royal Marines.

In April, 1915, *Baralong* sailed from Portsmouth to wander round the Channel and the Western Approaches in search of U-boats. It soon became apparent that some of the crew were not responding to Herbert's free and easy discipline in the right spirit. This was a secret mission and therefore shore leave was banned for the sake of security. But several times crewmen swam ashore against orders, and three stokers deserted altogether. There was trouble in Queenstown when some of the seamen jumped ship and came back on board drunk on poteen. On a visit to Dartmouth, the cradle of naval etiquette and his own *alma mater*, Herbert was persuaded to allow some official shore leave. He regretted it immediately. *Baralong*'s sailors went on a rampage of drunken brawling in the sedate town, completely wrecking one public house. Several of them were arrested and hauled off to the local chokey. Herbert, fearful that the secrecy surrounding his ship would be destroyed by the publicity, put up the bail to release them from custody. But in the morning none of them returned to court. They were unable to do so. Herbert had made sure of that. They were aboard *Baralong* and he had upped anchor and sailed during the night. He was more cautious when they tied up at Southampton. No leave was allowed. Instead, he went ashore with C.P.O. Dickinson, bought a large barrel of beer and had it delivered on board for the men.

All these events, plus Herbert's habit of carousing with his juniors, appalled Steele, who had been schooled to observe strict maritime protocol, and to whom such behaviour was taboo. He was completely aghast when Herbert told him to stop calling him 'sir'. When asked how he should be addressed, Herbert replied mysteriously, "Captain William McBride." That exchange was to be an important factor, in due course, when it came to an examination of the dramatic events that were about to unfold.

June and July came and went, and half of August too. *Baralong* had been 'operational' for over four months. Still discipline was well below standard. Indeed, one of the stokers was now languishing in prison in Falmouth. And the crew were bored. Their only moment of excitement had been their dash to offer help to the *Lusitania*, and that had been three months ago. The U-boats had been on an orgy of sinkings in the Western Approaches. Freighters, colliers, sailing ships, had met their doom all around *Baralong*. She had seen the blazing wrecks and towering columns of smoke, heard the explosions and watched the flotsam of this massacre floating by her sides, but her crew had yet to catch even a glimpse of a German submarine. They had steamed thousands of miles. All for nothing.

On 19 August, a beautifully clear day, she was patrolling up and down off the Scillies. It was 9.15 a.m. when her wireless hummed and pipped into life. It was an SOS call from a 16,000-ton passenger liner out of Liverpool, SS *Arabic*. She had been attacked by a U-boat. In fact, not only was the liner in distress herself, but she was calling for help for another ship nearby, the freighter *Dunsley*, which had also been torpedoed. Lieutenant Swinney plotted the position of the stricken ships. They were just twenty-five miles away. By dint of some more hard sweat by her stokers, *Baralong* could be there in a couple of hours.

Shaking herself up to her full twelve knots, she raced to the scene, with hidden gun crews at Action Stations and Corporal Fred Collins with a dozen marines crouching behind their screens clutching .303 rifles. The sea was calm and visibility was perfect. But there was nothing there. From horizon to horizon, nothing was to be seen. No liner, no submarine, no wreckage, no life-boats, no flotsam. Nothing. Herbert was furious.

"We're bloody well too late again!" he almost wept. What he did not know was that the liner's wireless operator, doubtless in panic, had keyed out the wrong position when sending out his SOS call. The two ships had gone down about thirty miles away, not far from where the *Lusitania* already rested on the bottom. As it was, eighteen of the *Arabic*'s 186 passengers, including two Americans, and twenty-one of her crew had lost their lives. Dejected, Herbert turned *Baralong* eastwards, to plod slowly towards the Bristol Channel, hoping, as ever, to find something on the way. Mid-afternoon came, finding her about eighty miles west of Bishop Rock and due south of Queenstown, when the wireless sang for the second time that day and the operator ran to Herbert on the bridge with the message on his pad.

It was another SOS. The signal was loud, indicating that it came from a ship probably no more than twenty miles away. "Am being chased by enemy submarine." At that moment one of the look-outs shouted that he could see steam right ahead. It was a large freighter. Herbert could see her with his binoculars. Minutes later, another signal was received. "Captured by enemy submarine. Crew ready to leave. Lat. 50.32N Long. 8.12W." At 3.15 p.m. a third signal blipped out, "Crew all left. Captured by two enemy submarines".

Two enemy submarines! It turned out to be false information, because in fact there was only one. However, Herbert was not to know that. He rang down for Full Speed, and sent *Baralong*'s crew to Action Stations. Unfortunately for the Germans, only a few hours before, the Q-ship's men had been listening to the distress calls from the *Arabic*. And now their wireless operator had just received what was to be another last call. "Help, help. For God's sake, help." The throbbing *Baralong* ploughed nearer to the freighter, churning a creamy wake out of the calm blue-green sea, with gun crews hidden behind their screens and marines lying with loaded rifles on her after well-deck. Mutters began to be heard among the tense waiting men. Angry, gritted-teeth, blood-thirsty mutters. They were about to exact revenge for the *Arabic*. And the *Lusitania*. And all the rest. Herbert hoisted the Stars and Stripes and two huge boards were lowered from *Baralong*'s rails, one on each side, which read "ULYSSES S. GRANT. U.S.A." Four stewards and two galley-boys waited in the galley. It was to be their job to haul the boards up when the US flag was dropped to be replaced by the White Ensign.

In twenty minutes *Baralong* was only a couple of miles from the tall-funnelled black-painted 6,250 ton freighter. She had stopped. Approaching astern of her was the *U-27*, long and very low in the water, like a grey crocodile about to snatch a drinking wildebeest. The big ship's life-boats had been lowered and were full of men, pulling away from her as hard as they could. She was the *Nicosian*, owned by the Leyland Line, master Captain Charles Manning, out of New Orleans, USA, for Liverpool, England, with a cargo of cotton, timber, steel rods, and tinned meat; plus 750 mules for the British Army, and their fifty tons of fodder.

The carnage of the First World War was not restricted to human beings. Horses, too, died in their thousands, as well as that other favourite beast of burden, the mule, in the sea of mud that was Flanders. The British Army could never get enough mules. A major source of supply of these sometimes fractious animals was the USA. The task of transporting them across the Atlantic was carried out by ships like the *Nicosian*. They were not pleasant ships in which to go to sea. In fact, they were little more than floating cess-pits. The volume of dung and urine produced by 750 mules is quite considerable and no matter how often the stalls were mucked out, these ships always carried an acrid eye-stinging stench about them which managed to percolate itself into every compartment, and contaminated the clothes and skins of all on board. And feeding and mucking-out several hundred terror-stricken, kicking and rearing, sea-sick mules on a three-week ocean voyage was a daunting enough job in itself.

The job of tending the animals on the crossing fell to men who were signed on for that specific task. They were known as muleteers. They were paid very little, somewhat less than what the ship's sailors drew. Around $15 'all found' seems to have been the going rate for the voyage, paid when the ship docked in Liverpool or Avonmouth. Their food and accommodation on board was basic, to say the least. They slept on thin paliasses alongside the animals in rough partitioned-off booths. Their diet did not consist of much more than bully beef and potatoes.

The life of a muleteer did not come particularly hard, or indeed as much of a surprise, to the unwashed hobo types who signed on. For them, it made a welcome change from riding as half-starved stowaways in rail-road box-cars around the vastness of America. But there was a sprinkling of another sort of individual for whom the idea of adventure as a muleteer seemed attractive. Indeed, with a war going on 'over there', it had become almost fashionable for some of the more educated types of young men to make their way to New Orleans or Newport News and sign on the first mule-ship that was due to leave for England. Some were even prepared to pay a sizeable handful of greenbacks for the privilege of making the trip. For them, accustomed to a very different style of life, the world of the muleteers often came as an unpleasant surprise.

When the *Nicosian* left her wharfside berth in New Orleans on Sunday, 1 August, 1915, to slide down the Mississippi to the Gulf of Mexico, she had several such young men among the forty-eight muleteers on board. There was big Jim Curran, a thirty-two-year-old university educated Irish-American. Curran had been a travelling salesman for ten years, although not a hugely successful one. One day he happened to pitch up in Fort Worth, Texas. He was nearly broke and needed a job badly. Fort Worth was one of the marshalling centres for mules that were to be shipped to England, and the smooth-tongued Curran managed to talk himself into the job of overseeing a train-load of 600 mules from the C.B. Team Mule Barn down to New Orleans. All arrived safely, and on the strength of this Curran convinced the cargo-master of the National Shipping Co. to sign him on as the muleteer-foreman for the *Nicosian*.

Curran took a horse-drawn cab to the wharf and heaved his baggage up the gangway. On deck was the quartermaster, sitting at a table on which there were several knives and a couple of pistols. Despite his protests that he was the foreman, Curran was made to turn out his pockets to check for weapons before being shown to his cabin on the main deck.

He then went below to inspect the stable-deck where the mules were housed and where the muleteers were to sleep. The animals were already up to their fetlocks in excrement. The overwhelming pungency stung Curran's nostrils and the knowledge that his men would be living in such conditions rankled him. He returned to the upper deck to stand by the rail and greet his team as they reported for duty. Of the forty-eight muleteers, only two were British. The rest were American. They came from all walks of life. There was Charles Hightower, a Texan church minister's son, Bud Emerson Palen, a Canadian actor; Ed Clark, son of a Detroit millionaire, Bob Cosby, a Texas banker's son, and two young men from Tennessee, an ex-US soldier, Tom Carson, with his side-kick Bill Dempsey.

Curran reported to the ship's American veterinary officer, William Banks, who acquainted him with his firm requirements. The animals were to have fresh straw and water at regular intervals and be kept on a strict diet. Mucking-out would be an endless task. These voyages were not, Banks warned him, the pleasure cruises that many young American rich-boys thought they would be. He had not been referring simply to the insanitary work with the mules. Curran realized this when he heard the British crew taunting the muleteers. "Just wait, you Yanks. You'll see some action when we reach U-boat alley!"

Before sailing from Liverpool on the outward trip, Captain Manning had applied, unsuccessfully, for the *Nicosian* to be fitted with a stern gun. Therefore, in mid-Atlantic on the homeward voyage, he decided to make a dummy wooden gun and mount it on the after-deck. This might, just might, he reasoned, deter a U-boat captain from chancing an attack. The Americans were furious. This was only inviting trouble, they protested. They threatened to take the "gun" and throw it over the side. It took all of Curran's salesman's patter to dissuade them from doing so. Then there was some trouble over lifebelts. Manning instructed lifebelts to be placed amidships, port and starboard, with the strict order that they were not to be touched without permission. He promised that ample warning would be given if an emergency arose. In the morning every lifebelt had disappeared. A search was made, and they were all found stashed in the Americans' quarters. After that, a guard was put on them.

The question of food rations became a running sore. The Americans felt that the ships' crew were enjoying better fare than the muleteers, which led to a clash between Hightower and the chief steward, Billy Musker. Fights had started to break out with surprising ease. In one, the normally easy-going Bob Cosby had a dust-up with the ship's carpenter. Feelings were running high. So high, in fact, that there had been talk of mutiny. Such were the conditions on board as the *Nicosian* drew near the Western Approaches, the dreaded U-boat alley.

The dummy gun on the *Nicosian*'s poop did not fool Korvetten-kapitän Bernard Wegener as he peered at the mule-ship through his binoculars from the conning-tower of *U-27*, mainly because there was nobody manning it. Wegener was already a U-boat ace, having sunk the

British submarine *E-3* near the mouth of the Ems, (the very first sinking of one submarine by another), the seaplane carrier HMS *Hermes* in the Channel and an armed merchant cruiser off the Mull of Galloway. He had a mission to perform; and that mission was to sink Allied ships. There was one now, a couple of miles off his port bow.

The *U-27*'s three-inch gun cracked out, sending a shell flying over the *Nicosian*'s mastheads to splash into the sea. The mule-ship's look-outs had, in fact, already spotted the submarine, and Manning had set off on a zig-zag course to try to outpace his assailant. But when the shell was fired, he panicked, rushing from the bridge to the wireless office, screaming at the operator, "For God's sake send SOS, SOS, SOS!"

Wegener ordered his gunners to aim for the merchant ship's aerials to silence it. Bam, again! It was a dead shot. The aerials came snaking down and draped themselves over the starboard rail. By now the panic had spread to the *Nicosian*'s muleteers. They charged over to the port-side lifeboat and started to climb into it, only to be prevented from doing so by a revolver held in the hand of Second Officer Williamson. Manning then realized that his thirteen knots would be no match for the U-boat on the surface. He rang down to Stop Engines. There was an excited yell from the heir to an automobile fortune from Detroit, Ed Clark, who had spotted the *Baralong* in the distance. But in the chaos nobody heard him.

Now astern of the stationary *Nicosian*, the *U-27* was only a few hundred yards off. Wegener hoisted a string of flags ordering Manning to abandon ship, and as soon as the British captain had assured himself that everyone on board was assembled, he gave the order, "Away all boats". He had regained his composure now, and was the last to leave his ship, sliding down a rope into a lifeboat. Wegener opened fire again, but, rather than stitching a line of holes along the mule-ship's water-line, most of the shells exploded almost harmlessly among her upper-works. Meantime, those men in the lifeboats who were not cowering down out of sight rowed them, frantically, round to the bow-end of their defenceless ship, from which could be heard the braying and hoof-stamping of 750 terror-stricken mules.

Baralong was coming up on the starboard beam. Herbert could see Wegener in his conning tower, looking towards him through his binoculars, obviously checking his identity. The Stars and Stripes and the big boards seemed to have convinced the German, but, as an additional bluff, Herbert ran up the international distress code flags for "am saving life". The U-boat now slid slowly out of Herbert's vision as it went along the port side of the mule-ship, continuing to pump shells into her, many of which missed completely and passed clean over the top of her to straddle the Q-ship itself. Herbert grabbed his chance. He brought the *Baralong* hard round to starboard. All three vessels now faced in the same direction, and he yelled, "Clear away guns!" Down went the US flag on its staff over the stern. Up came the White Ensign. Down dropped the rails to expose the three 12-pounders with crews at the ready and Corporal Fred Collins and his marines with levelled rifles. Up came the port name-board. (The starboard name-board stayed down, because the two stewards and the galley-boy on that side had run below, but that was out of sight of the Germans.) In less than half a minute the harmless American tramp had become a British man o'war. And it was all perfectly legal.

Herbert called through his megaphone, "Marines concentrate fire on forward gun. Guns' crews aim at conning tower and hull. Range six hundred yards." It seemed an age before the submarine's bows peeped from behind those of the *Nicosian*. At the instant her gun appeared the marines opened fire and a vicious rain of 0.303 bullets whined and ricocheted from her casing. The gun-layer jerked backwards like a puppet on strings, dead, into the sea. The others around the gun ran to hide behind the conning tower. Then the conning tower itself came into view and the Q-ship's 12-pounders crashed out in unison. The first two salvoes missed. (In fact, Sub-Lieutenant Steele's gun had a shell jammed in the breech and he risked both his life and a court-martial by snatching it out and hurling it into the sea. Regulations decreed a thirty-minute wait before touching a jammed shell, but Steele had waited long enough to catch his first U-boat already.) Then the *Baralong*'s gunners got the range. One shell hit U-27's conning-tower, blowing two men high into the air, and another struck the perfect blow, catching her amidships, just below the waterline. She heeled over and then an explosion seemed to lift her clean out of the water.

Herbert screamed, "Cease fire!" But his men's blood was up. They were avenging the *Arabic* and the *Lusitania*. For them this was no time to cease firing, even as the survivors of her crew appeared on the outer casing, struggling out of their clothes to swim away from her. There was a mighty hiss of compressed air from her tanks and the U-27 vanished from sight in a vortex of giant rumbling bubbles, leaving a pall of smoke over the spot where she had been. It had only taken a couple of minutes to fire the thirty-four shells at her.

Meanwhile, the *Nicosian*'s men sat in their lifeboats, witnessing the furious onslaught which screamed past them, literally under their very noses. Suddenly it was quiet, and as they pulled towards the *Baralong* they broke into crazy cheering, beside themselves with relief, not least Captain Manning himself, who jumped up shouting, "If any of those bastard Huns come up, lads, hit 'em over the head with an oar." Herbert was elated and beamed broadly. But within seconds of ordering tots of Navy rum for the men and inviting the officers for drinks in *Baralong*'s saloon he was giving the order for the marine riflemen to open fire again.

The *Nicosian* was not sinking, despite a pair of shell-holes near her waterline. Some water had entered her hull, but the timber content of her cargo had been enough to keep her afloat. And now several of the German submariners had swum towards her and were climbing up the *Nicosian*'s ladder and dangling lifeboat lines. Herbert explained what happened next in a secret report to the Admiralty. "I observed about a dozen Germans, who had swum from their boat, swarming up ropes' ends and the pilot ladder which had been left hanging down. Fearing they might scuttle or set fire to the ship with her valuable cargo of mules I ordered them to be shot away. The majority were prevented from getting on board, but six succeeded. As soon as possible, I placed my ship alongside and put a party of marines on board under Corporal Collins, warning him to be careful of snipers in case they had found the rifles, which I was informed by *Nicosian*'s captain had been left in the chart-house. A thorough search was made which resulted in six of the enemy being found, but they succumbed to the injuries they had received from lyddite shell shortly afterwards, and were buried at once."

The last sentence of that report is hardly believable. To suggest that six men, all seriously wounded by shell-fire, had made their way on board the freighter by swimming to her and then shinning up ropes, and then all died of their injuries simultaneously a few minutes later, is stretching the imagination. We will leave a closer examination of Herbert's words and the furore that stemmed from the killing of the unarmed German submariners until a little later. For the time being let us simply record that there was now not a single survivor from the *U-27*.

Herbert took the damaged mule-ship in tow and they wallowed on towards Avonmouth, but the line parted in the middle of the night. Manning was confident that his ship, even with over twenty feet of water in one of her holds, could make it into port safely. The *Baralong* left her near Lundy Island and headed across the Bristol Channel for Pembroke Dock. Before parting company, Herbert, who had maintained the phoney name of McBride throughout, wrote a letter to Manning, which presumably was sent over in a boat. It stressed the need for the mule-ship's men to keep silent about the encounter with the U-boat and the Q-ship's use of the US flag.

Manning read out "McBride's" letter to his crew and passed it to Banks, the veterinary surgeon, to show to the muleteers. In his reply he expressed the gratitude of all on board the *Nicosian* for the "magnificent way" in which the rescue had been conducted. He assured "McBride" that he had impressed upon his own crew and the muleteers the need for silence about the matter.

The Americans, now back aboard their own ship, spent a nauseating nightmare of a night. They had returned to find twenty-four mules lying dead amid a stinking quagmire of dung, urine, guts and blood, and set about cleaning up the sickening chaos. Shovels and brooms and buckets of disinfectant were wielded with much cursing. The animals, driven berserk by the gunfire, had reared and kicked in their stalls so frenziedly that some had battered themselves literally to death against the bulkheads. Others were so badly injured that Banks ordered them to be shot.

The *Nicosian* finally tied up in Avonmouth just after dawn on 21 August, but the muleteers were not allowed ashore. Manning had been convinced that there was another German hiding somewhere on board and a platoon of soldiers and a police squad were waiting on the quayside to carry out a search. Nothing was found. And then, even before work had started on her essential repairs, the ship was ordered to sea again, to ditch the bloated corpses of the dead mules. The stench had been overpowering the whole dockside, but Curran had needed to agree the tally with the waiting officer before disposing of any of them. It was agreed – 750 mules, dead and alive. (Strangely, in his later affidavit Curran gave the number as 354.)

Temporarily repaired, the *Nicosian* sailed for Liverpool, where some of the American muleteers, including Tom Carson and Bill Dempsey, declared themselves to be Canadians and joined the British Army. The others, thoroughly peeved, hung around in dockside seamen's rest homes for a week or so waiting to return home in the *Nicosian* when she went back for more mules. When they signed on again, they were formally warned by a police inspector not to talk to anybody, particularly US newsmen, about the *Baralong*. But it was too late, because three of them, Bill Roberts from New Orleans, New Yorker Henry Christie and a nineteen-year-old Kentuckian steward named Herbert Young, had already hurried ashore in Liverpool to see the American Consul and had provided him with signed statements in which they complained bitterly about the cold-blooded way in which the Germans had been slaughtered.

But it was Banks, the vet, who "spilled the beans" in a big way. And he did it almost instantly. He was due to return to the States aboard the White Star liner *Lapland* and, while kicking his heels in Liverpool waiting for her to sail, he had written a letter to a relative in Massachusetts in which he told about the U-boat attack and *Baralong*'s involvement, even the fact that she had been flying the American flag. By the time the *Lapland* berthed in New York the press had got hold of the story and Banks's letter had already appeared in the *New York Times*. Surrounded by reporters on the dockside, the surprised Banks tried to play things down, although he did agree that the British ship had been flying the US flag.

To an undecided America, with its freshly arrived cosmopolitan population split in its loyalties to the various participants in the World War that was raging all around it, this was big news. A wavering President Wilson had blown hot and cold on whether or not to toss America's mighty hat into the ring. In fact, since the *Lusitania* affair, it had looked as if America was at last edging herself towards a declaration of war against Germany. But the letter that William Banks sent from Liverpool had sparked such controversy that she climbed back on the fence.

After riding out a hurricane in the Gulf of Mexico, the *Nicosian* berthed at New Orleans on 1 October with her cargo of timber and wool. The disgruntled muleteers swarmed ashore to live it up in the bars and red light honky-tonks after their ordeal. Tongues loosened by drink, and no doubt revelling in their image as war-veterans, Curran, Clark, Palen, Hightower and Cosby took to flaunting a blood-stained shirt around, saying it had belonged to one of the German submariners. The German Assistant Consul in New Orleans, Dr Paul Roh, took little time to realize that here was an invaluable source of propaganda. He urged the five men to make sworn affidavits, affirming their experiences. They were only too pleased to comply, as eventually did a sixth ex-muleteer, J.M. Garrett, and another American, Larrimore Holland, who claimed to have actually been serving in the Royal Navy aboard the *Baralong*.

Roh passed the stories on to the *New York World*, which was delighted to obtain such a scoop ahead of its competitors. A scornful Captain Manning, who was about to sail from Ninth Street Docks with another load of mules, countered this with a short statement of his own to the Press, saying "They're trying to get revenge for imagined ill-treatment aboard my ship". But the German propaganda machine had moved into top gear. Their information bureau sent the muleteers' stories to over 1,000 newspapers, to be published in full. Meanwhile, the British population knew little, if anything, about it until a protest note, to which transcripts of the affidavits were attached, was received in London via the American Ambassador. The British Government issued a White Paper on Tuesday, 4 January, 1916, which was published in *The Times* the following day under the heading – "The *Baralong* Case – German Charge of Murder." It ran:

The memorandum from the German Government sets forth that six citizens of the United States had been examined on October 5 and 8, 1915, before the public notaries Mr E. Ansley of Hancock, Mississippi, and Mr Charles J. Denechaud, of Orleans, Louisiana, and made sworn depositions concerning the murder of the crew of a German submarine by the commander of the British auxiliary cruiser *Baralong*. The names of these witnesses are:-
> J.M. Garrett, aged 22, of Kiln, Hancock, Mississippi.
> Charles D. Hightower, 22, of Crystal City, Texas.
> Bud Emerson Palen, 27, of Detroit, Michigan.
> Edward Clark, 21, of Detroit, Michigan.
> R.H. Cosby, 21, of Crystal City, Texas.
> James J. Curran, 32, of Chicago, Illinois.

All are said to enjoy a good reputation; Curran was for a considerable time employed as commercial traveller in various large American business houses. According to the unanimous statements of these witnesses, the occurrence took place as follows:-
In August, 1915, the British steamer *Nicosian* was on her way from New Orleans to Avonmouth. She carried about 350 (sic) mules for war purposes, thus being laden with contraband. The witnesses were shipped

as muleteers and superintendents. On August 19, about 70 nautical miles south of Queenstown (Ireland), the steamer was stopped by a German submarine and fired on, after the whole crew, including the witnesses, had first left the ship in the lifeboats.

When the witnesses were outside the line of fire from the submarine, a steamer which had already been noticed by the witnesses Garrett, Hightower, Clark and Curran when still on board the *Nicosian*, approached the spot. This, as afterwards transpired, was the British auxiliary cruiser *Baralong*. As this steamer approached, all the witnesses noticed clearly that she was flying the American flag at the stern and that she carried on her sides large shields with the American flag painted on them. As the steamer carried the distinguishing marks of a neutral ship and had shown signals which according to the seafaring members of the crew of the *Nicosian* meant that she was willing to assist if desired, and as there was nothing in her outward appearance to indicate her warlike character, the crew in the lifeboats presumed that she was merely concerned with their rescue.

While the submarine was firing at close range on the port side of the *Nicosian* the steamer came up behind the latter and steamed past her. When she was a short distance ahead of the *Nicosian*'s bow she opened fire on the submarine at first, as all the witnesses, with the exception of Garrett, affirm, with small arms, and immediately afterwards with cannon, which had been hidden up to that time by screens, and were only visible when the latter were removed. The witness Curran also deposed that the American flag flying at the stern of the unknown ship was only lowered after the rifle fire. He repeated this statement in the enclosed affidavit made before the public notary Robert Schwarz at New York on October 21, 1915. As the submarine, after being struck several times, began to sink the commander and a number of seamen sprang overboard, the seamen having first removed their clothes. Some of them (the number given by the witnesses Garrett and Curran as five) succeeded in getting on board the *Nicosian* while the remainder seized the ropes left hanging in the water when the life-boats were lowered. The men clinging to the ropes were killed partly by gunfire from the *Baralong* and partly by rifle fire by the crew while the witnesses were boarding the *Baralong* from the lifeboats or were already on her deck. With regard to this the witness Curran also testifies that the commander of the unknown ship ordered his men to line up against the rail and to shoot at the helpless German seamen in the water.

Next the commander of the *Baralong* steamed alongside the *Nicosian*, made fast to the latter, and then ordered some of his men to board the *Nicosian* and search for the German sailors who had taken refuge there.

The witnesses Palen and Curran testify regarding this incident that the commander gave the definite order "to take no prisoners". Four German sailors were found in the *Nicosian* in the engine-room and screw tunnel and were killed.

The commander of the submarine, as the witnesses unanimously testify, succeeded in escaping to the bows of the *Nicosian*. He sprang into the water and swam round the bow of the ship towards the *Baralong*. The English seamen on the *Nicosian* immediately fired on him, although, in a manner visible to all, he raised his hands as a sign that he wished to surrender, and continued to fire after a shot had apparently struck him in the mouth. Eventually, he was killed by a shot in the neck.

All the witnesses were then temporarily ordered back onto the *Nicosian*. There the witnesses Palen and Cosby each saw one body of a German sailor while the witness Curran – who remained on board the steamer with members of the crew absolutely necessary to man her – saw all four bodies which were thrown overboard in the afternoon.

The commander of the *Baralong* had the *Nicosian* towed for a few miles in the direction of Avonmouth and then sent back to the *Nicosian* the remainder of the crew who were still on the *Baralong*. At the same time he sent a letter to the captain of the *Nicosian* in which he requested the latter to impress on his crew, especially the American members of it, to say nothing about the matter, whether on their arrival at Liverpool or on their return to America. The letter, which the witness Curran has himself read, was signed "Captain William McBride, HMS *Baralong*". That the unknown vessel was named *Baralong* was discovered also by the witness Hightower from a steward of the steamer, when he was on board that ship, while the witness Palen deposes that he, when he was leaving the ship, saw this name indistinctly painted on her bows.

The statements by the six witnesses are corroborated by the 18-year-old witness Larrimore Holland, whose sworn statement before the public notary Frank S. Carden in the county of Hamilton, Tennessee on October 12, 1915, is also annexed. The witness, who was a stoker on board the *Baralong*, was on board that ship when this unparalleled incident occurred. According to his statement also, the *Baralong* hoisted the American flag and, covered by the *Nicosian*, steamed towards the scene, where, as soon as the submarine was visible, she opened fire on the latter and sank her. He further states that about fifteen men of the submarine's crew sprang overboard as she sank and were killed by rifle and gun-fire from the *Baralong*, some while they were swimming in the water and others as they were trying to climb up the ropes of the *Nicosian*. If his statement differs in details from the statements of the other witnesses this evidently is caused by the fact that he himself only witnessed some of the incidents, and that he apparently only knows by hearsay of the other incidents, notably those which occurred on board the *Nicosian*.

By reason of the above evidence there can be no doubt that the commander of the British auxiliary cruiser *Baralong*, McBride, gave the crew under his command the order not to make prisoner certain helpless and unarmed German seamen, but to kill them in a cowardly manner; also that his crew obeyed the order and thus shared the guilt for the murder.

The German Government inform the British Government of this terrible deed, and take it for granted that the latter, when they have examined the facts of the case and the annexed affidavits, will immediately take proceedings for murder against the commander of the auxiliary cruiser *Baralong* and the crew concerned in the murder, and will punish them according to the laws of war. They await in a very short time a statement from the British Government that they have instituted proceedings for the expiation of this shocking incident; afterwards they await information as to the result of the proceedings, which should be hastened as much as possible in order that they may convince themselves that the deed has been punished by a sentence of corresponding severity. Should they be disappointed in this expectation, they would consider themselves obliged to take serious decisions as to retribution for the unpunished crime.

Berlin, Nov. 28, 1915.

As regards the annexed statements, they differed in some considerable detail, although some of the differences might be considered to be irrevelant. Nevertheless, despite the question of relevance, such differences, even if minor in detail, must detract from the overall reliability of the combined testimonies. None of the affiants was aboard the *Nicosian* when the search squad went aboard her to flush out the Germans, and their attestation in that regard was based upon hearsay, which they admitted. However, they did all provide versions which were, to all practical purposes, in mutual accord regarding the Germans who were shot at and killed while trying to climb up the side of the *Nicosian*.

Encouraged by German agents working in America, Curran was to emerge as the most vehement of the complainants. His account of the affair was published in a five-part serial in the *Chicago American* magazine, expressed in emotive terms which left no doubt as to his strong antipathy to the British. In fact, egged on by a leading Sinn Fein sympathizer named Jeremiah O'Leary, who "milked" the *Baralong* affair as hard as he could, Curran even went on to tour a number of US cities giving lectures designed to whip up anti-British feeling.

36

The evidence of young Larrimore Holland can be discounted entirely. It was little more than a tissue of easily proven lies. The truth was that he had run away from home in Chattanooga, Tennessee, and sailed on the mule-ship *Antillian* from New Orleans in mid-April. Ashore in Liverpool, he and his crew-mates had run out of money. A lot of them joined the British Army, but Holland decided that he would enlist in the Royal Navy. Putting himself down as a Canadian, and under an assumed name of "Tom Hicks", he was sent to Portsmouth to train as a Stoker Second Class. According to official records, on 11 August he admitted that he was an American and he was put into 'safe custody' while his discharge from the Royal Navy was arranged through the US Embassy. It was finalized on 24 August, 1915, on the same day that a patched up *Nicosian* was making her way gingerly from Avonmouth to Liverpool. Not only was Holland never on board HMS *Baralong*, but he never went to sea in any Royal Navy ship during his four months' service. The likelihood is that he made up his story in an attempt to soften his return home to Chattanooga, where an irate father awaited him.

Foreign Secretary Sir Edward Grey's reply on behalf of the British Government appeared alongside *The Times* report of the German protest. Sent via Walter Hines Page, the American Ambassador in London, it read:

Your Excellency,
I have had the honour of receiving your communication of the 6th instant, covering a memorandum of the German Government in regard to incidents alleged to have attended the destruction of a German submarine and its crew by HM auxiliary cruiser *Baralong* on 19th August last.

The German Government base on these alleged incidents a demand that the commanding officer and other responsible parties on board HMS *Baralong* shall be brought to trial for murder and duly punished.

His Majesty's Government note with great satisfaction, though with some surprise, the anxiety now expressed by the German Government that the principles of civilized warfare should be vindicated and that due punishment should be duly meted out to those who deliberately disregard them. It is true that the incident which has suddenly reminded the German Government that such principles exist is one in which the alleged criminals were British and not German. But His Majesty's Government do not for a moment suppose that it is the intention to restrict unduly the scope of any judicial investigation which it is thought proper to institute.

37

Now it is evident that to single out the case of the *Baralong* for particular examination would be the height of absurdity. Even were the allegations on which the German Government rely accepted as they stand, (and His Majesty's Government do not accept them), the charge against the commander and crew of the *Baralong* is negligible compared to that which seems to have been deliberately committed by German officers, both on land and sea, against combatants and non-combatants.

Doubtless the German Government will urge that the very multitude of these allegations would so overload any tribunal engaged in their examination as utterly to defeat the ends of justice. If, for example, a whole army be charged with murder, arson, robbery and outrage, it is plainly impossible to devote a separate inquiry to all the individuals who have taken a share in these crimes. These practical considerations cannot be ignored and His Majesty's Government admit their force. They would, therefore, be prepared, for the present, to confine any judicial investigations to charges made against British and German officers at sea, and even if this restriction were thought insufficient, they would be content to call attention to three naval incidents which occurred during the same forty-eight hours in the course of which the *Baralong* sank the submarine and rescued the *Nicosian*.

The first incident relates to a German submarine which fired a torpedo into the *Arabic* and sank her. No warning was given to the merchant vessel; no efforts were made to save its unresisting crew; forty-seven non-combatants were ruthlessly sent to their deaths. It is understood that this act of barbarism, though in perfect harmony with the earlier policy of the German Government, was contrary to orders recently issued. This, however, if true, only increases the responsibility of the submarine commander, and His Majesty's Government have received no information indicating that the authorities have pursued in this case the course they recommend in the case of the crew of the *Baralong*, by trying him for murder. The second incident occurred on the same day. A German destroyer found a British submarine stranded on the Danish coast. The submarine had not been pursued there by the destroyer; she was in neutral waters; she was incapable of either offence or defence. The destroyer opened fire on her and when her crew attempted to swim ashore the destroyer fired upon them also with no apparent object but to destroy a helpless enemy. There was here no excuse of hot blood; the crew of the British submarine had done nothing to rouse the fury of their opponents. They had not just murdered forty-seven innocent non-combatants. They were not taking possession of a German ship, or committing any act injurious to German interests. So far as His Majesty's Government knows the facts, the officers and men of this destroyer committed a crime against humanity and the laws of war, which is at least as worthy of judicial inquiry as any other which has occurred during the course of recent naval operations.

The third incident occurred some forty-eight hours later. The steamer *Ruel* was attacked by a German submarine. The ship, which had made no resistance, began to sink, the crew took to their boats, and while endeavouring to save themselves were fired upon both with shrapnel and rifle fire. One man was killed, eight others (including the master) were severely wounded. The sworn testimony on which these statements are based shows no reason whatever which could justify this cold-blooded and cowardly outrage.

It seems to His Majesty's Government that these three incidents, almost simultaneous in point of time, and not differing greatly in point of character, might, with the case of the *Baralong*, be brought before some impartial Court of investigation, say, for example, a tribunal composed of officers belonging to the United States Navy. If this were agreed to, His Majesty's Government would do all in their power to further the inquiry, and to do their part in taking further steps as justice and findings of the Court might seem to require.

His Majesty's Government do not think it necessary to make any reply to the suggestion that the British Navy has been guilty of inhumanity. According to the latest figures available, the number of German sailors rescued from drowning, often in circumstances of great difficulty and peril, amounts to 1,150. The German Navy can show no such record – perhaps through want of opportunity.

I have, &c,   E. Grey,
                                    Foreign Office, December 14, 1915.

Grey's reply was a good one from Britain's point of view. One can imagine the Foreign Secretary reading it over to himself with grim satisfaction, thinking that he had produced a trump to Germany's ace. But his attempt to involve America back-fired on him badly.

Reuters reported from Washington, dateline January 5th. "The United States Government, adhering to the policy of non-intervention in the controversies of belligerents, will not permit American naval officers to investigate the *Baralong* case under Sir Edward Grey's suggestion."

The German Press sizzled with venom. The *Kölnische Volkszeitung* urged the German Government to carry out the threat it had made in the final sentence of its protest note and "to take the reprisals demanded by the German people".

In the Reichstag there were furious scenes. Count Westarp said that England was guilty of "a cowardly murder" and that the *Baralong* affair was "a monument to England's shame". The Socialist, Herr Noske, spoke in vitriolic terms of how the submariners had been killed in "a simply bestial fashion". Working himself into high passion, his tirade of invective had little to do with the point of the debate, but he was now in top soap-box gear. "The German soldiers are not descended from Africans," he ranted "whose fathers ate human flesh, and who are now led against us in the field by France and England. Our soldiers come in great part from our midst, and went through the schooling of our politics and trade unions".

By this stage the debate had wandered so far from its original theme that it almost seemed as if the *Baralong* question had been forgotten altogether. It was left to Herr Fischbeck, of the Radical Party, to drag the delegates' minds back onto the point. England had sunk "step by step", he jeered, and she was employing new weapons which "deserve the contempt of the world". The German Government had promised reprisals and he was convinced that the German army and navy possessed the power to carry them out, although, he concluded darkly, "We are not permitted to discuss here in public the method of the reprisals that are to be made."

After all this international rhetoric, the question that remained was this. "It is accepted that the submariners in the water were shot at and killed, but exactly how, and by whom, were those Germans on board the *Nicosian* put to death?"

When the marine boarding party jumped across on to the stern of the *Nicosian*, they were accompanied by Chief Engineer Brown and a carpenter (who has never been named), both members of the mule-ship's crew. They were both armed with pistols, and it is probable that one or both of these men killed at least one German. But again, the precise facts are unknown.

Gossip abounded. According to one story, told by an old Liverpool stoker who had been a member of the *Nicosian's* crew, the Germans had been "bashed on the head, lashed to planks, and stuffed up the fires". This grisly account was endorsed by a Dane named Moller. He had been an apprentice on board the mule-ship and said that they had been hoisted up and dropped head first into the ash chute several times before being thrown into the furnaces to burn alive.

Statements were made by several men which entirely refuted the accusations of the American muleteers. Two of the most forceful came from their own countrymen, Carson and Dempsey, who had joined the British Army in Liverpool. Carson said he went back on board the *Nicosian* with the marine party. He saw no Germans shot. The sound of gunfire was the shooting of wounded mules. Dempsey had nothing but praise for "Captain McBride", who had kindly given him some ointment for the burns on his hands which he had sustained when sliding down a rope into the lifeboat.

The British Consul in New Orleans, Thomas Erskine, managed to obtain statements from six other men who had sailed on the mule-ship. One, John Alexander, who, it should be noted was a carpenter, swore that "the crew of the *Nicosian* went down into the hold with a marine from the *Baralong* and found four members of the crew of the submarine dead and about an hour and a half or so later they threw the bodies overboard". Significantly, Alexander made no comment as to how the Germans had died. They were simply found dead. The other five Americans, Fred Fisher, assistant vet to Banks, Richard Goodman, Curran's assistant foreman, two seamen, Walter Coker and John Cooper, and yet another carpenter, James Lowrie, all verified Alexander's words. Was there a conspiracy of silence within the circle of carpenters?

Another story altogether was put forward by the famous author of *The Thirty Nine Steps*, John Buchan, in his book *Naval Episodes of the Great War*, and articles in both the *News of the World* and the *Daily Telegraph* agreed with him. Buchan contended that the Royal Marines had killed nobody on the *Nicosian*. What had happened was that a boatload of Germans had arrived on the *port* side of the mule-ship, i.e., out of sight of the *Baralong*, intending to place bombs on board the steamer to sink her. Several muleteers had not gone into the lifeboats, contrary to the affidavits, but had remained on board. As the Germans had climbed aboard the mule-ship, they had had their heads stove in with iron bars by these men.

Against that was a heavyweight admission of British guilt from ex-Marine Corporal Fred Collins, who made no bones about the fact that Herbert had ordered him to "take no prisoners" when he took his party on board the *Nicosian*. Collins suggests that one of the Germans was shot by either Chief Engineer Brown or the obscure carpenter, but confesses that the rest were killed by his marines and himself.

And so the tangle of stories, truths, half-truths and lies, becomes a

Gordian knot. Probably the most serious attempt to untangle it has been made by Alan Coles in his intriguing book *Slaughter at Sea*. In it he tells how he managed to obtain an interview with the man who had been Herbert's First Lieutenant, Gordon Steele. Steele had gone on to win the VC in 1919 in an operation against the Bolsheviks, accompanied by Claude Congreve Dobson, who, it will be recalled, had captained the submarine C-27, towed by the Q-trawler *Princess Marie Jose* when they sank the U-23 in July, 1915. Steele was approaching ninety years of age when he spoke to Coles in 1981. Indeed, he died only a few months later. The old man was a little vague about many of the things that had happened on that sunny day in the Western Approaches sixty-six years before, but he was perfectly lucid on others. When Herbert had given the order for a party to be formed to board the *Nicosian*, Steele had prepared himself to lead it. However, Herbert would not let him go, for some reason, and insisted that Collins take charge of the operation. As the marines departed, Herbert said to Collins, "Take no prisoners". On that fact, Coles said, Steele was definite. It was on those few words, which formed a major common factor of so many 'versions' of the truth, that Coles based his conclusion and consequently laid the blame fairly and squarely on the head of Herbert. But Steele, perhaps unknown to Coles, was contradicting himself here. On 18 August, 1960, twenty-one years before he spoke to Coles, when he was twenty-one years younger, and with a less senile memory, he had written, "Herbert called the sergeant up to the bridge, and gave him his orders, *which I do not know*, for the recapture of the *Nicosian*." (author's italics)

Herbert always insisted that he had merely advised Collins to be careful of snipers and to be sure to get in the first shot. But that is not the same as saying, "Take no prisoners," which was what Steele said he heard him say (according to Coles), what the muleteers said they heard him say and, most telling of all, what Collins not only said he heard him say but later confessed to having carried out the order.

Indeed, it may well have been the strictly legal position that Herbert was accountable for the murders of the Germans, having issued such an order. But then it follows that he could point to the fact that he, himself, was only carrying out instructions. Had not Captain Richmond of the Admiralty Special Service Branch sent for him last May, after the *Lusitania* was sunk, to tell him "take no prisoners from U-boats"?

The sub-title of Coles's book is "The Truth Behind a Naval War

42

Crime". An admirable work it may be, and it certainly makes an engrossing read, but it only goes as far as pointing the finger of *blame*. To that end, it may be technically fair, arguably, to indict Herbert (and his superiors) because of the fact that he, as the commanding officer, was *accountable*. But it does not establish any *truth* as to what actually *did* happen in the *Nicosian*. Far from it.

Corporal Collins, although he confesses to killing one of the Germans, stated that "I saw somebody disappear through an alley and into a cabin. I kicked the door open, the bloke shouted out and I shot him. He toppled over the side the moment he was shot. Herbert was standing on the bridge and saw him floating past. Herbert had a revolver in his hand and threw it in the face of the man in the water, and said, 'What about the *Lusitania* you bastard?' I don't know anything about any of them being shot in the water swimming."

Steele, who had, after all, boarded the *Nicosian*, painted an entirely different picture. He said that "Wegener ran to a cabin on the upper deck – I found out later it was Manning's bathroom. The marines broke down the door with the butts of their rifles, but Wegener squeezed himself through a scuttle and dropped into the sea. He still had his life-jacket on and put up his arms in surrender. Corporal Collins, however, took aim and shot him through the head."

Moller, the Danish apprentice, added even more contradiction with his story. According to him, Collins had simply walked up to a group of six Germans, standing with their hands up, on the upper deck of the *Nicosian*, near No. 3 hatch, and shot one of them dead. As regards the German hiding in the cabin, a marine had "battered his way in with his rifle butt and the German knocked him down and slipped out, rushing to the rail and jumping overboard. While swimming around, he was shot dead alongside a lifeboat full of jeering men."

It follows that at least two of the three, Collins, Steele and Moller, if not all three, must be lying here. Such variations render every one of the statements valueless. And as the eye-witnesses are now all dead, we are limited to what they may have said or written in their lifetimes. We can never know the truth. Not for sure.

That said, apart from Collins, Steele and Herbert himself, not one of the sixty-five men who made up the rest of the ship's company of HMS *Baralong* appears to have ever uttered a word about the affair. Sixty-five is a lot of men to keep silent. Maybe that should tell us something. Maybe Herbert had passed on to them the advice that the devious

Admiral Reginald Hall, Director of Naval Intelligence, had given him. "Look here, Herbert," Hall had said, "If you get mixed up with civilians, they'll have your guts for a neck-tie."

*　　*　　*

The wartime Q-ship adventures of the former Mercantile Fleet Auxiliary No. 5, now known as HMS *Baralong*, were not over. There was more scandal to follow, to which we will return.

The sinking of *U-27* earned Herbert the DSO but in fact, just prior to *Baralong*'s encounter with the U-boat, he had already applied to return to submarines. He was delighted when his request was granted and he was appointed to command the new boat *E-22*. Again, he took a willing Steele with him as his No. 1 and handed *Baralong* over to her new captain, Lieutenant-Commander Andrew Wilmot-Smith.

From then on Herbert's war career continued to consist of a mixture of extraordinary luck, both good and bad, plus a good measure of uncanny coincidence. He had always seen himself primarily as a submariner and went enthusiastically to work in *E-22* to prosecute the war "against the Hun". But the ill-fortune which had dogged him in *D-5* in 1914 seemed to be set to continue in *E-22* in the winter of 1915. Patrolling the German coast off the Elbe, he spied a prize of gargantuan proportions. It was nothing less than four German battle-cruisers! All were unaware of his presence and they were sitting ducks at a range of a mere 300 yards. One can imagine him with his forehead rammed to the periscope, his knuckles white as they gripped the handles, and scarcely able to breathe with the tension as he lined up the target and gave the order to fire the first torpedo. It was impossible to miss. And he did not miss. What happened was that the torpedoes would not fire at all, due to a faulty valve lock. Such opportunities rarely come twice. His exasperation must have been unbearable.

In the spring of 1916 he passed *E-22* over to Lieutenant-Commander Dimsdale and went back to Q-ship work. It was here that his luck took another strange turn. The very next day *E-22* was torpedoed by Korvettenkapitän Steinbrinck in *UB-18* and Dimsdale was killed.

Herbert's new command, HMS *Carrigan Head*, alias *Q-4*, was a 4,201-ton cargo ship, built in 1901. She had a 4-inch Mk VII gun, two 12-pounders and two 13-pounders. Her peacetime Master had been Captain Pickford, brother of Sir John Pickford of the famous removals firm. Pickford stayed on to act as Herbert's navigating officer, presumably with a temporary commission. They sailed on 10 July, 1916, to patrol the waters that Herbert knew so well – the Western Approaches. For seven weeks they scoured the sea for U-boats, but saw not a trace of one. It was a repeat of the endless plodding around that he had done the year before.

All that changed on 9 September. *Carrigan Head* was engaged on her usual trudge up and down the threshold to the Atlantic and was about sixty miles west of Brest when a U-boat surfaced and shelled her, putting her wireless out of action and killing one sailor and wounding two others, including the Engineering Officer, Jim Purdy. It was *UC-65*, commanded by none other than Steinbrinck, who had sunk *E-22*. Rashly, Herbert dropped his disguise by giving the order to open fire at a range of about a mile. In showing his hand, he lost his chance, because the U-boat dived, as far as is known, undamaged. *Carrigan Head* raced to the spot and mounted a depth-charge attack. But yet again Herbert was to display his proneness to disaster. The explosion erupted too close to the ship, with such jarring force that one of her guns fired itself accidentally, wrecking much of her upper-works and wounding another sailor.

His career continued to oscillate between submarines and Q-ships. In September, 1916, he took command of the submarine *K-13*. These 1,800-ton steam-driven boats, the K-class, were notorious death-traps, and to tempt providence, Herbert had drawn number 13. On 29 January, 1917, she was on trials in the Clyde estuary and failed to surface after a practice dive. She rested on the bottom, sixty-odd feet down, and by the next day the air supply was running low. Herbert and his friend Lieutenant-Commander Goodhart tried a method of escape which they had worked out together. It involved Goodhart shooting through a hatch and Herbert quickly closing it behind him. But in the event both of them were sucked out of the boat in a giant bubble of air. Herbert rocketed to the surface, but Goodhart was killed as he hurtled upwards and his head smashed against *K-13*'s bridge. It was the second time that Herbert had been in a crashed submarine, the third if one includes the mined *D-5*. It was amazing that he had such love for them when they had brought him so much failure and so near to death.

Their Lordships agreed that Herbert was better off staying away from submarines and, in yet another swing of the pendulum, he found himself in his sixth command in less than three years. It was back to surface sub-hunting again, this time operating a flotilla of trawlers. Patrolling off The Lizard in June, 1917, their hydrophones picked up a telltale note. It was *UC-66*, commanded by Pustkuchen. Herbert laid an enormous pattern of dozens of depth-charges, making the sea erupt into huge white mushrooms over a wide area. One depth-charge, from the trawler *Sea King*, hit the submarine, almost certainly square-on. Six loud explosions were heard, which probably meant that *UC-66*'s unlaid mines had detonated in their chutes. Not surprisingly no wreckage came to the surface, although a large lake of oil did appear. In May, 1919, Herbert was officially credited with the 'kill' and awarded a bar to his DSO.

But to return to the story of the *Baralong*, Herbert and Steele departed to their submarine and Wilmot-Smith took command, but little else changed. She still carried much the same crew, with Fred Collins in charge of the marines, and she still patrolled much the same waters to the west of the Scillies, where the U-boat piranha packs continued to feast on rich commons.

The morning of 24 September, 1915, found *Baralong* cruising about sixty miles to the south-west of Bishop Rock. The sea was calm and visibility was perfect, just as it had been when the Q-ship had met up with the *U-27* and the *Nicosian*. Now, of course, the mangled submarine was in her tomb on the ocean floor and the *Nicosian* was thousands of miles away, approaching the hurricane-threatened Caribbean on her way to New Orleans for more mules.

Wilmot-Smith was heading west. *Baralong*'s deck crew were enjoying the warmth of the late summer morning sun on their backs when suddenly a shout went up. Dead ahead, six miles off, was a blazing ship. And she was sinking. They could see lifeboats full of men pulling away from her. Nearby, sitting admiring its handiwork like a smug artist looking at his finished painting, was a German submarine. She was the *U-41*.

Kapitänleutnant Klaus Hansen had had three exciting cruises in *U-41*. On the first, in mid-July, he had almost been rammed by the minesweeper HMS *Speedwell* when she had tagged him north of the Shetlands. No serious damage had been done, at least not to the boat's hull, but he could not operate unseen without a periscope, and both of *U-41*'s twin "eyes" had been put out of action by *Speedwell*'s keel. In an admirable display of seamanship, Hansen had been forced to sail her "blind" back to Wilhelmshaven for repairs.

The second foray, less than a fortnight later, had also brought its share of danger, incurred by Hansen's own impatience. This time it involved a Q-ship, the tiny 198-ton steam trawler HMS *Pearl*, GY 1121, alias *Ruby*, GY 1136, which operated out of Stornoway under Sub-Lieutenant Allman, RNR, armed with a single 6-pounder.

Pearl was off the southern tip of the Outer Hebrides when Hansen spotted her. Once more on his way to richer pickings farther south, he should have left alone such an unattractive target. Instead, he decided that he would take her, and fired a shot across the bows of the trawler. All that earned him was a return shot which splashed unpleasantly close. Hansen was scornful. The British ship probably had nothing more than a 'popgun', he thought. He decided to have some fun with her and ordered his gunnery officer, Oberleutnant Iwan Crompton, to pepper her with a few more shells. But then a shout went up from the U-boat's helmsman that her steering had jammed and *Pearl* was charging towards them, flat out at seven knots, spitting out a venomous stream of shells as she came. She was little more than half a mile away when two of them struck the submarine, severely wounding Schmidt, the officer-of-the-watch. Unable either to steer or to dive, U-41 was a sitting duck. With seconds to spare before *Pearl*'s stubby bows would have rammed her, somehow or other the U-boat's crew got the steering back into operation and she crash-dived. But her plates had been damaged by the shell-fire and she was letting in water badly. His pumps were unable to cope if he dived deeper than periscope depth, because the increase in pressure forced the water in all the more quickly. Hansen decided simply to sit still and hope that the little Q-ship would go away. He risked a peep, but the *Pearl* was still there. Indeed, when her gunners saw his periscope, they managed to shoot it off. Once more, Hansen was "blind".

Still at periscope depth, he turned away, but he was leaving a trail of oil on the water, and it was easy for Allman to track him. For eight hours *Pearl* dogged U-41, waiting for her to surface and to receive the inevitable *coup de grace* that awaited her. But Lady Luck was on Hansen's side again. Allman's engineer insisted that he abandon the chase to enable a faulty pump to be fixed. The German had got away, but the hue and cry was up for him. Hansen managed to elude the Royal Navy and made it back to Wilhelmshaven. But this time it was not only the boat which needed attention. Her crew, including Hansen himself, was in such a state of nervous exhaustion that they were ordered to take special leave to recuperate.

It was not until 12 September that they were able to sail on their third attempt to reach the Western Approaches, where they were to relieve *U-20*, sinker of the *Lusitania*. This time they made it to the hunting ground, but they were almost baulked again. The Kaiser had called off the U-boat campaign, but *U-41* was by then beyond wireless range and the order was never received. Or did Hansen choose not to hear it? After so many setbacks, he was told to come home just as he was about to start work! It would have been tempting for him to have been 'deaf'. If, in fact, that is what he did, it was a decision which was to cost him his life.

23 September had been a field day in "U-boat Alley" for *U-41*. In mid-morning she had sunk the horse transport ship *Anglo-Columbian*, 4,750 tons, about seventy-five miles south-east of the Fastnet Rock. In early evening the steamer *Chancellor* was dispatched to the depths, and just before nightfall a 3,500-ton freighter, the *Hissione*, gave Hansen a hat-trick.

Brimful of confidence, and not of course knowing that Admiral Sir Lewis Bayly was about to dispatch *Baralong* from Falmouth with special orders to Wilmot-Smith to hunt down the killer of the three merchant ships, Hansen ran south through the night. Dawn found him seventy miles south-west of the Scillies, ready for another day's work. It started well. Along came the Wilson Line's 6,500-ton freighter *Urbino*, on her way to Hull from New York. Was it really this easy after all? The complete British merchant fleet now seemed to be falling straight into Hansen's lap. He ordered the steamer's master, Captain Allanson Hicks, to stop and abandon her prior to sinking. From a distance of two hundred yards Crompton had no difficulty in hitting the target. Five shells were all that it took to set the *Urbino* on fire and start to sink. She was rolling over, ready to go down, when Hansen spotted another ship approaching from the east. Yet another victim! This was all too good to be true. On *U-41*'s outer casing, her crew gave a final round of abusive jeers to Allanson Hicks and his crew of forty-two as they pulled away in their lifeboats. Then they ran to throw themselves down the conning-tower hatch. The last one of them disappeared and the lid slammed down. Hansen had ordered a crash dive. *U-41* vanished from view and steered a course which would close the distance with the stranger. Hansen, of course, was unaware of the ironic fact that he was setting off to stalk the very ship that had been sent out to kill him. Surfacing a couple of miles from her, he could see her more

48

plainly. She was wearing the black and brown livery of the Great Eastern Railway Company, although it is unlikely that he would have been familiar with such a technicality. And even if he had been aware that he was approaching a Q-ship, the fact that it was the *Baralong* would have had no special significance for him, because the scandal surrounding her sinking of *U-27* had not yet erupted. He raced *U-41* towards her, noting that she was flying the Stars and Stripes of the still neutral USA. He signalled her to stop and she lowered a boat, ostensibly to bring an officer over with her papers. The two vessels sat riding the swell, while Hansen waited patiently in his squat conning-tower. The U-boat had swung, conveniently presenting a broadside view to the cargo ship, when suddenly all hell broke loose.

A torrent of concentrated rifle-fire spewed down from Collins and his marines, high on the after well-deck of the freighter. Hansen shouted, "It's a trap-ship! Dive! Dive!" *Baralong*'s big guns then opened up as Crompton and his gun's crew tore along the deck in frantic haste for the shelter of the conning-tower, but before they could get there two shells crashed into it, ripping a gaping hole in its base. Hansen and six men were blown to smithereens by the blast, and Crompton, who had somehow managed to get halfway into the conning-tower, lay stunned. His left eye had been shot out and he had a great yawning gash across his forehead. *U-41* was doomed. At that precise moment the valves had been opened to flood her ballast tanks in response to Hansen's order to dive. She plunged towards the bottom within seconds, bows first, taking the unconscious Crompton with her.

Not many men can have been as close to death as Crompton was that day and lived to tell the tale. In the darkness of the deep, the mutilated submarine's diving tanks suddenly emitted a huge billow of compressed air, creating a giant bubble within which she shot back up to the surface like a cork. Such was the impetus of her rise that it thrust her fore-part completely out of the water. Crompton was jettisoned clear and into the sea, and she disappeared again. It had all taken place in a matter of moments.

By now Crompton had recovered enough of his senses to arouse his survival instinct. He tried to swim towards the *Baralong*, but she was already turning away. The White Ensign now hung from her stern. Kept afloat by his life-jacket, and barely conscious, he waited to die, but after about an hour, or so it seemed, he heard the steady drumming of a ship's engines. She had come back! He raised his arms to attract

49

attention, but she surged straight past, with her crew hurling cat-calls down at him, just as his own men had done to those of the *Urbino* only a few hours before. Buffeted by the residue of her bow-wave and wake, he watched her go. Now he was sure he was going to die. But then something caught the corner of his one remaining eye. It was a boat, empty and drifting aimlessly, with the gentle wavelets of the calm Atlantic quietly smacking its sides. It was one of *Urbino*'s lifeboats, abandoned after the *Baralong* had taken her survivors on board. It took his last ounce of energy to heave himself over her side and he lay there gasping, faint from loss of blood and the effects of shock. Then he heard another sound. It was a cry. Painfully hoisting himself up to peer over the gunwale, he saw that it was Godau, *U-41*'s helmsman, who, as it turned out, was the only other survivor. The weakened Crompton could do little more than dangle his arms over the side for the man to pull himself aboard.

Baralong did eventually rescue them, but not before she had provided them with another fright. They heard her returning. She was steaming at speed. They stood up, shakily, and waved their arms. She turned towards them, but did not slow down as she drew nearer. Crompton could see a sailor in her prow waving his arms. The German was unsure what message the man was trying to convey. Was the sailor directing his helmsman so as to run them down? The bows of the freighter loomed huge as they surged towards the helpless pair. "Jump!" yelled Crompton, and the two Germans hurled themselves into the sea. The long ship swept on and they were sucked down under the twisting foam created by her wash. Gasping as they surfaced, they managed to grab the side of the lifeboat and hung there as she bobbed and danced until the turbulence subsided. Slowly they managed to haul themselves back into the boat. A little while later *Baralong* returned yet again. This time she was steaming at a more sedate pace and slowed as she drew alongside them. Voices called out, ropes were thrown down and the two Germans were hoisted aboard.

Marine Corporal Fred Collins was to play a major part in the aftermath of the sinking of *U-41*, just as he had done in that of *U-27*. Only now it was a very different Fred Collins from the one which had shot unarmed Germans just five weeks before. He was ordered to take charge of the two prisoners and lock them in the sheep-pen on *Baralong*'s upper deck. Crompton, in particular, was in a hideous state. His empty left eye-socket was a dark staring hole and the deep furrow across his temple still oozed blood, which covered his face like a scarlet veil. Collins brought hot Bovril from the galley and applied Vaseline, good and thick, to Crompton's injuries. The narrow sheep-pen was open to the chill of the night and Collins wedged himself on the mattress alongside the wounded man to shield him as best he could.

Just before midnight an officer awoke Collins to enquire whether Crompton was dead. Collins replied that the man was alive, but would not survive much longer without treatment. The officer then told Collins that Wilmot-Smith did not intend taking the Germans into port and if Crompton was not dead by midnight Collins was ordered to shoot them both. Collins was not averse to killing the enemy in battle. He had been trained, as a marine, to do just that. But the awareness of what he had done on board the *Nicosian* now affected him greatly. He bridled at the officer's words. "I can't do it, sir," he said firmly, "And what's more I shan't give the order to any of my men." It came as a relief when the officer returned later and informed him that Wilmot-Smith had decided, after all, to take the Germans into Falmouth.

The south Cornish coast was lagged with a thick fog as *Baralong* arrived off Falmouth in the early hours of the next morning. A trawler was awaiting her in the roads with two intelligence officers on board. They delivered sealed orders to Wilmot-Smith. He was instructed that HMS *Baralong* had made her last voyage as such. With immediate effect she was to operate under a new name. She was now HMS *Wyandra*.

Crompton was in no condition to be interrogated, but a terrified Godau, convinced that he was about to be shot, blurted out all he knew about *U-41*. Meanwhile Collins requested permission to take Crompton to the captain's bathroom to clean him up. "That bloody German's not using my bath," was the reply.

Eventually, after all *Urbino*'s wounded sailors had received medical attention, the doctors came to look at Crompton at about midday. They patched him up, but he was retained on board until it was deemed that he was in a fit state to be questioned. Two days later he was brought before a captain from Naval Intelligence, but steadfastly refused to give more information than his name and rank. He then stayed in a military hospital in Falmouth for nine days before being taken to Devonport naval detention quarters.

It was reassuring to find Godau already there, but Crompton's wounds were troubling him, and as yet he had only received the most cursory medical attention. He complained about this, and a fuller investigation revealed that he had, in fact, sustained worse injuries than had been realized. Besides the loss of his eye and the wound in his head, his jaw was fractured. And X-rays revealed a brass screw still embedded in his skull and several bits of glass lodged in his eye socket. These were removed and he spent the next month in Devonport Naval Hospital. Later he was taken to a prison in York, and then just before Christmas to Dyffryn, on the Welsh coast on Barmouth Bay, which was the main camp housing U-boat prisoners. From there he wrote to the American Embassy in London, alleging that the *Baralong* had misused the US flag in her attack on *U-41*, and complaining about the shabby treatment he had received from his captors. Despite repeated letters, he never received a reply.

The second *Baralong* episode, although known of at senior Government level, was kept firmly under wraps. But languishing in Dyffryn there was Crompton, pestering to be repatriated under an arrangement whereby certain German officers could be sent for intern-ment in Switzerland if their medical condition were considered sufficiently grave. A team of Red Cross doctors visited the camp in May. They recommended that Crompton be interned in Switzerland, but after he was examined by a further medical board (composed mainly of British doctors) a fortnight later, it was decided that he was not unfit enough to go. For reasons which are not entirely clear, the mind of officialdom was eventually changed and it was finally decided to release Crompton to Switzerland after all, where he arrived in early November, 1916. It did not take long for the bitter German to contact his country's Press, and the very next day saw the resurrection of HMS *Baralong* as a hot news item.

The German Press seems to have given up hope, by this time, of ever getting the Americans to condemn the British for improper use of their flag. Their clarion headlines made almost no comment on this running sore of an issue. Instead, they devoted themselves to firing acerbic broadsides, peppered with words such as "atrocious", "brutality" and "savage", based on the allegations that the Royal Navy had been given orders not to rescue U-boat crews in distress, and that the imprisoned Crompton, having failed to oblige the British by dying from his wounds, had been intentionally obstructed from communicating his complaints to the outside world. In other words, they had withheld his letters to the US Ambassador.

From Whitehall the Admiralty rumbled out an instant reply. "The facts are perfectly simple," their Lordships growled, "On the morning of 24 September, 1915, in the western Channel, the *U-41* was engaged in sinking a British merchant steamer. While she was so engaged, a converted merchant vessel, commissioned as one of HM auxiliary ships, approached the submarine and the sinking vessel. Her character was not at once recognized and in order that the submarine would not submerge before she was within range, she hoisted neutral colours – a perfectly legitimate *ruse de guerre*. When within range, she hoisted the White Ensign, as all British ships of war are required to do, fired on and sank the submarine. The immediate preoccupation of her commander was to rescue the crew of the British vessel sunk by the submarine, who had been compelled to take to their boats fifty miles from the nearest port. When this had been done, HM ship closed one of the boats of the sunken steamer, which had broken adrift, into which two survivors of the submarine's crew had climbed. These were rescued in the same way as, but after, their victims . . .

The statement that the Admiralty has ever issued orders that survivors of German submarines need not be rescued is an absolute lie and was explicitly denied in the note of His Majesty's Government on the *Baralong* case dated 25th February 1916."

Wilmot-Smith himself made two written reports on the incident. In the first he said, "One of the *Urbino*'s boats when cleared got loose and drifted astern. On going to it later, we discovered that two Germans had got in. There were no signs of them in the water previously. Unfortunately, having got all of the crew of the *Urbino* on board, and not knowing if they (Crompton and Godau) were to be trusted we had to pick them up; they could not have been left in the boat in case they should have been picked up by a neutral ship."

His second statement was made in reply to the accusations of ramming the lifeboat which were hurled at him by the German Press. "On approaching this boat," he declared, "my attention was temporarily distracted from the work in hand, and I suddenly realized that the ship had too much weight on. I immediately reversed engines, at the same time putting the helm hard a port. The boat was not struck by the ship and came past along the port side. The prisoners, however, when the boat in which they were was some twenty yards from my bows, both dived overboard. The boat was in no way damaged."

He went on to insist that the Germans had been treated fairly. The sheep-pens in which they had been confined had never been used as such, and the doctor who visited the prisoners in Falmouth had considered them to be suitable accommodation. The Germans had been given dry clothing and ample blankets and bedding. Godau had behaved in a compliant way, but Crompton had acted in a surly fashion "probably due to the seriousness of his wounds".

The ex-*Baralong*, now *Wyandra*, was transferred to the Mediterranean to assist in combating the growing U-boat problem in that theatre. The Navy finally discharged her from its service on 9 November, 1916, and she resumed life as a merchant vessel known as the *Manica*.

As for Herbert's decision to adopt the *nom de guerre* 'Captain McBride' when in command of the *Baralong*, what are we to make of it, if anything? In *Slaughter at Sea* Alan Coles goes to some lengths to add it to a welter of circumstantial evidence which is all slanted towards drenching Herbert with a deluge of guilt in connection with the killings of the Germans on board the *Nicosian*. But is it possible that he may have read too much into Herbert's use of the name? Did Herbert ever seriously intend it as a subterfuge? Consider these facts. We do not know exactly when Herbert told Steele to address him as 'McBride', and Steele was understandably vague about many things. Herbert was certainly 'McBride' to Captain Manning and the crew of the mule-ship. It follows that Herbert's conversation with Steele must have taken place *before* the encounter with the *Nicosian*, which was only three months *after* the sinking of the *Lusitania* off the Old Head of Kinsale, which in turn had been only weeks after the *Baralong* had been commissioned. And revenge for the *Lusitania* had been sworn by many a British sailor. Remember that Herbert commanded a decoy ship, and the annals of naval history contain many mentions of decoys. One, in particular, is of special interest.

Sometime in the 1780s a 64-gun man o' war, HMS *Bienfaisant*, came across a convoy of British cargo ships. Among them was a French warship, the *Comte d'Artois*, also of 64 guns, which was about to embark on a feast of destruction. The French captain, a certain Monsieur Clonard, tried to decoy HMS *Bienfaisant* by hoisting the Union Jack. This did not fool the British captain. He placed his ship in a position on the Frenchman's bow, where Clonard could not bring his guns to bear, and opened a raking fire with such effect that the latter was compelled to strike his colours, with a loss of twenty-one killed and thirty-five wounded. The place? Off the Old Head of Kinsale. The name of the British captain? McBride. A coincidence? Maybe. Herbert's career had already seen many strange coincidences. Why not one more? Or could it be that the Dartmouth-educated Herbert had recalled his naval history lessons well and that his grim humour was as lost on Steele as it has been with others?

Chapter 5

1916
Twelve Months of
Hide-and-Seek.

All through the winter of 1915–16 the Q-ships rolled around the grey heaving wastes of the seas of north-western Europe, hoping to be attacked by U-boats, but not a sign of one was seen. The Germans were lying low, although in fact the Kaiser lost four submarines without the Allies even needing to fire a shot. In October *UC-9* blew herself up when laying mines off the Long Sand Light Vessel. On 4 November *UC-8* was on her way from Emden to the U-boat pens at Zeebrugge when she ran aground off Terschelling, on the neutral Dutch coast, and was interned. On 29 November *UC-13* was on patrol out of Constantinople when her compass failed during a storm and she ran aground on the north Turkish coast. And in broad daylight on the afternoon of 16 March, 1916, the submerged *UC-12* was laying mines in Taranto harbour, on the southern coast of Italy, when she too blew herself up. When divers went down later to examine the wreck in 100 feet of water, they found papers which, somewhat ironically, had warned the U-boat captain, Frohner, about the danger from British decoy ships. The loss of four submarines had to be seen as a setback, but Germany had ordered 100 more during the previous year of which fifty-two were completed.

On 4 March, 1916, the Kaiser relented to pressures from the Reichstag to permit the unleashing of unrestricted submarine warfare. The date was fixed for 1 April, but the campaign was not carried through because of the enthusiasm of the trigger-happy captain of *U-29*, which torpedoed and sank the cross-Channel packet *Sussex* on 24 March with considerable loss of life, including that of some American passengers. This brought another bout of indignation against Germany from the USA. The upshot was that, under American diplomatic threats, orders were issued to U-boat captains on 24 April that the formal Prize Laws must be strictly observed. Before enemy merchant ships could be sunk in future they must be stopped, have their papers examined and all passengers and crew taken off safely. The German Navy chiefs, especially Admiral Scheer, objected, saying that it would put their submarines in unwarranted danger, given that a British patrol vessel could easily come on the scene while the U-boat was carrying out this unnecessary ceremony. Nevertheless, during that month the U-boats had already sunk another 141,000 tons of British merchant shipping.

At last Campbell's men were suddenly jerked into action after their cold, wet and windy winter of excruciating boredom in the wilderness of the Western Approaches. On the morning of 22 March *Farnborough* was cruising to the west of Ireland. Campbell had just finished his cup of coffee in the saloon when the Officer of the Watch announced, "Torpedo coming, sir." A straight streak of bubbles was about to cross *Farnborough*'s bows. Campbell rang the bell for 'action stations'. A submarine's grey conning tower rose into view astern. It was *U-68*. Her gun's crew were out on the gleaming wet casing and ready to fire almost before she had fully surfaced. A shot splashed into the sea. Campbell stopped immediately and blew off steam, while the panic party clicked into their well-rehearsed theatrical routine, scrambling hither and thither and falling into the lifeboats. It worked perfectly. The U-boat captain, Guntzel, moved closer and from about 800 yards fired another shot which was barely short of where it would have hit the Q-ship's magazine.

For Campbell the classic instant had arrived; the fate of all concerned in the drama would swing on the cusp of his decision. *U-68*'s shot had been perilously close and the panic party had not yet even left the ship. "Let go!" came his words down the voice-pipes and immediately *Farnborough*'s guns were flashing as they hurled 12-pound shells at the grey shape in the water. Guntzel tried to dive, but it was too late. *U-68* had been holed several times within seconds and she sank, stern first. The Q-ship raced to where the submarine had disappeared and dropped depth charges. The sea boiled white and a column of water shot into the air, bringing with it *U-68*. It hung there in the water, with its bows pointing up at the sky like a giant angler's float, until more shells from the after-gun of the Q-ship sent it back, almost mercifully, to the bottom of the Atlantic.

Only a matter of hours earlier *Farnborough*'s crew had been composed of some of the darkest pessimists in the human race. All winter they had not seen a single U-boat. They had become convinced that they never would. In a flash all that had changed. Campbell mustered the ship's company and read the Prayer of Thanksgiving for Victory from the Prayer Book. Then he called for three cheers for His Majesty King George the Fifth and sent everybody back to 'cruising stations'. From down below wafted the wobbly strains of a gramophone record. It was 'Down among the Dead Men let him Lie' (see over).

The rest of the year 1916 proved to be fairly quiet for the decoy ships, although in other areas many memorable events were shortly to take place – the Easter Rising in Dublin, the Battle of Jutland and the Battle of the Somme, to name but three.

However, that is not to say that everybody went into hibernation. On 12 April a torpedo narrowly missed HMS *Zylpha*. Her lookouts spied a periscope, but the submarine dived and did not reappear. McLeod knew that his ship had obviously undergone close inspection by the enemy and hurried to a quiet anchorage in Bantry Bay, off Whiddly Island, where he hurriedly altered her disguise. The little 59-ton Lowestoft smack *Cheerio*, alias *Mascot*, or actually the *Energic*, LT 1195, caught a U-boat in her mined nets, possibly *UB-13*, on 24 April. The following day a U-boat sank the *King Stephen*, GY1174, a little Grimsby trawler which had infuriated the Kaiser earlier by refusing to pick up the survivors from a crashed Zeppelin.

The *Redbreast*, a 1,300-ton Fleet Messenger, had an exchange with a submarine in the Cerigo Channel in the Mediterranean on 16 July. The Dutch-built *Helgoland*, a 182-ton brigantine, now owned by Messrs H & G Grayson of Liverpool, actually engaged two U-boats with her four 12-pounders and a Maxim off the Lizard on 24 October. Two torpedoes passed beneath her, but the old sailing ship escaped damage with her shallow draught of only eight feet.

With November came a flurry of action. On the 2nd the *Saros*, alias the *Bradford City*, or the *Ballistan*, a big 3,483-ton collier, carrying two 4-inch guns, one 3-pounder and a Maxim tackled a U-boat in the Mediterranean. One of the purpose-built convoy sloops, the *Viola*, had duels with unidentified U-boats twice, on 23 and 29 November. And on the 29th the steamer *Wileyside* had the distinction of being saved from a German submarine by the intervention of a famous Q-ship HMS *Penshurst*.

It was the start of an action-packed war for *Penshurst*. She had waited ever since the previous autumn for action, as had most of the other decoys. But now her captain, Commander F.H. Grenfell, had received reports that a U-boat had been seen proceeding down-Channel and set a course which he hoped would bring him into contact with her. It was a fine morning, just after half-past seven, with the sun starting to push its way through the grey late-November dawn and with barely a ripple on the surface of the sea. Grenfell was aware of the presence, fine on his port bow, of the *Wileyside*. She was about seven miles off and heading up-Channel, on the opposite track to *Penshurst*. There was also a sailing ship, hull-down on the starboard bow, which would put her somewhere off the Lizard.

Suddenly the lookout reported a small object on the port beam some five miles off. It was difficult for him to identify it against the shimmering sheen of the calm Channel, but at 7.52 a.m. it saved him the trouble by introducing itself with a couple of shells, one well over, but the other only a few yards short of the Q-ship. That put paid to any doubt. It was a U-boat.

Grenfell slowed to about five knots and changed course away from the submarine, as if making for Falmouth, hoping to induce it to chase him. But the German had decided that he had easier pickings in the *Wileyside* and turned towards her.

Grenfell changed course yet again, this time by a full ninety degrees to port, to bring his ship back on a path directly towards, and between, the submarine and the *Wileyside*. This brought an instant reaction from the German captain and another shell splashed into the sea 200 yards short of the *Penshurst*. Grenfell stopped his engines and the panic party went into their clumsy act. It was 8.12 a.m. The U-boat closed to 3,000 yards, with three of her officers perched in the conning tower, carefully studying *Penshurst* through their binoculars. They seemed uncertain. After eight minutes, which seemed a hundred times longer to the Q-ship's stock-still gun crews, it was clear that the sub was not going to come any closer. It was a stand-off. There was only one thing that Grenfell could do. He opened fire. The *Penshurst*'s 12-pounder, 6-pounder and 3-pounder all barked in unison, but they only had time to loose off a few rounds before the U-boat disappeared, presumably

DOWN AMONG THE DEAD MEN.

Words by
DYER.

Music
About 1700.

Here's a health to the King, and a last-ing peace; To
Let charm-ing beau-ty's health go round, In

fac-tion an end, to wealth in-crease; Come, let's drink it
whom ce-les-tial joys are found, May con-fu-sion

undamaged. Grenfell raced his ship to the spot where his adversary had submerged and dropped depth-charges, but no wreckage or oil came to the surface. She had escaped. As had the fortunate *Wileyside*.

But the German captain had had a good look at *Penshurst* and she had now revealed that her true purpose in life was not to hump cargo but to sink U-boats. He would have made careful note of all her various characteristics, and radioed out a full description of her.

By now Grenfell had had a further report of the sighting of another German submarine five miles off the coast of Alderney. Presumably it was lurking there hoping to attack merchant shipping bound for Cherbourg and Le Havre. He headed off in that direction. But it was imperative to do something about his identity before being spotted by any inquisitive periscopes, and when darkness fell he slowed to a crawl and all hands set-to. It was a completely different ship which sailed into the mid-Channel dawn on 30 November, 1916. Her funnel was a different colour, her collapsible mizzen mast had disappeared and she now wore a white canvas apron around her lower bridge.

Shortly before noon a wireless message was intercepted from the Weymouth-Guernsey packet-boat *Ibex* warning shipping that she had just spotted a submarine diving twenty miles north-west of the Casquets, an outcrop of rocks to the west of Alderney. Grenfell crammed on speed and at 1.50 p.m. the lookout reported a submarine on the surface, five miles to the south. She was chasing a fleeing steamer. Before he could do anything, a sea-plane appeared overhead. It circled above the U-boat, its engine throbbing, and dropped a bomb, whereupon the submarine dived. The aircraft was British Seaplane No. 8379, out of Portland, piloted by Flight-Sub-Lieutenant J. R. Ross with his wireless operator/observer J. Redman. It was 2.22 p.m. Grenfell signalled his identity to the sea-plane and Ross brought her down to sit on the water alongside the *Penshurst*. From the air it was likely that Ross would be able to see the outline of the submerged U-boat. They arranged that the sea-plane would act as 'spotter' and guide the Q-ship into a position to drop her depth-charges. The sea-plane roared off across the water to take off, but almost immediately disaster struck, and it crashed into the sea, breaking a wing and snapping off its floats. It began to sink. Luckily *Penshurst*'s gig was on the spot within minutes and rescued Ross and Redman. *Penshurst* was in the process of grappling the 'plane, to swing it inboard, when three rapidly fired shells splashed into the water about 200 yards ahead. The submarine had resurfaced and was sitting about 6,000 yards away on the port quarter. The little sea-plane was unhooked from the derrick and sank within seconds. It was 3.14 p.m.

In his report, Grenfell said,

"The submarine overhauled slowly, firing at intervals, and at 4.12 p.m. when she was within 1,000 yards of us, I stopped engines, the boat party abandoned ship and the two boats pulled away to starboard. The submarine now took a sheer out to port and came round in a sweep on our port beam, passed clear under the stern (with the object, I learned later from her officers, of obtaining the ship's papers from her Master, whom they assumed would be in one of the boats, before boarding the ship and sinking her with explosives) and at 4.26 p.m., when she was on our starboard quarter and all our guns were bearing, I opened fire at 250 yards range.

"As the attention of all on the deck of the submarine was directed to our boats, no one was by her gun, and no attempt was made to return our fire. I was told that our second shot, fired from the starboard three-pounder, penetrated the engine-room and prevented diving. At this short range our guns were able to work at their maximum rapidity, nearly every shot took effect, the hull was riddled with holes, large parts of the conning tower and hull plating were blown away by the twelve-pound lyddite shells and the submarine sank, bows first, at 4.36 p.m.

"The survivors of the crew on board were taken off by the boats just before the submarine foundered, and those who had jumped overboard were picked up.

"I desire to bring to your notice the admirable steadiness displayed by all hands during the rather trying time (nearly an hour) we were being shelled without replying. Fortunately, we were not hit, though a shell cut the whistle lanyard."

The submarine was the *UB-19*, one of the newly developed little 260-tonners, specially designed for coastal operations and working out of Zeebrugge. Her captain, Niemeyer, had slipped out of the pens on 22 November, with four torpedoes nestling in her bow tubes, and winkled his way past the Dover Barrage to begin a three-week patrol. *UB-19* had already disposed of a Norwegian steamer with one of her torpedoes before her fatal meeting with *Penshurst*. Grenfell rescued sixteen of her crew, including three officers, Noodt, Bartel and Eigler, but the remaining seven were presumed either drowned or killed by gunfire. Indeed, no fewer than eighty-three shells had been fired at

UB-19. HMS *Penshurst* had chalked up her first success, which earned Grenfell the DSO.

The year 1916 was drawing to a close. There had been some mighty events in its course, which were to be well-chronicled and remembered for ever. But, stupendous as they were, these localized battles were as mere cymbal clashes in the symphony which was being played around the globe. It was these mundane affairs, in their dozens, which provided the continual bass-voiced rumble of the general grind of the conflict. The Royal Navy's campaign against the U-boats was part of this.

During 1916 more and more commercial ships of all shapes and sizes had been requisitioned by the Navy, some of which were to enjoy very short lives. There was the Elders and Fyffes banana boat, *Barranca*, Herbert's *Carrigan Head* and *Princess Ena*, the *Wonganella* and the *Perugia*, which was torpedoed and sunk by *U-63* in the Gulf of Genoa on 3 December; the big colliers *Djerissa*, *Maresfield*, *Dunclutha*, and the *Harmonic*, out of Cardiff, the *Hartside*, from Tyneside, all 3,000–4,000 tonners, and the cargo liner *Intaba*, pushing 5,000 tons, from the Union Steamship Co. of New Zealand, which had a tussle with a U-boat off Murmansk, far away from the usual Q-ship track, on 8 December. There were the little smacks, the *Telesia*, which destroyed *UC-3* in its mined nets off Zeebrugge on 23 April, 1916, the *Fame, I'll Try, Holkar*, (which was lost in a collision on 19 November) and the *Thalia*, only 32 tons, all from Lowestoft, the *Fizzer* out of Leith, the *Strumble* and the *Kemes* from Milford Haven, the steam trawler *Asama*, belonging to Neale & West of Cardiff, the tug *Earl of Powis* and the coaster *Lady Olive* from Teesside.

The Admiralty had had some evolutionary ideas. Some were good, others were not. They took several sloops that had originally been designed as convoy escorts and converted their appearances to resemble 1,000-ton tramp steamers. They were the famous Flower Class corvettes. HMS *Aubretia, Heather, Salvia, Tamarisk, Tulip* and *Viola* were among the first, with many more to come. Another idea, which was astonishingly ill-conceived, was to allocate a number of the decoy ships with a Q "name". Now, despite all the painstaking care taken by the captains and crews of the decoys to preserve the cloak of secrecy which was so absolutely essential to the success of their efforts, the whole world and his proverbial wife knew who they were. The *Perugia*, *Intaba*, *Barranca*, and *Carrigan Head* became HMS *Q-1, 2, 3* and *4* respectively. Campbell's *Farnborough* was HMS *Q-5*. And so on. The idea was soon dropped and the frequently-changed-name system was re-adopted. But by then the damage had been done. Hitherto, they had been known as decoy-ships, or mystery-ships. The Germans called them "trap ships". But now they would be known to history as Q-ships.

The fundamental principle of the Q-ship was to deceive the enemy. The object was to present him with an apparently harmless prey. And the more apparently harmless the prey, the more effective the deception. What better, then, than an old sailing-ship as the prey?

And so, during the course of 1916, a tidy little armada had joined *Helgoland* and the other sailing Q-ships. There was the 224-ton barquentine *Gaelic*, Q22, belonging to W. Thomas & Sons of Amlwch, Anglesey. There was the Boulogne lugger *Bayard*, Q20, the three-masted schooner *Result*, Q23, owned by Clark's of Barnstaple, Devon, which had two torpedo tubes in addition to her guns, the brigantine *Ready*, Q30, already fifty years old, which sailed out of Granton, Edinburgh, and the modest little 150-ton coasting ketch *Sarah Colebrooke*, which went to war under the name of HMS *Bolham*, from the ancient Sussex sea-port of Rye. And there were two that were to become renowned U-boat fighters. They were the *Mary B. Mitchell*, Q9, and the *Prize*, Q21.

Almost certainly, there can never have been a ship which, in the course of its life, boasted as many names and identities as the 210-ton three-masted steel schooner *Mary B. Mitchell*. Owned by Lord Penrhyn, she had been built in 1892 at Carrickfergus, and happened to be at Falmouth in mid-April, 1916, picking up a cargo of china clay, when the call came from the Admiralty saying that she was required as a Q-ship. They gave her a 12-pounder, which was hidden beneath a false deck-house on the poop deck, two 6-pounders, one under each of the hatch-covers on swinging mountings, two Lewis guns, rifles and hand grenades.

Such was the perfection of her disguise on her first patrol out of Falmouth, now painted black with a fancy yellow line around her midriff and the legend, *Mary y Jose* Vigo, written on her stern, that when she was stopped by a British patrol trawler for inspection the boarding officer was totally deceived and allowed the 'Spaniard' to pass on her way. When she sailed at midnight on 3 August, 1916, to embark on her second patrol, she had become the French schooner *Jeanette*. Over the next few months she wandered around the Bristol

Channel, the Channel Islands and the Bay of Biscay. Sometimes she would be the *Mary y Jose*, at others the *Jeanette*, or the *Brine* of St. Malo, or even the Russian *Neptun* of Riga. Her gunners could bring the guns into action within *three* seconds, although it was never known for sure that she ever sank a U-boat. Three 'possibles' was her final score.

The *Prize*, another 200-ton steel schooner, was of German birth. Her name had been the *Else* when she was built in 1901 by the firm of Smit & Zoon. She had been unlucky to find herself at the western end of the English Channel on the day that war was declared in 1914, several days sail from her home port of Leer, a little riverside town fifteen miles up the Ems from Emden. Less than half a day into the biggest conflict the world had ever seen, she was captured by the British and taken into Falmouth, never to be German again. At a Government auction, she was bought by the Marine Navigation Company, who changed her name, appropriately, to *First Prize*. In November, 1916, she was lying in Swansea when the Admiralty requisitioned her. She was still being fitted out at the year's end. Her action-packed future had yet to unfold.

For HMS *Farnborough* much of 1916 had brought little but fruitless frustration, as it had with so many of her Q-ship fellows, although in her case there had been a welcome change of scenery. In the autumn she had returned to Queenstown to find fresh orders awaiting. She was to proceed to Bermuda, of all places! It had been decided to replace her 'cargo' of coal with timber to give her buoyancy if struck by a torpedo. Her coal, 5,000 tons of it, was required for use by the ships based on Bermuda. From there, Campbell was to sail in ballast to Quebec, load up with timber, and then return to Home Waters.

It was an enjoyable cruise, at a steady 7.5 knots, to Bermuda. Not a single ship was seen on the way, and the crew could relax on deck in the sunshine. There was much hard work to be done, however, before they reached their destination. The discharging and loading of cargo would bring her into contact with many dockside people, which posed a serious security risk. Therefore, all her guns had to be demounted and stowed away out of sight with their ammunition. There was no such ship as a *Farnborough* in Lloyd's Register, but there was a *Loderer*. And so it was with her old name painted on her stern that she arrived in Bermuda.

Campbell was to face many ticklish situations regarding his true identity in the course of this trip. One harbour pilot was anxious to talk about Cardiff. It was supposed to be Campbell's home port, but he had never been to the place! And one Port Officer, an old acquaintance, assumed that the scruffily dressed Campbell had been discharged from the Navy and was eking out a living on this old rust bucket. Nothing was said, but the man was clearly sympathetic.

In Quebec all the talk was of the German submarine U-53, which had had the temerity to appear off New York and sink much Allied shipping. Campbell received orders from the C-in-C, Halifax, Nova Scotia, Admiral Sir Montague Browning, that as soon as the holds of the *Farnborough/Loderer* had been stuffed with the thousands of twelve-foot-long planks of 9" x 3" spruce, he was to patrol in the Gulf of St Lawrence for as long as he was able, in the hope of luring the U-boat to destruction, then to sail for Halifax and a re-fit, before returning home. Obviously this meant that Campbell would have to re-mount his guns, which would then be seen by the river pilot. Although it was strictly against regulations, he decided to dispense with the services of a pilot. He weighed anchor during the night and groped his way on a hair-raising trip down the fog-bound St Lawrence, to plod around the freezing Gulf for twenty-three days in bitter weather without seeing or hearing anything of U-53. It was with only a couple of tons of coal in her bunkers that the Q-ship finally arrived in Halifax.

Major repairs were required, but they could not be carried out at Halifax, and so it was back to Bermuda, with hoses playing on the main shaft bearings the whole way, to keep them cool. For some reason, Campbell was ordered to return home via Sydney, on Cape Breton. His departure from that port was delayed at the last minute by the discovery that 'Darky', the ship's black cat, had disappeared. It is a well-known fact that sailors are superstitious, but Campbell had not realized quite how seriously this was taken until the cat went a.w.o.l. There could be no question of sailing until the animal was found. The dockside had to be searched with the proverbial fine-toothed comb before the pet was located and taken on board, much to the relief of the lower deck. And then a signal arrived from the C-in-C to say that the Admiralty had informed him that the German decoy raider *Möwe* was again at large in the Atlantic. Orders were that all merchant shipping was to remain in port.

Campbell had already been away from his home hunting grounds for many more weeks than he wanted. And here was the fascinating possibility of out-decoying another decoy. He called the ship's company together and told them about the *Möwe*. They too were amused by such thoughts. He replied to the signal, saying that he had already sailed. Then he closed down his wireless for reception and slipped his moorings. But the Atlantic is a big place and no sign was seen of the German raider, or any U-boats, on the uneventful crossing. It was Christmas Eve, 1916, when *Loderer* berthed again in Queenstown, to become once more HMS *Farnborough*. She had been away for three months.

Chapter 6

Spring, 1917
The U-Boats Run Rampant

The New Year opened with some filthy weather in the seas around the British Isles. On the night of 7 January the *Mary B. Mitchell*, now known simply as the *Mitchell*, was pitching and rolling off the coast of South Devon. The north-east wind, rising in a steady crescendo to a howling roar, carried away both her mainmast and foremast. They, and their spars, crashed down over the sides and the helpless schooner was blown away to the south-west. It blew ferociously all the next day, and the next night too. By the morning of the 9th she had drifted all the way across the wide western end of the Channel, which brought her dangerously near to the point of Ushant, on the Brittany coast. It was not until the evening that her flares were spotted by the Norwegian steamer *Sardinia*, who took her in tow. They had not gone far when a French torpedo-boat came on the scene. The Q-ship's captain, Lieutenant John Lawrie, thinking quickly, gave the French captain a glimpse of his White Ensign by dangling it over the stern, out of sight of the Norwegian. The Frenchman understood immediately and signalled the Norwegian to cast off, indicating that he would take over the tow. By noon the dismasted *Mitchell* was safely in Brest Harbour undergoing repairs. For once the Admiralty reacted quickly and positively. They fitted her with an auxiliary motor. She would not be blown a hundred and fifty miles off course again.

Another thirteen Flower-class convoy sloops were ordered in January, 1917, and the numbers of vessels joining the ranks of the

Q-ships from all walks of maritime life grew rapidly. Records are far from dependable, but 1917 would appear to have seen at least another 100 new Q-ships. However, the Germans were building more and more U-boats. They now had over a hundred available, and work was rushing ahead on the construction of more of the improved UB coastal submarines, as well as the mine-laying UCs. And the rate at which they were sinking British merchant shipping was causing grave alarm. In the first month of the year alone their 'haul' was not far short of 400,000 tons.

In fact, the early part of 1917 was the point at which Germany threw its all into an effort to win the war by cutting Britain's supply lines completely. On 1 February they announced that unrestricted submarine warfare was to begin. Admiral Scheer wrote in his diary, "We now enter a new stage of the war in which the submarine arm is to bring the decision by strangling British economic life and sea communications. Every means of naval warfare must be put into the service of our U-boat operations." The monthly tonnage totals of sunken British shipping rose from 540,000 in February to 594,000 in March, to peak at 881,000 in April. In that first quarter of the year, however, the Q-ships had quite a run of successes, albeit against the rising tide of U-boat victories.

On 14 January UB-37 was patrolling in the Channel, midway between Portland Bill and Alderney, when she came across a 1,000-ton tramp steamer. She was typical of her hard-working breed, with her one tall funnel and not-too-smart appearance. Gunther, UB-37's captain, saw some easy pickings and made towards her on the surface. It was about five minutes to four, with the winter afternoon light on the wane, when the German fired a shot across the tramp's bows from about 3,000 yards. The merchant skipper stopped his engines immediately and his crew took to their boats. Gunther approached to within 700 yards of the tramp's starboard bow, firing intermittently as he came. He stopped dead ahead of her and loosed two shells at her bridge. This was a sensible move; a wise precaution against being decoyed. If there were still men on board the steamer they would surely be commanded from the bridge. The awning had been shot away and the corner of the bridge itself hung drunkenly. But there was no sign of life and no sound except for a faint hiss of steam.

Gunther did not know it, but there were men on board – several of them – and two of them were dead. Nor did he know that he had taken on HMS *Penshurst*. The German's shells had killed the gun-layer and loading-number of the 6-pounder gun's crew and wounded both the breech-loader and the signalman waiting to hoist the White Ensign. This was the supreme test for a Q-ship's crew. To maintain absolute silence until the order came to fire, when men had been killed around you and you were yourself severely wounded, required discipline and courage of a very special brand. Not a groan or even a whisper could be allowed to escape your lips, and you may have to endure this agony for hours.

Mercifully the waiting was short. At 4.24 p.m., with the submarine presenting an inviting broadside silhouette, Commander Grenfell pressed the bell for action. The sides of the dummy lifeboat on the main hatch of the Q-ship fell away, the false deck-houses abaft her funnel collapsed, up fluttered the White Ensign and her guns belched flame and smoke. It was the very first shot from the 12-pounder which spelt the end of the *UB-37*. It hit her squarely at the base of the conning-tower, blowing much of it away. Clouds of black smoke poured from the stricken U-boat as more and more shells savaged her. *Penshurst*'s starboard 3-pounder alone claimed four hits. The submarine sank quickly by the stern. There were no survivors.

On 17 February *Farnborough* had been on patrol in the Western Approaches for seventeen days. It looked like being a fine day. The Atlantic was as calm as it ever gets in February. All was peaceful until, at about 9.45 a.m., a torpedo was seen streaking towards them on the starboard side. After *Farnborough*'s victory over the *U-68* nearly a year ago Campbell had given much thought to the question of his tactics in future. The upshot was that he had entered in the ship's Order Book the following statement, which all officers were required to sign:- "Should the Officer of the Watch see a torpedo coming, he is to increase or decrease speed as necessary to ensure it hitting."

What better way to lure a U-boat, Campbell reasoned, than to present her captain with the sight in his periscope of a direct torpedo hit and a 'helpless' victim? The Q-ship's holds were now crammed with timber to keep her afloat and, as long as she could avoid a hit in the engine-room or steering gear, she would still be a powerful force. All the same, it called for a degree of raw courage which bordered on the reckless. Every man on board was aware of the order. Every man had been given the opportunity to return to General Service. Every man had declined the option to leave the ship. And every man had sailed. The torpedo kept coming. It had been fired from long range and *Farnborough*'s lookout had spotted it in ample time for Campbell to have avoided it if he had so chosen. But it was heading straight for the engine-room! Cleverly, he put his helm hard over at the last moment, and the torpedo hit just abaft the engine-room with a mighty explosion. Unfortunately, it also burst through the bulkhead between the holds and thus two-thirds of the ship instantly flooded. They had drilled and drilled this particular exercise. The laid-down routine was that Campbell would shout, "Torpedo coming!" to alert everybody, and then either "Torpedo missed!" or "Torpedo hit!", in which case the panic party would go into its comic boat-lowering act. On this occasion, with *Farnborough* already visibly down at the stern, Campbell noticed that, although the men had rushed towards the boats, they had not as yet tumbled into them and were lounging around, chatting and smoking. He roared at them, demanding to know why they were not abandoning ship. The reply was that they were waiting for him to shout, "Torpedo hit!" After he had stopped laughing and shouted "Torpedo hit!", the usual mayhem started. The lowering ropes of the first boat jammed half-way down, so everybody rushed for the next one. Eventually two boats and a dinghy shoved off, the last man in being the corpulent Chief Steward, whose arms would not support his weight on the ropes and he fell the last few feet into the boat, squashing several of his shipmates.

And 'Darky', the lucky black cat, which had been sitting on the fo'c'sle, and had been blown into the water by the explosion (or jumped overboard in fright), swam the whole length of the ship and climbed aboard near the stern, which was now well awash.

As the boats pulled away from *Farnborough*, the submarine crept nearer and nearer, still submerged but with raised periscope, until it was only about fifteen yards from the ship's side. Campbell, lying flat on his belly on the bridge, squinted through his peephole down at the sinister cigar-shape just beneath the surface as it slid past him on its cautious tour of inspection of its 'kill'. It was an eerie moment. He would have loved to open fire there and then, but his guns would not bear at such short range. All the time *Farnborough* was settling down. In fact the water was creeping towards the feet of the crew of the after-gun in their fake deck-house. If anybody had panicked, the whole show would have been ruined. But every man remained absolutely silent and stock-still.

The U-boat continued up the starboard side and crossed the bow to proceed back down the port side. On the bridge Campbell changed places with the signalman, using their well-practised belly-crawl. The

HMS *Farnborough*'s 'panic party'. Note the stuffed parrot. One of a series of sketches by Lieutenant J.E. Broome, RNR.

German surfaced and made for the *Farnborough*'s boats, which were sitting a little way off on the port quarter. He seemed satisfied and was now going to get the ship's papers from the "Master", who, he assumed, was in one of the boats. The submarine was about 100 yards away on the port side. The captain was climbing out of the conning-tower. Campbell's guns could bear now. He was not going to get a better chance.

At precisely 10.10 a.m. – twenty-five minutes after the torpedo had struck – the White Ensign flew with a jerk to the masthead, there was a clatter of falling screens and three 12-pounders, the 6-pounder, the Maxims and rifles all thundered out together. The *U-83* never had a chance. Her captain, Bruno Hoppe, had his head taken off by the first salvo. The first inkling his crew had that anything was wrong was when his decapitated body fell back down through the hatch. Forty-five shells were fired at the sub, nearly every one on target. The conning-tower was nothing but a mass of twisted metal as she sank. The survivors, about eight men, poured out through the open "lid" and jumped into the lake of oil on the surface of the icy sea. *Farnborough*'s boats found only two of them, one of whom was in a bad way and died shortly afterwards.

As soon as the Q-ship had opened fire her wireless operator had started to transmit signals to the C-in-C, asking for assistance. *Farnborough*'s two after-holds, the engine-room and boiler-room were all filling rapidly. If help did not arrive quickly, her fate was sealed, despite the buoyancy of the timber in her forward compartments. Campbell called for twelve volunteers to stand by the ship and the rest to take to the boats. The whole crew volunteered, so he selected twelve, plus himself, to stay on board. He busied himself with the destruction of secret documents and the sending of a coded signal which has become as famous in Q-ship folk-lore as Nelson's "England Expects . . .":

"From Q5. To Vice-Admiral Queenstown, via Valencia. 11.00 hours, Feb 17th. Q5 slowly sinking respectfully wishes you goodbye. 1100"

But she did not sink. By midday she had stabilized, and at last help arrived when the destroyer HMS *Narwhal* and the sloop HMS *Buttercup* arrived on the scene, to be joined later by another sloop, HMS *Laburnum*. The destroyer took most of the Q-ship's crew on board, leaving Campbell and his damage control party to be towed home by *Buttercup*, with *Laburnum* as escort. There was a following swell, which continually broke over the stern of *Farnborough*. At about 2.00 a.m. she suddenly heeled over. It was 18 February, 1917.   ✺

Campbell went below with the Engineer Officer, Lieutenant Loveless, to investigate the problem. They had only a couple of spluttering candles, which kept going out (presumably because of a strong draught of air) to find their way around in the pitch blackness. Most of the coal had been washed out of the starboard bunker. This had been preventing more ingress of water, but now the compartment was steadily filling. It had become impossible to re-light the candles and they were concerned that they would become trapped. But before they could make their escape, an important job had to be done. It was the lucky black cat! They could hear it miaowing plaintively and spent some time trying to locate it. But a black cat, even a lucky one, is a difficult thing to find in the unlit coal bunker of a sinking ship in the middle of the night. It proved to be an impossible mission and sadly they had to leave it. Perhaps there was something in the sailors' superstition after all. (There was a happy conclusion to the story of the cat. Stuart, in a letter written years later, recorded that 'Darky' somehow survived. According to him, the cat's luck continued to hold good, and it "retired from naval life to a peaceful rural existence".)

In the morning HMS *Laburnum* took over the tow. They made Berehaven, in Bantry Bay, Co. Cork, by 9.30 that evening, and beached the *Farnborough* in Mill Cove, her days of action over. Berehaven was one of many little harbours, normally quiet and sleepy, which had been transformed by the war. Its single street contained a dozen pubs which rarely closed. Every night swarms of rowdy, sometimes brawling, off-duty sailors bought buckets of beer and raced on donkeys up and down the road while searchlights swept back and forth across the harbour entrance. When peace came Berehaven went back to sleep.

Campbell was summoned to the presence of the King a few days later and awarded the Victoria Cross. His Majesty expressed the wish that every man who had remained on board after the torpedo attack should receive some recognition for his bravery. In addition to Campbell's VC, the list was as follows:

Distinguished Service Order. Lieutenant R. Stuart, RNR, Engineer-Lieutenant L.S. Loveless, DSC, RNR.
Distinguished Service Cross. Acting-Lieutenant F.R. Hereford, RNR, Sub-Lieutenant R.P. Nisbet, RNR, Assistant-Paymaster R.A. Nunn, RNR.
Distinguished Service Medal. Petty Officer F.J. Horwill, Stoker Petty Officer S.J. Pollard, Leading Seaman H. Day, RFR, Seaman B. Samms, RNR, Seaman A.S. Morrison, RNR, Leading Stoker R.E. Davidson, RNR, Stoker A. Hopkins, RNR, W/T Operator T.E. Fletcher, RNR, Seaman W. Williams, RNR.
Bar to DSM. Chief Petty Officer G.H. Truscott.
Mentioned in Dispatches. Acting-Lieutenant F.G. Russell, RNR, Wireless Telegraphist A. Andrews, RNR, Petty Officer E. Pitcher, Shipwright W.S. Smart, Able Seaman C.E. Hodder, Able Seaman R.W. Sheppard, Seaman A. Davies, RNR, Able Seaman E.A. Veale, RFR, Seaman P. Murphy, RNR, Seaman R. Jenkins, RNR, Seaman J. Martindale, RNR, Seaman M. Connors, RNR, Able Seaman B.R. Harris, Seaman R. Dryden, RNR, Able Seaman N. Britton, Seaman J. Orr, RNR, Signalman C.W. Hurrell, RNVR, Seaman F. Dodd, RNR, Seaman W.H. Bennison, RNR, Engine Room Artificer A.W. Morrison, RNR, Leading Stoker T. Davies, RNR, Stoker W. O'Leary, RNR, Stoker G. Rees, RNR, Armourer's Crew S. Woodison.

While they were beaching the poor *Farnborough*, the little 700-ton steam-coaster *Lady Olive*, Q18, was on the hunt in the western reaches of the Channel. She had only been in commission since being brought down from Teesside some eight weeks before. They had armed her well. With a 4-inch gun and four "long" 12-pounders, she packed a weighty punch.

It was at 6.35 a.m. on the morning of 19 February that she was fired on by a submarine which was approaching astern of her, about three miles off. The panic party went into its usual routine and the boats pulled away as the U-boat drew nearer. The German came up close to the stern of the Q-ship, presumably to read her name. At ten past seven she was at a mere 100 yards, and *Lady Olive*'s captain, Lieutenant F.A. Frank, RNR, decided to open fire. The first shots holed the conning-tower and put the sub's gun out of action, killing the gun crew. The British gunners managed to get in another half-dozen shots, most of which hit the target and killed a man in the conning-tower, before the submarine dived. In Robert Grant's *U-Boats Destroyed*, which is a painstakingly researched work, he credits *Lady Olive* with the destruction of the submarine. According to him, it was the *UC-18*.

Frank rang down for Full Speed Astern, intending to drop depth-charges, but there was no response. Going below to investigate, he found that his engine and boiler-rooms were flooded with rapidly rising water and his wireless had been smashed. Clearly the *Lady Olive* was beyond rescue. There was only one thing for it and that was to take to the boats.

Frank threw overboard the steel box with the ship's papers in it and they clambered into the three boats and two rafts. The sea was calm, but there was a bite in the February breeze as they pulled away for the French coast. They rowed all day, but had made poor progress by five o'clock in the afternoon. Frank decided to abandon the rafts, which were hampering the efforts of the tired rowers. They all crowded into the boats, twenty-three men in each, and set off again. But a strong current was sweeping down the Channel, like a sluice, and it was impossible to make any real headway. Men were beginning to faint with the cold and exposure. In the evening a thick mist came down and it started to drizzle. They saw lights now and again, but no ship saw them. At about ten o'clock Frank noticed that they had lost touch with one of the boats. Drawing on reserves of strength, they rowed all night, spurred on by the thought of seeing a welcoming beach at daybreak. But dawn came and there was no land in sight. By now some of the shivering men were beginning to fall asleep with fatigue and the sea had developed a nasty choppiness. Frank, sitting in the stern-sheets, tried to raise their spirits by insisting that he could see land in the distance. By noon the weather had moderated and the day had brightened, which was a blessing, but Frank could see that to pass another night in an open boat would probably be fatal for some of them. He took his own turn at the oars, and tried to stir them up by telling them that their only chance was to row for all they were worth. Just after five o'clock a steamer passed them by to the westward. Their hearts all felt a little heavier at the sight of her stern moving into the distance. But wait! She was turning to come back. It was the French destroyer *Dunois*. She was actually chasing a U-boat at the time, but broke off for a moment to lay alongside *Lady Olive*'s boats. They landed at Cherbourg to find their shipmates in the 'lost' cutter already there.

While *Lady Olive*'s men were rowing through the foggy drizzle in mid-Channel another drama was being played out a few miles to the west. *Penshurst* was about to have a busy couple of days. She was at latitude 49.21 N, longitude 6.16 W. on 20 February when a U-boat surfaced a couple of miles away and opened fire. The panic party went into the boats and Grenfell managed to close the range somewhat without alarming the German into diving. At 1.04 p.m. *Penshurst*'s guns barked out. Several hits were scored by the Q-ship, but all were above the water-line and none penetrated the hull or ballast tanks. The U-boat crash-dived and, although *Penshurst* plastered the spot with depth-charges, it seems that she escaped.

Only two days later, on 22 February, a few miles away off the coast of southern Ireland, *Penshurst* spied a U-boat and gave chase. But her lumbering gait was no match for *U-84*'s surface speed of nearly seventeen knots. Just before noon they lost sight of it, but half an hour later its periscopes appeared about a quarter of a mile away on the port beam, and a torpedo streaked through the water, narrowly missing the Q-ship. Grenfell turned away to the east, as if running away, and the panic party made a great show of lining the rails with their lifebelts on, ready to abandon ship. *U-84* re-surfaced and began to shell *Penshurst*, and the panic party took to the boats, whereupon the submarine dived again. The German captain approached at periscope depth and made a close and cautious inspection. He said later that he took her for an oil-tanker. When he was satisfied that this was no decoy, he surfaced again,

77

and an officer and some ratings appeared in the conning-tower. The officer yelled for the "Master" in the lifeboat to produce his papers, but the petty officer who was acting this role pretended not to understand and continued rowing towards the stern of the stopped Q-ship. This was astute, because the U-boat was, at that moment, sitting broadside on to the guns in the *Penshurst*'s false deck-houses, and now they had a clear shot at it. Crack! The submarine was hit in several places, but yet again the shells failed to cause fatal damage. The men vanished from the conning-tower and *U-84* crash-dived. After a few minutes, her bows shot out of the water at a steep angle, and the waiting Q-ship hit her with more shells. Still they could not kill her, and she dived again, to sixty-five feet.

Grenfell tried a depth-charge attack. The explosions shook the U-boat, knocking out her gyro-compass, main rudder and most of her electric lighting. And she had started to leak, which forced her to the surface again, where she found that *Penshurst* had been joined by HMS *Alyssum*, one of the Queenstown sloops. Both British ships poured more shells at her, but *U-84* was a credit to her builders. She was still able both to float and to fight, even after the pounding she had undergone.

In fact she was one of the biggest and most powerful U-boats built up to that time, at 800 tons, with a surface range of 4,500 miles, a 4.1-inch gun and ten torpedoes. But again her captain was mistaken. He took *Alyssum* to be a destroyer. If she had been, he would have been sunk for certain. But she was not. She was designed for slow minesweeping, not high-speed submarine chasing. In fact *U-84* could have done for both British ships with her torpedoes and far greater speed. Instead, the German elected to turn away. They chased him all afternoon, but he drew steadily away. At a quarter past five, with the light fading, they lost sight of him for good. On top of all the problems in steering and navigating, *U-84* was now leaking badly. The German sailors managed to plug the worst of these with rags, spare clothing and the tricolour of the French sailing ship, *Bayonne*, which they had sunk five days before. They got home safely.

These two incidents serve to show that for a Q-ship to sink a U-boat with shellfire was not as simple as may be imagined. A conning-tower, protruding from the water like the dorsal fin of a giant shark, is relatively easy to hit but it is not crucial to the survival of the submarine because it is nothing but an adjunct to the integral body of the boat. It was only the hull and ballast tanks of a U-boat which constituted its Achilles Heel. Even then, much of the hull was below the water-line, thus presenting a pencil-slim target to gunners who only had a few rounds with which to hit it. And a submarine's body is composed mainly of curved surfaces. Any shells striking her obliquely tend to ricochet and their effect is greatly reduced. A killing 'hit' had to be a square-on shot, somewhere near the waterline. As we have just seen, a U-boat with severe but superficial damage could continue on the surface, and still outrun any ship but a destroyer or fast patrol boat.

HMS *Privet*, an almost brand-new 800-ton steamer, was another recent Q-ship recruit. She also sailed under the aliases *Alcala*, *Island Queen* and *Swisher*. To the Admiralty, she was more commonly known as *Q-19*. On 12 March she was making her unhurried way towards the Channel Islands when, in the middle of the afternoon, somewhere off Start Point on the Devon coast, the lookout was just in time to see a torpedo arriving. It was heading for the engine-room, but it was running too deep and passed beneath her keel. *Privet*'s captain, Lieutenant-Commander C.G. Matheson, RNR, pretended not to notice and kept steadily on his course. After a few minutes a U-boat rose to the surface fine on the starboard quarter and began shelling. It was *U-85*. She fired nine times, rapidly, with her 4-inch gun, and scored five hits, which caused many casualties among the 'panic party' assembling near the boats, destroyed the falls of the boats themselves, and badly holed the Q-ship's hull. Matheson put out an SOS, saying that his engine-room was disabled and rapidly filling with water.

Luckily for the *Privet* her 4-inch gun and port battery of 12-pounders could now bring a full broadside to bear on *U-85*. There was the usual clatter as the screens fell down and all the guns began to blaze away together. The U-boat was hit several times and tried to dive. But Petz, the commander, with his boat leaking badly, managed to thrust his way back to the surface. As soon as it re-appeared, however, it was met with more shells from *Privet*. It lifted its bows into the air and slid backwards beneath the waves, not to be seen again.

Meanwhile, the Q-ship herself was in serious trouble. The chief engineer reported to Matheson that the water in the engine-room was approaching danger level. They tried to plug the hole with hammocks and pieces of timber, but it was no use. (Who knows how many lives have been saved over the centuries by the lashed-up sausage of a Navy hammock, now only of fond and distant memory?) Matheson ordered 'abandon ship' and they took to the boats. But *Privet*, although in a sorry state, did not sink, and before long two destroyers, HMS *Christopher* and HMS *Orestes*, were racing to the scene in response to the SOS.

They watched over her, a crippled derelict, for another hour and a half, and when it was clear that she was not going to sink Matheson went back on board with a working party and secured a tow. *Orestes* hauled her towards Plymouth, slowly and painfully. They had almost made it into the Sound when the last of her bulkheads collapsed under the weight of water inside her and she went down in Cawsand Bay, opposite the Picklecomb Fort. Luckily, it was only in four and a half fathoms of water, and it was not many days before they had salved her, taken her into Devonport, and repaired her. The Germans had not seen the last of HMS *Privet*.

The little 113-ton schooner *Glen* had only been on active service as a Q-ship for six weeks when, in the early evening of 17 May, 1917, she was about thirty-five miles south of the Isle of Wight. She was trotting along before a Force 4 wind, with all sails set, when suddenly gunfire was heard, flashes were seen to the south and her lookouts reported a submarine on the surface about three miles away. *Glen*'s captain, Lieutenant R.J. Turnbull, RNR, backed his sails and the 'panic party' prepared to perform their act. The U-boat approached rapidly to about 800 yards and then submerged to periscope depth. She came even closer, to within 200 yards of the schooner's starboard side. So quickly had this happened that the 'panic party' had not yet pulled away in their boats. Then, with astonishing rashness, the German captain, Küstner, surfaced. Now the U-boat was only eighty yards from the waiting muzzles of Turnbull's 12-pounder and 6-pounder. Within five seconds the first twelve-pound shell was screaming towards the submarine. It missed. But then another amazing thing happened. A man appeared in the conning-tower, just as the *Glen*'s second shot hit the U-boat amidships. He disappeared and the submarine went into a crash dive. As her stern rose two more shells from *Glen*'s 12-pounder burst on the hull, aft, punching great holes in it. The smaller gun got off six rounds, five of which found their mark all along her waterline. She rolled over on her port side and sank amid a surge of oily bubbles. There were no survivors.

Glen was given no chance to rest on her laurels, however, because at that instant another submarine was seen about 4,000 yards away, approaching on the starboard bow. Turnbull opened fire immediately, there being little point in continuing the pretext of being a harmless sailing ship. This caused the stranger to dive, but she reappeared minutes later, this time on the port bow. Turnbull fired again. She dived again and surfaced on the port quarter, half a mile off. Anticipating a torpedo attack, Turnbull started his auxiliary motor to boost his sail power and made off northwards as fast as he could. But the day's work was still not done. At about 7.30 p.m. yet another submarine appeared, on the starboard beam, evidently on a course to take her down Channel into the Western Approaches. She exchanged several shots with *Glen* but did not stop. Obviously she had a more important mission to perform elsewhere.

There are several incidents in the Q-ship story about which researchers have produced differing versions of events, and this is one of them. Chatterton is quite clear that HMS *Glen* sank *UB-39* on 17 May, as we have just seen. Indeed, he describes the fight in vivid detail. However, according to Grant, this particular U-boat was lost on the night of 14/15 May, presumably hit by a mine. When she became overdue at Zeebrugge, the commander of *UB-12*, which had been on patrol with her, reported that he had heard a loud underwater explosion 'in the direction of No. 3 Buoy in the British Field', which suggests a British mine. Grant says with confidence that this 'presumably marked the end of the *UB-39*', although he offers no particular reasons for this presumption. Interestingly, Gordon Campbell, writing in 1928, thirty-six years before Grant, also excludes the *UB-39* from his list of Q-ship victims.

Altogether, eighteen U-boats were sunk in the first five months of 1917, including those claimed by the Q-ships. But the Wilhemshaven slipways were easily keeping pace to ensure that there was no net deficit. And the Q-ships themselves were not without loss.

On 30 January the gallant little Lowestoft smack, *Inverlyon*, LT687, which had attacked a U-boat in August, 1915, and was now 'retired', was herself sunk by shellfire whilst peacefully fishing off Trevose Head. Another ex-Q-ship, the tiny 45-ton Brixham smack *Strumbles*, M135, which fished out of Milford Haven, was captured and later sunk by *U-65* off the Welsh headland which bore her name, Strumble Head. And the *Warner*, Q27, a 1,293-ton freighter, had a fatal encounter with *U-38* off the west coast of Ireland on 13 March.

HMS *Bayard*, Q20, a former Boulogne lugger, had the misfortune to be run down in the dark by the British steamship, SS *Tainui*, in the Channel on 29 March. *Bayard's* commander, Captain Keith Morris, DSC was very lucky. As the steamship's towering bows ploughed into the little lugger, Morris saw a mooring rope hanging down from her side, swarmed up it and stepped aboard her without getting his feet wet. But others were not so fortunate. Among those killed was Lieutenant W. Scott, RNR. The *Tainui* was sailing as a merchantman and the Court of Inquiry held that she was responsible for the disaster, which meant that claims for compensation were instituted. The representatives of Scott's estate listed the following items of lost property. Given that an essential factor in the disguise of a Q-ship was the 'rough and ready' appearance of its crew, it may have caused some raised eyebrows: 3 plain-clothes suits; 4 sets of underclothes; 3 pairs of boots; 1 pair of thigh boots; 1 pair of knee boots; 6 flannel shirts; 6 white shirts; 1 bridge coat; 1 overcoat; 1 oilskin; 3 pairs shoes; 3 sweaters; 12 pairs socks; 2 pairs stockings; 2 doz. handkerchiefs; 2 doz. collars; 1 suitcase; dressing-gown; 1 diamond ring; 1 pair cuff-links; 1 sextant; 1 pair binoculars; 1 Masonic apron; 1 watch; 1 silver mounted walking-stick; a velours hat. Total - £102. 6s. 6d. One of the deck-hands, Archibald Dupre, had lost his tools which included "two roping palms, two seaming palms, pair of rigging screws and a mallet".

The ex-banana boat *Barranca*, Q3, was torpedoed on 26 April, although they managed to tow her into Portsmouth. HMS *Lady Patricia*, Q25, alias *Anchusa*, *Paxton* or *Tosca*, was torpedoed by *U-46* in the Atlantic on 20 May. And the following day the big 3,049-ton collier, *Ravenstone*, alias *Donlevon*, was also torpedoed, but was fortunate in that the rescue tug *Flying Spray* was on hand to tow her into Queenstown.

The sinking of HMS *Tulip*, Q12, one of the Flower class sloops, was not without interesting incidents. On 30 April she was on patrol 200 miles west of Ireland, when the lookout reported a periscope. *Tulip's* captain, Lieutenant-Commander Norman Lewis, turned towards the submerged submarine, intending to ram, but at that instant a torpedo exploded amidships, killing several men in the engine-room. The damage was such that Lewis immediately ordered a genuine 'abandon ship' and the survivors hurriedly took to the boats. As they pulled away Lewis's steward, who in civilian life was a professional butler, apologized that he had left the captain's cabin in a very untidy state! The submarine, *U-62*, came to the surface to find debris from the now-

1. "Admiral Sir Stanley Colville had assembled another group of decoy ships... at Longhope, a bleak little inlet off Scapa Flow" (p.8).

2. "*Prince Charles*, armed with two hidden 6-pounders, two 3-pounder Hotchkisses and rifles" (p.8).

3. "Lieutenant William Mark-Wardlaw....accompanied, even to sea, by a faithful spaniel friend called Rover" (p.8).

4. The bulldog-faced captain of the *Baralong*...Lieutenant-Commander Godfrey Herbert, was somewhat of a maverick"(p.20). Here he is seen on the bridge, wearing a wig, disguised as a Dutch pilot.

5. One of *Baralong*'s 12-pounders, hidden behind a fake lifebelt locker. The Royal Marine in the foreground is dressed as a merchant seaman.

6. *HMS Penshurst* showing some of her repertoire of disguises. The mizzen mast has been lowered, the funnel given a white collar and a canvas screen placed around the bridge. The "lifeboat" under the boom hides a 12-pounder gun (see p. 61 *et seq*).

7. *Penshurst*'s Captain, Commander F. H. Grenfell, shows how the "lifeboat" fell apart to reveal the gun.

8. *Penshurst*'s gun-layers

9. *Penshurst*'s officers: Grenfell, with beard, third from the right.

10. HMS *Farnborough* meets her end, still flying the White Ensign (see p. 74).

11. "The submarine surfaced dead astern and began shelling the *Dunraven*" (p.109). Captain Gordon Cambell inspects the damage. Note the peppered bridge-screen which saved his life.

12. Campbell (see p.75) and Lieutenant Charles Bonner (see p. 112) at a Buckingham Palace garden party for winners of the Victoria Cross.

13. Petty Officer Ernest Pitcher, VC (see p. 112) at a naval exhibition in 1918 with King George V, Queen Mary and Queen Alexandra.

14. Lieutenant William Sanders VC (see p. 85) and Seaman William Williams VC (see p. 95).

15. "...resulted in a monumental celebration in the sand-floored taproom of the 'Village Maid'" (p.118). The inn at Lound, in Suffolk, where Edward Fenn's celebration was held. The photograph was taken 81 years later.

16. Leading Seaman Ross, DSM and bar, with Skipper Tom Crisp, VC (see p.120).

vanished *Tulip* floating all around. Among this was a sailor's ditty-box and inside was a post-card addressed to him c/o HMS *Tulip*. There would be no difficulty in identifying the 'kill'. An officer appeared in the conning-tower. He called to the men in the life-boats, asking which one of them was the captain. Lewis raised his hand in the air, resigned to his fate, but he was pleasantly surprised when taken before the U-boat's captain, Korvettenkapitän Hashagen. "Good afternoon, Captain," said Hashagen, "Do you have any weapons or papers?" The answer was "No." "In that case," the German replied, "Please sit down. Let us have a drink."

On the same day that Hashagen sank the *Tulip*, one of the most famous of the Q-ship dramas was being played out about 350 miles away to the south-east. Lieutenant William Sanders RNR, the lean, quiet-mannered, thirty-four-year-old son of a New Zealand boot manu-facturer, was now in command of the Q-ship *Prize*, a 199-ton three-masted schooner. Sanders had first gone to sea at the age of seven-teen and had gained his master's ticket after joining the Union Steamship Co. When war broke out he had 'worked his passage' to England in a troopship in 1915 to join the RNR. He had already been awarded the DSO after a Q-ship action 'in undisclosed circumstances' when he commissioned HMS *Prize*, at Falmouth early in 1917.

HMS *Prize*, originally the German ship *Else*, had had the distinction of being the first ship captured in the war, in August, 1914. The Admiralty put her up for auction and she was purchased by the Marine Navigation Co, who gave her the appropriate new name of *First Prize*, which was eventually shortened to simply *Prize*. The Director of her new owners, William Garthwaite, offered her to the Navy for decoy work, but was highly dissatisfied with the rates of hire suggested by Their Lordships. So much so, in fact, that he told them, with patronizing sarcasm, to keep their money and he would make no charge for the services of his ship. Furthermore, he would equip and man her, all at his own expense, but felt that he should be appointed as an Honorary Captain RNR in recognition of the gesture. They thanked him for his patriotic generosity, but regretted that his final suggestion was "out of the question".

Off the Scillies, in the early evening of 30 April, HMS *Prize*, or Q-21, now fitted with three 12-pounders and with 170 tons of copper slag in her bottom as ballast, was slowly ambling along before just a whiff of wind. A couple of crew members lounged on deck, enjoying a spot of leisure with their pipes. Her captain was on deck, aft, watching the set of his sails and checking his compass. All these men were actually keeping a very close watch on the sea around the little schooner. Suddenly somebody called out, "Object in sight astern!" Sanders turned. It looked like a rapidly approaching submarine, creating a white smile of greeting with its bow-wave. Shells started to splash into the sea around *Prize*. It was 8.40 p.m. Sanders brought her head into the wind to bring her to a stop, and ordered his 'panic party' away in the boats, under trawler skipper Brewer. The firing intensified as the U-boat's gunners found the range. The *Prize*'s auxiliary engine-room was on fire, her mainmast had been hit and she had three holes along her water-line. Several men were wounded by flying splinters as they lay flat, out of sight, waiting for orders to fire. Not one of them uttered a sound. They bit their lips or their fingers and waited.

It was twenty minutes before the submarine ceased firing at the apparently deserted schooner and slowly drew nearer, dead astern. The U-boat commanders had learned that this was the safest angle of approach, where they only risked being fired on by the small stern-gun that most British merchantmen now carried. Sanders, together with another trawler skipper member of his crew, Meade, was hiding under the steel companion cover amidships, peering through a slit. From there he was able to control operations by means of a voice-pipe which ran for'ard to the mainmast, at the base of which Lieutenant W.D. Beaton, in command of the forward gun, was lying. The rest of *Prize*'s suffering crew lay quiet, crouching behind her bulwarks.

The submarine was the big brand-new *U-93*, on her first patrol out of Emden. Her aristocratic captain, Kapitänleutnant Freiherr Speigel von und zu Peckelsheim, had good reason to feel pleased with himself. So far he had sunk eleven ships. This would make a dozen, a nice way to round off a patrol before popping home to see his horses run at the Berlin races in mid-May. Speigel steered towards Brewer's panic party, sitting in their boats eighty yards away. He said later that he had absolutely no reason to suspect he was being decoyed. It was 9.05 p.m.

U-93 proceeded across the port quarter of the Q-ship, towards her beam. She was about to present a perfect point-blank target, broadside on. Sanders whispered, "Stand by" to his crew and a couple of moments later he rapped out, "Let go", jumping to his feet to run up the White Ensign as the flaps fell down and the guns roared. One of the first shots from one of the 12-pounders blew the U-boat's 4-inch forward gun, and its gunners, into the sea. The Lewis guns blazed away. One of them was manned by a "hairy looking ruffian" who "leisurely steadied his gun on the bulwarks and proceeded to sweep the deck of the submarine with a hail of lead." Meanwhile the *Prize*'s larger guns were scoring hit after hit. No fewer than thirty-six 12-pounder shells blasted the U-boat at point blank range. Its conning-tower was a complete wreck and internal fires could be seen glowing through gaping holes in its hull.

Speigel managed to turn the sub towards the Q-ship in an attempt to ram, but it lurched away to starboard, apparently out of control, and disappeared. The 'panic party' rowed towards the spot and picked up three 'survivors'. Covered by Skipper Brewer's revolver, they were taken on board *Prize*. They were Speigel himself, his navigating officer and a stoker.

The amazing thing about this episode was that both vessels survived. *Prize* herself was almost sinking, but all hands, including the three German prisoners, turned to pumping out the water from her hull and plugging her leaks. They managed to nurse her towards the Irish coast, 120 miles away, and she was five miles off Kinsale when a motor launch took her in tow and brought her safely into harbour.

Even more astonishing was the brilliant seamanship of *U-93*'s First Lieutenant, Ziegler, in bringing the submarine home to Germany, all the way on the surface. This was confirmed within a few days by a request for information as to Speigel's whereabouts from Germany via the Swedish Red Cross. Everybody else believed that the U-boat had sunk, including Speigel himself, who had been blown into the water. But she had merely staggered into a convenient bank of sea-mist.

Sanders was awarded the VC for his gallantry in this action, although there was a sad ending to the story, as will be seen later.

As can be seen from several of these encounters, U-boat captains had become much more cautious in their approach to merchant ships, by attacking them from much greater distances. The Q-ships were no longer a secret weapon. As Admiral Lewis Bayly noted in March, 1917, "Torpedoing ships without warning has now become much more common, and even where a torpedo is not used, the ship is shelled at long ranges for a considerable period."

As the war at sea continued at an ever more furious pitch, with both sides grappling like wrestlers for a stranglehold around the throat of the other's supply lines, little consolation could be taken by Britain from the fact that her own blockade was forcing Germany herself to face starvation at home. Something had to be done to staunch the disastrous losses at the hands of the ever more efficient U-boats. The mightiest Navy the world had ever seen was not producing the result which was either desired or expected. Admiral Beatty, in command of the Grand Fleet which lurked at Scapa Flow, writing to Sir Edward Carson, First Lord of the Admiralty, in April, 1917, said, "I would like to scream at times, when I think of all the sacrifices that have been made, the gallant efforts of our glorious army, and the navy is losing the war as fast as the army is winning it. We are sitting on top of a volcano which will blow the navy and country to hell if we don't pull ourselves together."

Beatty was not exaggerating. In the first quarter of 1917 Britain had built 246,000 tons of new merchant ships, but this was less than 20% of the amount lost. Even with her gigantic merchant fleet of over ten million tons, she could not survive for long at such a rate of attrition.

There had been a niggling argument going on in top-brass naval circles for some time. It concerned the pros and cons of the convoy system. Convoys of merchant ships had been the standard practice in time of war for centuries. In fact, during the Napoleonic Wars it had been compulsory. The main opponent of convoying was the First Sea Lord, Admiral Sir John Jellicoe. He opposed it for several reasons, mainly because of the shortage of fast escort ships in proportion to the number of merchantmen; the log-jam of ships which would block Britain's ports by all arriving together, and the alleged inability of merchant skippers to keep station. There were very strong arguments against Jellicoe's stance. All the evidence pointed to the fact that the present system, i.e., patrolling the sea-lanes along which sailed lone merchant ships, simply did not work. The Admiralty's asinine answer to this, so far, had been simply to build more and more patrol craft to operate that unsuccessful system. And now that America had joined in the war, there would be even more of these available. In other words, the escorts which Jellicoe considered that Britain lacked were already at sea, but they were working ineffectively. The port congestion problems could be avoided by better organization. As regards merchant skippers keeping station, if they could do it in days of sail, they could certainly do it with engine-powered ships. At a conference held at Longhope in April it was agreed that Beatty should press the Admiralty to adopt the convoy system.

In truth, the advantages of convoying had been staring the Admiralty in the face. France was short of coal, because the Germans had captured her main coalfields early in the war. Ever since 2 January, 1917, four protected convoys of colliers *per day* had been leaving for France from British ports. As at the end of April there had been over 2,500 collier sailings, and only *five* of them had fallen victim to the U-boats.

Prime Minister David Lloyd George was already convinced of the practicalities of convoy and he was rapidly losing confidence in the 'palsied and muddle-headed' Admiralty. Finally, their Lordships agreed to give convoy a trial, but with in-bound ships only. The upshot was the tremendous success of a convoy of seventeen ships which sailed from Gibraltar on 10 May. They were escorted by three armed yachts out into the Atlantic, where two Q-ships took over. They were passed into the care of eight destroyers as they neared the Western Approaches, to divide off the Scillies towards various home ports. None was sunk.

Convoying was to extend in practice, and with growing success, throughout the ensuing months. The new tactics had changed the rules of the game almost overnight. As for Jellicoe, more and more confidence was lost in him. He was vilified in the press, particularly by Lord Northcliffe's *Daily Mail* and *The Times*. It was rumoured that Lloyd George said to Northcliffe, "You kill him. I'll bury him." They fired him on Christmas Eve, 1916.

In the end it was to be the convoy system which ensured Britain's delivery from starvation, and the convoy escort, the mine and the depth-charge, not the Q-ships, which defeated the U-boats. But in the early part of 1917 that defeat was still many months away and the German Admiralty was cock-a-hoop with the successes of their unrestricted submarine warfare campaign, which was re-started on 1 February. In reality, however, the German political leaders had committed a fatal error in abandoning the earlier unrestricted campaign in the spring of 1916 when they had bowed to American diplomatic pressure against the sage advice of old Admiral Tirpitz. Only the previous year, Tirpitz now pointed out bitterly, the U-boats had been well on the way to bringing Britain to her knees. But now, in 1917, the British had been given breathing-space, time in which to re-think their barrage techniques, time in which to lay more mine-fields, using an improved mine (which was shamelessly based on a German design) and time to build more attack submarines, fast patrol craft and anti-submarine destroyers. Furthermore, America was now in the war, and she had brought with her the escort ships which would swing the balance.

But in the meantime the Q-ships' 'private' war against the U-boats went on apace. From the spring onwards not many days passed without a skirmish between them. As we have seen, the Germans had learned how to deal with the British decoys, and they proceeded to sink them at a steady rate, including some of the most famous ones.

But for all that, the spring of 1917 marked the start of the slippery slope for the U-boats too. This was the point when the improved British mine-fields, depth-charge techniques and increased numbers of fast submarine hunters started to take a steady toll of their numbers. The Kaiser had lost no fewer than eighteen boats by the end of May that year. Only four of them had been lost to the Q-ships. Of the rest, four were rammed, either by British destroyers or merchantmen, three were torpedoed by submarines, one was depth-charged by a destroyer, three were destroyed by British mines and two of them blew up on their own mines. The fate of the remaining one, *UB-6*, lost on 13 March, is unknown.

Chapter 7

1917
A Fateful Summer

One of Admiral Lewis Bayly's Queenstown decoys, the 1,300-ton freighter *Mavis*, was hunting for U-boats in the wreck-littered Western Approaches on 3 June when at 9.45 in the evening, about twenty miles south of Wolf Rock, a torpedo was seen speeding towards her. It was less than fifty yards off when it was first sighted and there was not the slightest opportunity to steer the ex-freighter out of its path. There was a huge explosion as the torpedo hit amidships, immediately flooding the engine-room and stoke-hold. The wireless equipment was smashed and the only distress call that could be put out was by firing rockets. This brought the ever-dependable destroyer HMS *Christopher* and the trawler *Whitefriars* to the rescue. Together with a couple of tugs they towed the crippled ship into Plymouth Sound and beached her at that favourite resting place for several of the Q-ships, Cawsand Bay.

There cannot have been many more harmless-looking Q-ships than HMS *Bolham*, or to give her her proper name, the *Sarah Colebrooke*. She was a ketch-rigged sailing barge of 158 tons, 102 feet long and 24 feet across the beam. The Navy had taken her from the little port of Rye, on the Sussex coast, and commissioned her at Portsmouth only a month before. They gave her two 3-inch high-velocity guns, depth-charges, machine guns and a lot of ammunition. They packed sandbags inside her and reinforced her lee-boards with steel plates. They put Lieutenant C.W. Walters, RNR, in command, with three officers, three engineers, two wireless operators, three petty officers and a bluejacket crew. Walters said that she was 'the queerest craft' he had ever handled, but it was his proud claim that her gunners, by dint of hard practice, could load, train and fire her 3-inch guns within *five* seconds.

On 3 June, while they were towing the *Mavis* into Plymouth Sound at one end of the Channel, there was a skirmish going on at the other. It was about fifteen miles off Beachy Head to be precise. HMS *Bolham*, or rather the *Worrynot* of Littlehampton, which was her *nom de guerre* that day, was on her very first patrol. And she was being shelled by a U-boat. The exchange was short but sharp, and the ketch was severely damaged. Her stern had been lifted clean out of the water by a shell which exploded under the port quarter. Another salvo smashed her deck-house and put her auxiliary motor out of action, and she was only saved by her strengthened lee-boards from being holed in the hull. But she returned a hot fire with her forward gun, which forced the U-boat to dive. It was not seen again, although it was later confirmed that it had been only lightly damaged. Walters was awarded the DSC for this action, and two of his crew the DSM.

Admiral Sir Stanley Colville, now C-in-C Portsmouth, was extremely proud of the *Bolham*. In the course of her time in the Navy he showed her to no end of dignitaries, including members of the Royal Family, the US Navy Commander-in-Chief, the C-in-C of the South African Army, the Lords of the Admiralty and various visiting Generals.

In the end, her presence in the Channel became so familiar that she was retired from decoy work in the autumn of 1918. When they took her back to Rye, several of her war-time name-plates were found on board – *Bolham*, *Worrynot* and *Meryl*. But she never went into action under her peacetime name of *Sarah Colebrooke*. That was the name of the wife of her first owner, W.E. Colebrooke. It seems that that name was kept in reserve, ready for the day when Alf Woods and 'Winky' Smith could take her up to Scotland again for another cargo of coal and back to Rye without meeting any unfriendly submarines on the way.

The following week saw more action for Commander Gordon Campbell, VC, DSO, RN. After beaching the mutilated *Farnborough*, her crew were "paid off" and sent into barracks in Devonport where Campbell joined them later. All Q-ship crews had the option to leave after each patrol, but almost all of the *Q-5*'s men volunteered to follow Campbell. He was only too happy to concur with that, and was given permission to select a ship for himself. Eager to get back to sea, he hurried to Cardiff. He knew exactly what he wanted. She was a

3,000-ton, ten-year-old tramp steamer named *Vittoria*. Campbell telephoned London right away. Within twenty-four hours the loading of cargo into the *Vittoria* in Cardiff Docks had come to a halt and she was the property of the Royal Navy.

The *Vittoria*, or the *Snail* as she became known officially on 28 March, 1917, was given a powerful punch, with a four-inch gun, four 12-pounders, two 14-inch torpedo tubes and an 11-inch bomb thrower. There had been several new "inventions" since Campbell had fitted out his last ship and these were now put to good use. One was the "tilting mounting", which enabled a 12-pounder to be laid down sideways when not in use, making it easier to hide. The gun could be brought into use by simply pushing it upright.

The four-inch gun was mounted aft, on the poop deck, under a false hatch-cover with a dummy boat upside-down on top of it. Occasionally, to change "identity", they dispensed with the boat and draped a few bits of laundry over a spar, alongside the gun barrel, which protruded slightly above the hatch. Two of the 12-pounders were mounted one each side, amidships, in fake cabins, the sides of which were designed to fall down under their own weight when the guns were required to come into action. The third 12-pounder was placed on the fo'c'sle. It was here, in such an exposed position, that the new tilting mounting was invaluable. The gun presented a flat enough "lump" for it to be disguised as a coiled hawser. The last 12-pounder was put on the boat-deck. It needed little concealment, being naturally hidden by the canvas screens on the rails and the wash-deck lockers and life-belt racks. The two torpedo tubes were fitted on the mess-deck, with invisibly hinged doors being cut in the ship's side, through which they would be fired. They were, in fact, a mixed blessing, because not only did they take up space on the already crowded mess-decks, but they required specially trained 'torpedomen' to look after them. Rather than take any additional bodies on board, Campbell sent some of his existing crew for torpedo training.

The gun on the fo'c'sle posed a difficult question. There was nowhere to conceal its crew while they were waiting for the order to 'let go'. Campbell had a special hatch cut in the fo'c'sle, through which the gun's crew would crawl, dressed in drab overalls to lie prone on the open deck on their bellies, absolutely still and rigid, with faces turned in-board! Hopefully, a German submarine captain would take them for baulks of timber or untidy coils of rope!

Eventually, towards the end of May, they sailed for Queenstown, but not before another mystery unfolded. The name *Snail* had been discarded, Campbell was informed. It is astonishing, perhaps, that anybody could have suggested such a name in the first place. His ship was now to be known as HMS *Pargust*. He searched through the naval histories of every major power, but found no trace of any ship with such a name. He pored over geography books, dictionaries and encyclopaedias, but he never did find out what it meant.

Within days they were back on their old beat in the Atlantic, trudging out to about sixteen degrees west, then turning about in the night to appear as if homeward bound the next day. The dawn of 7 June broke with the Atlantic in one of its cantankerous moods. The sea wore a grey choppiness, and the squalls were heavy and incessant. *Pargust* was buffeting her way eastwards through the weather, about ninety miles from the south coast of Ireland. At about eight o'clock a torpedo came streaking towards the starboard side. Nobody saw it until it jumped clear of the water a few yards off, before hitting her plumb in the engine-room. They could not have avoided it even if they had wanted to. It blew a great hole, thirty feet across, in her side and blasted through a bulkhead. Instantly the engine and boiler-rooms, together with No. 5 hold, were flooded and the starboard lifeboat was turned into matchwood.

The experience of being in the torpedoed stokehold of a ship in mid-ocean can only be imagined, because it is a miracle if any man survives it to tell the tale. The sudden roar of an explosion, only feet away, the metal debris zipping through the air in great jagged shards, maybe a torrent of scalding steam, a second or so of daylight through the gaping hole, and then the Atlantic Ocean falling on top of you, creates in the mind a scene from hell. If you are not killed by the explosion, and escape being scalded to death by the steam, and avoid drowning, trapped as you are in your rapidly filling steel tomb, there has indeed been a miracle. And it must have been a miracle which saved Engineer-Sub-Lieutenant John Smith, RNR.

Campbell was amazed to see him, wet through, staggering towards his station shortly after the torpedo hit. He had assumed that Smith, on duty below, would have been killed outright. It was plain that the young officer was disorientated, and Campbell had him locked in the saloon, this being the safest place for him, with *Pargust* about to go into action. (Later, when in hospital having several bits of metal and coal removed from his body, Smith was quite unable to explain how he had managed to get up on deck. As all the ladders had been blown away, it can only be assumed that he had been ejected up through the engine-room hatch by the blast.) Of the two stokers on watch, one, Petty Officer Isaac Radford, was killed, but the other was a lucky man. Smith had just sent him up on deck on an errand when the torpedo struck.

And there was a problem at the starboard gun position. The violent impact of the explosion, almost directly beneath it, had released the securing pins of the screen that hid the gun, i.e. the side of the fake cabin. If it fell down exposing the gun to the U-boat, all would be lost. With great presence of mind, twenty-six-year-old Royal Naval Reservist Seaman William Williams jumped forward and took the whole weight of the screen upon himself to stop it from falling. There was no sign of the submarine, but Campbell ordered the boats away, and the best 'panic' act in the business went into play. Every well-rehearsed item was included in the drama, right down to the terrified fireman who had been left behind and yelled for the boats to come back and fetch him, and Lieutenant Hereford, now wearing Campbell's battered gold-braided cap in his role of 'Master', clutched his adored stuffed green parrot in its luxurious cage as he went over the side as the 'last' man to leave the ship.

Campbell squinted through his observation slit on the bridge. He could now see a periscope about 400 yards off on the port side. The fo'c'sle gun's crew were lying prone on the deck by their gun, still as statues, each man facing inboard as instructed. Campbell was filled with admiration for these men, who had no protection whatsoever from any shellfire.

The U-boat crept nearer, its one-eyed stalk sticking out of the water. It inspected the boats, rocking on the waves out on the port quarter. It inspected *Pargust* herself from no more than fifty feet away, peering up and down both sides of her. It was *UC-29*. Her commander, Rosenow, had clearly heeded the advice for caution that he had been given before slipping away from his base at Brunsbüttel, opposite Cuxhaven on the Elbe, on 25 May. It was half an hour before he surfaced, only fifty yards from the crippled Q-ship, but nobody appeared in the conning-tower. *UC-29* was a sitting duck at that range, but Campbell was taking no chances. He wanted to catch it with its 'lid' open. All this time not a man on the fo'c'sle had moved a muscle and Williams was still holding up the screen.

Hereford, sitting calmly in his lifeboat on the port quarter, resplendent in his gold-braided cap, now used his initiative. The U-boat, very close on the quarter, was safe from *Pargust*'s stern-mounted 4-inch gun, which could not depress enough. Campbell would want the submarine to be on his beam before delivering his hardest punch. Hereford calmly started to pull towards the starboard side, around the stern of the Q-ship. Rosenow followed, naturally concerned to see what he was going to do. By now there was an officer in the conning-tower, shouting at Hereford through a megaphone, ordering him to hand over his papers, which the German captain would need to confirm his 'kill' when he got back to Brunsbüttel. Hereford feigned either deafness or an inability to understand the shouts, and the lifeboat did not stop. This roused the anger of the officer in the conning-tower. He was now furiously semaphoring to Hereford and had been joined by another man with a rifle. By now the submarine was presenting a nice angle on the beam, with its 'lid' open. And Hereford, although he had now pulled close to the side of *Pargust* and was safely beneath the angle of fire of her guns, was in danger of being shot by the German with the rifle. And for once the cast-iron self-control of the Q-ship men had cracked The men in the lifeboat were starting to laugh. That would give the game away for sure – shipwrecked mariners laughing. Campbell did not hesitate for another second. At 8.36 a.m. he gave the order to open fire.

At last relief came to the aching muscles of William Williams when *Pargust*'s guns' crews finally snapped into action. With a roar the three 12-pounders and the 4-inch blasted out a lethal broadside at the doomed *UC-29*. It was only fifty yards away. Campbell even fired one of his torpedoes as an afterthought, but it missed.

The submarine heeled over on her port side and lost way. Pools of oil were gathering on the surface of the sea around her as men came pouring out of her after-hatch and conning-tower, holding their hands in the air in surrender. But she suddenly surged ahead again, washing the men on her outer casing into the sea. Campbell could not take the risk of catching another torpedo from her and began firing again. This was where the fo'c'sle men came into their own with their 12-pounder. Theirs was now the only gun that would bear, with *UC-29* now fine on the bow. After a few rounds she exploded and sank about 300 yards away, stern first. Thirty-eight shells had been fired at her, point blank, in just four minutes. As she disappeared, the last that was seen of her was a man clinging to her bow. They found only two survivors.

Although *Pargust* was helplessly immobile, with no engines, she was in no immediate danger of sinking, as only the centre part of her was flooded. As long as her bulkheads held up, she could float, and help was not too far away. She only had to wallow around in the Atlantic mist for the rest of the forenoon until they came for her. The sloop HMS *Crocus* towed her to Queenstown, escorted by HMS *Zinnia* and the USS *Cushing*. It was 3 pm. on 8 June.

King George V approved the awarding of two VCs to the crew of HMS *Pargust*. One was to be to an officer and one to a man, as selected under Clause 13 of the statutes of the Victoria Cross. This states that if any "squadron, flotilla or ship's company ... having distinguished itself collectively in the performance of an act of heroic gallantry in the presence of an enemy ... in such a way that the Admiral is unable to single out any individual, then one or more of the officers ... seamen in the ranks ... shall be selected to be recommended to us for the award of the Victoria Cross ... the selection to be by secret ballot."

Campbell's officers pressed him to be the officer recipient, but he already wore the VC and he felt that even that one was a symbol on behalf of the whole crew, rather than for any act of his own. Their suggestion was expressive of the loyalty they felt for him and he was deeply touched by it, but he declined. The ballot was conducted and the officer VC went to the First Lieutenant, Lieutenant Ronald Stuart RNR. The thirty-year-old Stuart, a former Cape Horn windjammer man from Liverpool, was typical of his breed. He was tough, blond and red-faced, from a long line of sailors. Soon he was to be given a Q-ship of his own.

William Williams was elected to receive the lower-deck VC. He came from a poor family of half-a-dozen children in Amlwch Port on Anglesey. He had joined the RNR at the outbreak of war and was well-known to his shipmates as a cool customer when manning a gun. But for him holding up the gun-screen for those thirty-odd minutes of muscle-aching heart-stopping suspense, in Campbell's words, "the action may never have taken place".

Stuart and Williams received their medals from the King at Buckingham Palace on Saturday, 21 July, 1917. Williams' parents, summoned by Admiralty telegram, caught the train up from Anglesey for the ceremony. Some well-earned leave was due and they all went home to Amlwch. The local hero arrived to an understandably excited welcome. He was besieged by reporters, but judging by contemporary news comment, it seems that he shunned publicity. The *Holyhead Chronicle* stated on 24 August that he was "at home and indisposed".

Harold Auten's first Q-ship, in which he was the First Lieutenant, was the 1894 Sunderland-built, 2,900-ton collier *Zylpha*, Q6. She had had an eventful war. At about the same time as Campbell had taken the *Loderer/Farnborough* across the Atlantic in 1916, she too had been ordered there to discharge her coal and cram her holds with Canadian spruce for buoyancy. While on that side of the ocean, she had been dispatched to the Gulf of Mexico to try and find and destroy a U-boat that had been sighted there. It was obviously intent on attacking the oil-tankers which were so vital to Britain's war effort. But it turned out that the 'German' submarine was an obsolete boat that had been bought by an American film director, who was actually filming an 'attack' scene when it had been spotted by a British intelligence agent! Auten saw the funny side of it, wondering what it would have done to Anglo-American relations if he had sunk the sub with several famous actors and actresses on board!

In mid-April *Zylpha* had had a brush with a real U-boat. Her captain, Lieutenant-Commander McLeod, had held his fire, patiently waiting for the German to draw nearer, but it seemed that her captain was intent on following the new 'long range' rules. Fifty shells had already burst around the Q-ship and she had sustained some damage near the water-line. (The shots had been carefully counted by a signalman, sitting quietly in a corner with a note-pad.) McLeod saw that he was merely soaking up punishment unnecessarily. He ordered, "Let go", and at last *Zylpha*'s guns crashed out. The submarine was seen to be hit, but she made off at speed on the surface and was soon out of range of the Q-ship, with her painfully slow maximum eight knots.

One day in early June, 1917, HMS *Zylpha* sailed from Liverpool, headed south, rounded the coast of Ireland and passed the Fastnet Rock, as if she were bound for New York. The third day out dawned gloriously and blossomed into bright beautiful sunshine, with the merest lick of breeze. The morning watchmen felt good to be alive. They had just heard eight bells sound. The forenoon watch would be tumbling up to relieve them and they could enjoy a good breakfast and a smoke. But suddenly there was the almighty roar of an explosion and *Zylpha* seemed to leap clean out of the water in surprise.

Nobody had seen the torpedo coming. It had crashed through the Q-ship's hull on the port side of the engine-room. It was a perfect shot.

Almost instantly the ship's engines were flooded and she lost way. One man was killed. He was *Zylpha*'s peacetime Third Engineer and had been having a wash behind a condenser when the torpedo struck. The others on the engine-room duty watch were lucky to escape up the iron ladders and onto the open deck before they were trapped. The Chief Steward had just drawn some 'victuals' from the Purser and was walking aft with them when the torpedo arrived. He was thrown a good twenty feet along the deck and his stores disappeared over the side. For a minute confusion reigned, but soon everybody gathered their wits and doubled towards their gun positions.

Mcleod ordered the 'panic party' away and they rowed around aimlessly, hoping to entice the submarine to the surface. An hour and a half ticked away, but no sight or sound was heard of it. At long last McLeod's voice came down the pipes, "Submarine in sight. Dead ahead. Long way off. Moving away from us." Eventually, she disappeared altogether. Yet another U-boat commander had followed the 'long range' hit-and-run code. *Zylpha*'s crew were furious. They had lain doggo for nearly two hours without firing a shot, and the German had behaved most unsportingly in not showing himself. Even worse, he had abandoned the crew of a crippled ship 180 miles from land. And *Zylpha* was in a bad way.

It was only the Canadian spruce, hammered tight in her holds, which kept the Q-ship afloat. Her wireless, fortunately, was intact and McLeod was able to transmit a distress call which was picked up by an American destroyer, the USS *Warrington*. She was soon on the scene, but her captain was unwilling to stop for more than a minute in case the U-boat returned to torpedo the destroyer herself. Taking most of *Zylpha*'s crew on board, the destroyer took off on a zig-zag course, circling round the stricken Q-ship and transmitting a distress call for the assistance of an ocean-going tug. But even if one were to sail right away, it would take her at least a day to reach them. McLeod took stock of his situation. His ship was unharmed for'ard, but was badly down astern, with Nos. 3 and 4 holds flooded. He put the pumps into these compartments, and everybody left on board, including the doctor and the paymaster, turned to with the pumping. They worked for a solid twenty-four hours, with the steady clanks of the pumps producing rhythmic spurts of water which flowed over the decks and back into the sea.

At noon the following day *Warrington* signalled that she was low on fuel and was forced to return to harbour. Her crew gave McLeod and his men three hearty cheers as the low, grey shape swung away. It was with heavy hearts that *Zylpha*'s skeleton crew watched her grow smaller in the distance. With steadfast pumping they managed to contain the rise of water, but the weather was worsening. If the sea got up, making her take on too much of a roll, the weight of water still in her could make her bulkheads give way, which would seal her doom.

They tried to fashion some sails out of what canvas was available, but it was woefully inadequate to drive a 3,000-ton ship, especially one that was almost sinking. However, it did permit the helmsman to keep her head towards the nearest land – eastwards – which shielded her holed port side from the worst of the weather. It even seemed that they were making some headway, but each time the navigator got a glimpse of the sun through the greyness of the sky his calculations always came out the same. They were still about 180 miles from land.

All the time the weather was deteriorating and the wind had reached something like gale force. In the middle of the night the sea at last broke over the after-part of the wallowing *Zylpha*. The men working the pumps were held fast by lifelines, but McLeod realized that it was too dangerous for them to continue. They secured the pumps and retreated, cold and exhausted, to huddle beneath the bridge. She was rolling crazily and the water within her could be heard hurling its weight, with great booming slaps, against the bulkheads between the compartments.

In the following forenoon the First Lieutenant reported that the stokehold deckhead was giving way and there was danger of water flowing right for'ard through the 'tween decks, which would flood the fore-holds. It would also put the wireless office out of action. *Zylpha*'s transmitting range was only fifty miles, but her operator was able to listen in on the many calls, all beyond that distance, between the ships searching for her. It must have been soul-destroying listening to the would-be rescuers, whilst quite unable to utter a sound.

She would have foundered for sure but for the brave actions of the crew of volunteers, led by the First Lieutenant and the Chief Engineer, who went down into the watery hell of the stokehold and shored up the deck-head with great baulks of timber. She was still afloat the following noon, but only just. And then the lookout shouted, "Smoke ahead!"

Several ships had found *Zylpha* simultaneously. There, in front of their exhausted eyes, was salvation. It was the destroyer USS *Drayton*, with a couple of Queenstown tugs, and the sloop HMS *Daffodil*, which took her in tow. The sloop towed her most of the way home, but she was slowly sinking all the time and did not quite make it. They were just off the coast of Killarney when she slipped out of sight. It was 11.20 p.m. on 15 June, 1917.

The sloop *Salvia*, Q15, first saw action on 20 October, 1916, when she was torpedoed and left to grope her way home with her choking stokers working for all they were worth in a cauldron of steam and lyddite fumes. And on 30 June, 1917, it happened again. She was in the Atlantic, about 200 miles from the coast of Ireland, when she was struck on the starboard quarter. The concussion caused her own depth-charges to explode, which devastated her stern more or less completely, blew the 4-inch gun into the water and put her engines out of action. The submarine, *U-94*, then surfaced and began to shell her from long range from dead astern. Soon a fire had started in her wheel-house and spread rapidly to the bridge. Five sailors had lost their lives in the attack. The survivors took to the boats and Carley rafts, whereupon the U-boat closed with them, and took the Q-ship's captain prisoner. She watched the *Salvia* sink and then dived, leaving them to their fate, soaring and plunging over the rolling humps of the high ocean swell. In such conditions a small object such as a Carley raft can be invisible, even from only a short distance away, and it is not surprising that very soon the men in the boats lost sight of the rafts. After an hour or so, whilst poised at the top of a hill of black water and just about to slide into the deep valley on the other side, one of the boats caught sight of a mast. It appeared to be a tramp steamer. They hoisted their little sail and managed to steer close enough to her for them to be seen. They were in luck. It was the Q-sloop HMS *Aubretia*, commanded by the retired Admiral Marx, who had returned to the service as a Captain RNR. It was 11.20 a.m. when she picked them up. The sloop circled the area for another couple of hours before she found the other three boats and the rafts.

June, 1917, had not been short of action for both the Q-ships and the U-boats. *Pargust* had sunk *UC-29* on the 7th and, as we have already seen, Godfrey Herbert's depth-charges from the *Sea King* put paid to *UC-66* on the 12th. In July the barquentine Q28, (*Merops, Bellmore, Imperieuse, Maracaibo, Steady* or *Toofa*) caught fire and eight of her crew were badly overcome by the fumes from her burning lyddite ammunition. And HMS *Redbreast*, a 1,300-ton steamship working as

a fleet messenger in the eastern Mediterranean, was torpedoed by
UC-38 on the 15th.

But it was a bad month for the U-boats, too. UC-1 and UB-20 were
mined. U-99 was torpedoed by the British sub. J-2. UB-27 was rammed
and depth-charged by a patrol vessel. UC-61 was stranded at Boulogne
and UB-27 was mysteriously lost, probably off S.W. Ireland. The
Q-ships may have had a quiet month, but it was a lull before a storm.
The seas around the British Isles were to rumble with shellfire
throughout the whole of August as the pace of the battle picked up
again.

The Q-ship HMS *Chagford* was the 2,095-ton ex-Admiralty collier
Bracondale. The Navy had not stinted itself when arming her. She had
a 4-inch gun, two 12-pounders, a howitzer, two Maxims and two
18-inch torpedo tubes. Commanded by Lieutenant D.G. Jeffrey, RNR,
she sailed from her base at Buncrana, in Lough Swilly on the Donegal
coast, on 2 August to search for U-boats. By dawn on the 5th she was
125 miles into the Atlantic, north-west of Tory Island, where sightings
of submarines had been reported. Just after 4.00 a.m. an unseen torpedo
from an unseen submarine caught her directly under the bridge. It was
a fine shot by the U-boat captain. With one torpedo he wrecked both
her torpedo tubes and 4-inch gun, reduced her starboard life-boats to
firewood, shattered Jeffrey's cabin and chart-room, caused the engine-
room to flood, putting her engines out of action, and disrupted all her
voice-pipe connections. As the 'panic' boats were getting away, the
submarine surfaced about 750 yards off the starboard side. This was
far beyond an ideal range for Jeffrey to open fire, but he had no other
option because the damage done by the explosion had left his guns
exposed. The ship's 12-pounders and Maxims fired as many rounds as
they could at the U-boat and were gratified to see some of them strike
home, but of course the German dived immediately he realized that he
was facing a warship.

Half an hour later a second torpedo struck *Chagford* amidships on
the starboard side. Now was the time for a little more clever play-acting.
Jeffrey recalled the 'panic' boats and, together with rafts and a dinghy,
most of the remainder of the crew got away in them, leaving only the
captain himself, four officers and a petty officer hiding on board. But
the submarine's captain was reluctant to be fooled. He stayed
submerged. Another hour went by and he fired yet a third torpedo,
again at the starboard side of *Chagford*. She was now in a desperate

condition and only kept afloat by her wooden 'cargo'. Still the German did not show himself, at least not at close range. He took himself off to the horizon to surface for a while and then dived again. His periscopes reappeared, only a few yards away, to snoop all around the waterlogged *Chagford*. All day he kept this up, returning every hour or so to repeat his inspection. All day the Q-ship was gradually settling in the water. And all day Jeffrey and his men watched in suspense from their peep-holes, talking only in whispers.

When night came Jeffrey anticipated that the Germans would come aboard under cover of darkness. He issued rifles and bayonets all round. They did not come, but he could see that his ship was not going to stay afloat much longer. Probably the U-boat captain had reasoned that his prey was sinking anyway and had gone to seek fresh targets. At midnight Jeffrey decided that it was time to leave and the six of them took to an abandoned motor-boat they had picked up at sea a few days before. It had no fuel and they were faced with a long row. They were lucky to be spotted and picked up by a trawler, HMS *Saxon*, in the morning. They returned to *Chagford*, which still had not sunk, and took her in tow. Now barely afloat, she broke up under the tow and finally sank early the next day. It was 7 August.

But her last fight had probably not been totally in vain. It would seem that she was at least partly responsible for the U-boat eventually meeting her end. On 8 August, the day after *Chagford* sank, *U-44* rendezvoused with *U-84* off the Hebrides. Her captain, Wagenführ, reported that he had tangled with a decoy three days before. When he had crash-dived under the sudden shellfire, water had flooded his batteries and the sub had been filled with chlorine gas, which still lingered, making it impossible to dive for more than a few minutes. On the night of 11/12 August Wagenführ managed to contact Wilhelmshaven by wireless, saying that he would meet his escort at 0600 on the 13th off the coast of Norway. But he never made it. The British intercepted his wireless message and the Third Light Cruiser Squadron was alerted. It was the destroyer HMS *Oracle* which sighted the strange sailing-craft with a submarine's body on the horizon. It was a far from convincing disguise and, what was more, Wagenführ knew that he could not hope to outpace a destroyer, even on the surface. And so he took down his sail and dived. Inevitably the chlorine forced him to surface after only a few minutes, only to find *Oracle* waiting and ready to ram. The destroyer's sharp bow sliced into the hull of *U-44* and as she passed over she let go a depth-charge for good measure.

While the *Chagford* versus *U-44* drama had been taking place, Captain Gordon Campbell, VC and his intrepid decoymen had been in action again. They had stayed in Queenstown for only one night with the battered *Pargust* before being towed round to Plymouth. Once in dry-dock there, it became apparent that her damage was far more than had been realized and it was decided to pay her off. Even at the height of a major war, officialdom will always cause an obstruction to those whose only wish is to get on with the fighting and Campbell was faced with much dreary paperwork in dealing with all the formalities connected with a 'paying off'.

Nevertheless, the enforced break from the constant stresses of his particular brand of naval warfare was, no doubt, a blessing, although he would never have admitted it. His home in Saltash, on the Cornish side of the Tamar, was close at hand and he was able to spend time there relaxing with his family. His crew, too, temporarily housed in Devonport Barracks, were given time to unwind.

One of them, the loyal Leading Seaman Jack Orr, who had been with Campbell ever since they had first commissioned the *Loderer*, went over to Saltash one day to 'tidy up' the garden. The Captain returned to find that all the stones had been whitewashed, 'shipshape', and that no distinction had been made between weeds and flowers! Campbell was clearly fond of Orr. He described their first meeting. "I saw a man getting on in years sauntering about with a face like a sea-boot, and I casually asked him if he had ever steered a ship. He gave me a look I shall never forget, spat on the deck, and asked me if I realized he had been Quartermaster in the *Titanic*, and was now 'by rights' Chief Quartermaster of the *Olympic*. (He didn't tell me his chief duty was probably looking after the ladies' deck-chairs.) I asked him if he would come on a 'stunt'. He came and stayed with me till the end of the war, as Quartermaster and my servant in mystery ships, and then as my coxswain in light cruisers. Jack Orr was his name, and I have never met a more typical handyman. He was a brilliant helmsman and an excellent servant, the sort that puts your morning tea just out of reach, so that you either turn out and get it or go without. Hairdressing, tattooing, and carpentry were among his other qualifications. I never once saw him laugh during the three years he was with me. I tried hard to make him do so, but the most I could get was a faint smile combined with an agonized face."

With *Pargust* paid off, no time was lost in fitting out a replacement. Another Cardiff ship, the *Dunraven*, was selected. She was a 3,117-ton collier, 331 feet long, with a large poop and a double well-deck. By now the small tightly-knit Q-ship fraternity had acquired a rich pool of ideas and experiences which they readily imparted to each other. Many of these were applied to *Dunraven*. She was to be a showpiece; a 'top of the range' model of a Q-ship. As with *Pargust*'s 4-inch gun, the hatch concealing it was roofless, and the gun protruded slightly above the sides, to be hidden by some old bits of canvas draped over a derrick which lay along the top of the gun, as if drying. Just abaft the dummy hatch was a dummy hawser reel. It was simply a steel drum with ropes reeled round it, with observation slits cut in its sides, and a periscope. The officer of the gun entered it via a trap-door from below deck.

The large poop space was to play an important part when *Dunraven* went into action. Campbell had had the poop deck lowered to accommodate the guns and various decoy gadgetry. Beneath it sat four large depth-charges, each containing 300 lb of explosive ready to slide through the stern-ports. The rest of the space was taken up as a mess-deck for the gun's crew, and stores compartments. Most thought-provoking of all, at least for the guns' crews, were the 4-inch shells which lay in their racks in the magazines alongside the mess-deck space.

Campbell had just learned of the death of Hallwright, whom Harold Auten was to succeed as captain of the Q-sloop *Heather*. Poor Hallwright's naval career had been peppered with action and trouble. As a sixteen-year-old midshipman, he had gone ashore with the guns from HMS *Terrible* to blast the way through to Ladysmith during the Boer War. Immediately afterwards *Terrible* had proceeded to the China Station to help quell the Boxer Rebellion. At nineteen, Hallwright was fined ten shillings by the Portsmouth Magistrates for being drunk and disorderly, which also cost him three months' seniority. At twenty-eight, when serving on the Australia Station in the cruiser HMS *Psyche*, he was dismissed his ship for misconduct. In December, 1916, he was praised by Admiral Bayly for his handling of an incident involving the Sinn Feiners off Galway Bay and was awarded a 'red recommend' for his 'exceptional ability'. Promoted to Lieutenant-Commander as captain of *Heather Q-16*, he had distinguished himself in an action with a U-boat on 19 March, 1917. This earned him the DSO, but he never knew the honour of wearing the medal on his chest because only weeks later, on 21 April, he had been lying on his belly on the bridge, looking through the peep-hole at a U-boat, when a shell-splinter had torn its way through the screen and ripped into his brain. Thus cautioned, Campbell had the sides of *Dunraven*'s bridge lined with one-inch armour-plating. As will be seen, this almost certainly saved his life.

Around the new Q-ship's upper works was installed a perforated pipe, connected to the boiler-room. At the turn of a tap Campbell could make a generous wreath of steam hang over the ship, giving the appearance that she had been hit in the engine-room or boiler-room. With the U-boats now following the practice of firing at long range, hopefully this would fool the German gunners into thinking that their shooting had been more accurate than had been the case.

As a final touch Campbell had four fake railway trucks made out of canvas on wooden frames. Many of these were being carried as deck cargo by merchant ships outward bound for the Mediterranean at the time. It was a clever idea. They were easily collapsible, and by taking them down in the night, when turning for the in-bound leg of a patrol, Campbell was able to add another 'change of identity' item to his repertoire.

Dunraven's crew were nearly all ex-*Pargust*. All had volunteered to sail with Campbell again. Many of them had now been torpedoed twice already, which speaks volumes for the calibre of determination and *esprit de corps* that existed. The First Lieutenant, Stuart, had been appointed to command his own Q-ship, HMS *Tamarisk*, and Campbell promoted his Second Officer, thirty-two-year-old Lieutenant Charles Bonner RNR, to take his place.

Bonner, youngest son of a Midlands farmer, had joined the merchant navy training ship *Conway* when he was fifteen, and obtained his master's certificate at twenty-two. He had had a strange war so far, being interned in Belgium whilst serving as a petty officer RNVR in the naval division. Finding this unacceptable, he managed to make his way back to England by devious means, only to meet with official disapproval of his conduct! As a result he was drafted to a cruiser as an ordinary seaman! Eventually officialdom came to its senses, as it has sometimes done on other rare occasions throughout the ages, and Bonner was commissioned as a Sub-Lieutenant RNR. It had only been on 17 June, a few weeks before *Dunraven* sailed, that he had married Alice Mabel Partridge at St Matthew's Church, Walsall.

Campbell faced a heart-rending problem with John Smith. After the

Engineer Sub-Lieutenant's ordeal in *Pargust*'s engine-room, and his subsequent operations, he had been packed off from hospital to convalesce. Now he appeared in Devonport, having made the long journey from Scotland without official permission, to volunteer to sail again. Clearly, the man's nerves were still in tatters. Campbell could only admire his "pig-headed Scottish blood", as he put it, but it was obvious that Smith was in no fit state to sail. With much tact, and doubtless a few 'white lies', Campbell managed to 'decoy' him into returning to hospital.

Reports had been coming in of German submarine activity in the Bay of Biscay, and when *Dunraven* sailed, disguised as a steamer of the Blue Funnel Line, Campbell headed south from Plymouth with his four 'railway trucks' conspicuously displayed on deck as a bait. They spent an uneventful three days on this course, and were well down into the Bay when Campbell turned back homeward during the night, carefully remembering to collapse the trucks first.

The next day, 7 August, was still and hazy. The Bay of Biscay, flat as a puddle, was adorned with great patches of dense summer fog. In the afternoon they sighted a large white schooner in full sail, graceful as a swan, just before it vanished into a fog bank. At once the sailors' superstitions were aroused. One old salt was convinced that they had seen the Phantom Ship of the Bay of Biscay and that this was a very bad omen. Some laughed, but others agreed with him. Two of the wireless ratings said that they too had had premonitions that they would soon be in a fight, and both had taken a good bath so as to be clean in case they were wounded.

Dunraven continued northward and was about 100 miles off Brest by the morning of the 8th. It was at precisely 10.58 in the forenoon that a submarine was spotted on the starboard beam. It was *UC-71* and she was steering towards them. As usual they chose not to have seen it and continued innocently on their way. The submarine dived. Nothing happened for an agonizing half-hour; then it re-surfaced dead astern and opened fire. Campbell raised the Red Ensign and fired back with his little poop gun. The British gun crew, Leading Seaman Cooper, Seaman William Williams, VC, and Wireless Operator Statham were, of course, fully exposed to the U-boat's fire. Their act had been well rehearsed. All their shells fell well short of the submarine, in order to try to entice it nearer. The number of mis-fires they contrived to effect, and their knockabout clumsiness around the gun, would have caused a

Whale Island Gunnery Instructor to have had convulsions if it had been genuine.

Campbell made as much smoke as possible to give the impression that he was running away, but in reality he had reduced his speed by one knot. By doing this, and by making the occasional zig-zag, he brought the submarine into closer range. He started to transmit uncoded wireless signals: "SOS"; "Am being attacked"; "Help". This brought replies from the Lizard and other stations, asking the ship's position, but these received no answer. *Dunraven*'s operators, being in a 'panic', were not, of course, listening to incoming calls.

Campbell's tactics appeared to be working because, although the U-boat had been firing persistently for half an hour, all its shots were falling ahead of *Dunraven*. It ceased firing, approached at speed to a range of 1,000 yards, and from a position fine on the quarter restarted the attack. Campbell passed the order to stand by to 'abandon ship'. The German's fire was becoming more accurate and his shots were now falling uncomfortably close. When one splashed only a few feet away, Campbell turned on his new-fangled steam device and the Q-ship became enshrouded in a thick cloud, as if she had caught a shell in the engine or boiler-rooms. He ordered 'abandon ship'. Cooper, Williams and Statham ran from their gun on the poop and the usual confusion started with the 'panic party'.

As *Dunraven* came to a stop, UC-71's captain, Salzwedel, closed still further. The U-boat fired a single shot, which hit the poop with dire consequences. There was an enormous explosion and it seemed to Campbell that her magazines had blown up. This would mean that the Q-ship's secret 4-inch gun would have been revealed to the enemy. Momentarily unsighted by his clouds of steam, and concerned for the safety of his crew now that the game was up, he sent out a genuine call for assistance from any British man o' war. As luck would have it, there happened to be a battleship, homeward bound from the Mediterranean, in the vicinity, which answered his call to say that it was sending one of its destroyer escorts to assist. But then the steam cleared and he was surprised to see that the poop was still intact. One of the depth-charges had exploded, blowing Seaman Morrison clean through the poop doors. He was severely wounded, but was found by a shipmate trying to stagger back to his post. "I'm in charge of the depth-charges," he explained, "I must get back to them." Lieutenant Bonner had been blown out of his 'hawser reel' and was wounded in the process, but had managed to crawl along the deck and into the hatch with the 4-inch gun crew.

Dunraven's guns had not, after all, been exposed to the Germans and the 'harmless merchant ship' sham could continue. Campbell hurriedly sent out another call, "Keep away for the present." A thirty-knot destroyer slicing its way onto the scene would have been most unwelcome now that there was still a chance to decoy the U-boat.

UC-71 fired twice more, both shells hitting the poop again. Instantly there were clouds of black smoke and angry orange-red flames started to lick around the after-end of the ship. Campbell faced an agonizing dilemma. The magazine in the poop was soon certain to erupt and the sailors hiding there would be blown to smithereens. If he ordered them to leave the gun, he would reveal the fact that *Dunraven* was not 'abandoned' and the submarine would simply dispatch her with a torpedo and go on its way to sink more merchant ships. Or he could open fire on the U-boat. But he could hardly see it through the smoke, although it was moving towards a position which would give him a better sight. But it was not quite there yet and at any second now the magazines would explode.

It was a huge amount of explosives that the men in the poop were virtually sitting on and the disciplined bravery which they displayed can rarely have been matched in the history of sea-fighting. Choked and blinded by the smoke and fumes from the fire raging only a few steps away from them, they remained at their gun stations, hidden in their dummy deck-house awaiting the order to open fire on the U-boat. The deck beneath them was scorching hot. Beneath it was the magazine. And on it, all around their gun, were shells and boxes of cordite. Very soon, even if the magazine itself did not explode, this 'ready use' ammunition would do so as the deck grew hotter. In order to save the show, the cordite had to be prevented from over-heating, and so, with scarcely believable courage, they sat on the searing hot deck and lifted the boxes on to their knees. To call it a dramatic moment of high suspense must be an understatement. "To cold-bloodedly leave the gun's crew to their fate seemed awful," Campbell wrote, "and the names of each of them flashed through my mind, but our duty was to sink the submarine. By losing a few men we might save thousands not only of lives but of ships and tons of the nation's requirements."

And so he waited. *UC-71* slid past the stern of the burning Q-ship. In a mere fraction of a minute it would be well on the weather side of her and within the combined arc of three hidden 12-pounder guns. But at that very instant, 12.58 p.m., the poop went up with a deafening roar which shook *Dunraven* to her very rivets. The stern was blown out and the 4-inch gun and its crew were sent cartwheeling into the air. The gun, weighing several tons, landed on the well-deck, and its ready-use shells, which had been stacked on the deck around it, fell like gigantic hailstones all over the ship. Luckily none exploded. As for the men, one of them came down into the sea, together with a shower of tins of condensed milk which rained on to the panic party in their boat. The others were all saved by Campbell's canvas 'railway trucks'! These, being collapsed flat on the deck, acted as a merciful cushion as the men fell from the air on to them. By a miracle, they all landed on the canvas and they all survived. Bonner, severely stunned and with his hands badly burned, staggered up on to the bridge and apologized to Campbell for leaving the gun! Later, he could not remember having done any such thing.

Dunraven's true character as a warship had now been revealed to Salzwedel. There was nothing for it but for Campbell to order 'Let go'. The White Ensign shot up and the boat-deck 12-pounder got in a couple of rounds before the submarine crash-dived, although it was unlikely that she was seriously damaged. Salzwedel said later that the Q-ship's disguise had been immaculate. Until the explosion, he had had absolutely no reason to suspect that he was dealing with anything but another tramp steamer, despite all his patient caution.

It was now virtually certain that the German would torpedo *Dunraven*. Quickly Campbell took stock of his situation. It appeared that by some million-to-one chance the magazine had not, after all, exploded, it had been the remaining depth-charges, containing between them 900 lb of TNT. The fire was now raging furiously around the mangled stern of the stricken ship. The after-deck had been rolled back like the flap of an envelope, exposing the side of the magazine. Even where the deck was still intact, it was scorching hot. There was still a chance, albeit a faint one, that they could decoy *UC-71* by sending away another panic party in a seemingly 'genuine' abandonment of the ship as soon as the inevitable torpedo struck. Campbell turned all his available water hoses on to the burning poop and shifted all the wounded men to the saloon, or into the cabins, so that they could receive first-aid attention from Surgeon Probationer Alexander Fowler, who had joined the ship only five days before.

Then they settled down to wait. It was not long coming. At 1.20 p.m. a tell-tale streak was seen approaching them on the starboard side, and seconds later there was an enormous crash as the torpedo hit *Dunraven* just abaft the engine-room. The fake railway trucks and hatch-covers were splintered into matchwood and the plates in the engine-room bulkhead parted. Campbell sent his 'Q abandon ship' party away, some in the 'panic boat' which had returned to take them on board, and some on a rough and ready raft which they had lashed together from spars and empty casks to give another touch of realism.

Including the wounded, there were still thirty-six men on board the Q-ship. Campbell had kept back two guns' crews. One, under Lieutenant Nisbet, manned the fo'c'sle 12-pounder, and the other was huddled inside the dummy 'cabins' amidships, where they could fire either the port or starboard gun as required, with Sub-Lieutenant Frame in command.

UC-71 circled the helpless ship for nearly an hour at periscope depth. It was plain that Salzwedel was not prepared to rush in, but he frequently presented a good close target for Campbell if the latter had chosen to use his own torpedoes. Campbell admitted later that he had no great faith in his torpedoes and elected to wait on the chance that the German would surface to find Nisbet's and Frame's 12-pounder muzzles firing at him. Meanwhile *Dunraven* was seriously on fire. The shells and boxes of cordite below the poop deck were exploding sporadically all the time, as soon as each one reached the required temperature to set it off. And with water flooding into her engine-room, the Q-ship was slowly sinking.

At 2.30 p.m. the submarine surfaced dead astern and began shelling the *Dunraven* with its big deck gun. The first shell smashed into the bridge, ruining Campbell's little bathroom which the dockyard had installed there. A splinter ripped off Jack Orr's cap as he crouched at the wheel. There was no question but that all four men on that bridge would have been killed if it had not been for Campbell's last minute fitting of the armour-plating around it.

Campbell was powerless to reply, because he now had no guns that would bear astern, and the *Dunraven* had to endure nearly another half an hour of heavy shelling, although little more damage was done. At 2.55 p.m. the U-boat dived to periscope depth. She was only 150 yards away and now Campbell did use his torpedoes. He fired the port side tube personally, but at such short range it passed over the submarine, apparently unnoticed. Salzwedel started to circle the ship again, and Hereford, on the starboard side of the Q-ship's bridge, prepared to fire his torpedo when the German passed down that side. The U-boat was so close that the sound of Hereford's torpedo striking it was plainly audible. But it failed to explode.

UC-71 would have sailed from base with a full load of seven torpedoes, but Salzwedel now had none left. Campbell, of course, had no way of knowing this, and all he and his men could do was to await the *coup de grace* – which never came. Any intentions that the German may have had of surfacing to continue the assault by means of shellfire were frustrated by the timely and unexpected arrival of an American armed yacht, the USS *Noma*. The American fired a few shots at the U-boat's periscope, which forced it to submerge completely, not to be seen again. It was now 4.00 p.m., five hours after the action had started.

HMS *Dunraven* had lost her submarine and lost the fight. The gun crews emerged from their stations. The strain they had endured, tightening all the while like a wound-up clock-spring for five hours under continual threat of attack, had affected some of them to such a degree that they had gone, temporarily out of their minds. Two of them had to be physically restrained from diving into the sea to chase after the U-boat and 'get him'! In the saloon, where the wounded lay, one man was licking blood to quench his thirst.

Soon the destroyers HMS *Attack* and HMS *Christopher* arrived and the rescue operation began. The first task was to attend to the wounded and the Medical Officers of the *Noma* and *Christopher* came on board to assist Fowler. The two most serious, seamen John Martindale and Alex Morrison, required operations and were taken with all haste on to the *Noma* for hospitalization in Brest. Then there were the fires to put out and the tow cables to prepare on the fo'c'sle. And they had not eaten since breakfast that morning. The weather was getting up and *Dunraven* was shipping more and more water by the stern every minute. It was a sorrowful scene. Campbell transferred most of the men to the trawler *Foss*, which was standing by. Bonner pleaded with Campbell to be allowed to stay. They put him in a chair on the bridge, where he sat with a bandage round his head, keeping up a cheery patter with those around him.

Christopher took up the tow. This ship was manned by some of the unsung heroes of the war. Time and again her name crops up when stories of rescue in the Channel and the Western Approaches are recounted. They managed to make about one knot through the water, but by nine o'clock that evening *Dunraven* was two-thirds full of water. The tow was transferred to a couple of ocean-going tugs, *Atlanta* and *Sun II*, but by the early hours of the morning Campbell sensed that she was about to go under. He ordered the tugs to release the tow, signalled *Christopher* to come back alongside and mustered his skeleton crew. It was a pitch-dark night, with a stiff wind churning up a humpy sea. The men had fallen in on the sloping fo'c'sle and stood there in hushed silence, expressionless, just staring into the blackness. Speaking years later, Campbell was to describe what happened next as the most exciting – if unpleasant – moment of his life.

"I intended to remain on the bridge and go down with the ship," he said. "Why, I do not know, as there was no sense in doing so, but I had a sort of feeling that a captain should go down with his ship, a no doubt worthy but erroneous idea. However, Hereford eventually persuaded me to go down with him, having pointed out that I could do no good to anyone by going down with the ship for no good reason. I therefore walked for'ard with him to the forecastle deck and the ship was so far gone that we had to wade through water to get there. The destroyer's boat had not yet arrived when I joined my crew and I realized that when it did, it would not be safe for more than four men to go in her, otherwise she would capsize.

"It was obvious that our ship was sinking fast and that there would be time for the boat to make only one trip. I gave orders for 'only four men to get into the boat when she arrives'. There was still deadly silence, only broken when the senior hand said to me,' No one wants to be saved before the others, sir. Will you please mention four men by name?'

"I mentioned four men by name. They got into the boat and not another man moved. The boat never came back, for by this time the water had worked so far for'ard that we were standing in it and so we had to 'fall in' on the forecastle head. Lieutenant-Commander Peters of HMS *Christopher* then bumped the bows of his destroyer against our bows, being carried away by the waves and then closing again. The crew jumped from our deck into the darkness on to the deck of the destroyer, (one by one, each time she bumped) but no man jumped until I personally told him to do so. By the time I got on to the deck of the destroyer, *Dunraven* had gone end up and sank in a perpendicular position."

Dunraven had gone on her reluctant way to rest sixty fathoms down. It was 3.17 a.m. The destroyer made for Plymouth, where they found their shipmates who had arrived in the *Foss*. They were a sorry sight to behold, having lost everything but the clothes on their backs. Campbell was surprised to find that he still wore his whistle and binoculars round his neck.

Admiral Bayly summoned Campbell to Queenstown. It had been decided that it was time for him to be given an indefinite rest from Q-ship work, having done more than his fair share of it. His protests that he wished to continue fell on deaf ears, even when a telegram was delivered during his interview with the Admiral which read, "Crew of *Dunraven* all volunteer for further service under your command".

They had failed in their last fight, but it had been an astounding display of sheer cold-blooded bravery, steadfast discipline and grim determination. Plaudits came in from all around, from Their Lordships at the Admiralty, other officers and men of the Royal Navy, various dignitaries and ordinary members of the public. Even Salzwedel, in his report to his superiors, paid tribute to them. Admiral Sims, of the U.S. Navy, wrote to Campbell, "Long after we are dust and ashes, the story of this fight will be an invaluable inspiration to British and American naval officers and men. I know of nothing finer in naval history than the conduct of the men of the after-gun crew, or indeed of the entire crew of the *Dunraven*."

The greatest honour was bestowed on them by the King, who presented the Victoria Cross to Bonner and to the after-gun crew under Rule 13. Petty Officer Ernest Pitcher, P/227029, the 4-inch gunlayer, who had supported cordite on his knees in the oven-heat of the poop, was elected by ballot to receive the VC. The other members of the gun's crew received the Conspicuous Gallantry Medal, and most of the rest of the lower deck, were decorated in one way or another. Campbell himself received a second bar to his DSO, Hereford, Grant and Loveless Bars to their DSCs, Nunn the DSO and Andrews, Fowler and Frame the DSC, whilst Nisbet was Mentioned in Dispatches.

After the war Bonner specialized in marine salvage work with the Leith Salvage & Towage Co. for the rest of his working life. He was involved in several major projects in the course of his career, including the salvage of the *Caledonia* in the Firth of Forth during World War Two, and in 1948 he went to Norway to advise on the salvage of the German battleship *Tirpitz*.

Pitcher, the wiry twenty-eight-year-old son of a Swanage, Dorset, coastguard, had joined the Navy at fifteen. He volunteered for Q-ship

CERTIFICATE FOR WOUNDS AND HURTS

These are to Certify the Right Honourable the Lords Commissioners of the Admiralty that

(Name in full) (Rank or Rating) (Official or Regimental No.)

William Henry Bennison Seaman RNR 7495 A.

belonging to His Majesty's Ship *Dunraven*

being then actually upon His Majesty's Service in Special Service.

Here describe the particular duty

"Injured" or "Wounded" Date

was wounded on 8th August 1917 by explosion on board during encounter with enemy submarine. He received a scalp wound two inches long over left supra-orbital ridge, abrasions & contusion left elbow, and severe sprain left right ankle.

Here describe minutely the nature of the injury sustained and the manner in which it occurred :- as required by Articles 1207, 1318 and 1354 of the Kings Regulations

A. E. Fowler
Surg. Prob. R.N.V.R.

"Sober" or not sober

He was sober at the time.

Personal Description

Age about 20 years. Born at or near Hartlepool Height 5 ft. 7½ ins
Hair Brown Eyes Blue Complexion Fair

Particular marks or scars.

Tattoo marks as follows. Ring on right middle finger
W.H.B. on left forearm posteriorly. Sailor and arm on left forearm anteriorly. Flag surrounded by wreath & clasped hands below "on" and "abreast" right forearm

Date 15 August 1917

Signature of Commanding Officer of Ship or of Coast Guard or Marine Division. Gordon Campbell

Rank Captain

Signature of Person who witnessed the accident Gordon Campbell

Rank Captain

Signature of Medical Officer [signature]

Rank Staff Surgeon General.

NOTE:- The grant of a Hurt Certificate to a Petty Officer or Man is to be noted on his Service Certificate.

C. P., Ltd.

The wound Certificate of Seaman William Bennison, of the *Dunraven*'s after gun-crew.

service while serving in the super-dreadnought *King George V*, and had been a member of Campbell's crews since August, 1916. He was also honoured by France, receiving the French Médaille Militaire and the Croix de Guerre.

Clearly, and understandably, the memory of their fight against *UC-71* that day in August, 1917, and their affection for the *Dunraven* never left Bonner or Pitcher. Bonner's son was christened Gordon Dunraven, while Pitcher's house at 4 Richmond Road, Swanage, was called Dunraven, and his daughter was christened Ruth Mary Dunraven.

Bonner died at his home in Edinburgh on 7 February, 1951. Pitcher died of tuberculosis in the RN Hospital, Sherborne, on 10 February, 1946. There is a memorial tablet in his honour in the parish church at Swanage.

The other lower-deck honours were as follows:-

Conspicuous Gallantry Medal. (The after-gun crew).
Able Seaman Dennis Murphy, D/J 25416.
Able Seaman Richard Shepherd, D/J 25419.
Seaman William Bennison, A7495.
Seaman John Martindale, A8556.
Wireless Telegraph Operator Thomas Fletcher, WTS404.
Seaman James Thompson, A6029.
Seaman Alex Morrison, A5848, (posthumously)

Bar to Distinguished Service Medal.
Seaman William Williams, VC, A6224.
Leading Seaman John Orr, D2434.
Signalman Charles Hurrell, Z2181.

Distinguished Service Medal.
Stoker John Cook, S4704.
Wireless Telegraph Operator William Statham, WTS34.
Leading Seaman Edward Cooper, D/J —7225
Stoker William O'Leary, S8352.
Petty Officer Samuel Nance, D/185134.
Seaman Benjamin Haynes, A8476.
Stoker Robert Thomson, S4031.
Seaman David Dow, A8593.
Stoker Thomas Owen, S8362.
Steward 2nd Class William Trickey, D/L4900.

17. "...the wiry, and sometimes fiery, Commander Maurice Blackwood" (p. 123) seen here as a midshipman in 1902, convalescing after being accidentally shot in the foot while serving in HMS *Andromeda*.

18. Lieutenant Harold Auten, VC, disguised as the skipper of a merchant ship (see p.140).

19. "Korvetten-Kapitan Graf Nikolaus zu Dohna-Schlodien... a classic example of one of the Kaiser's Navy's wealthy officer class" (p. 152) addressing the crew of the *Möwe*.

20. SMS *Möwe* (see p. 179 *et seq.*) leaving Kiel on her first cruise, still in her "banana boat" colours.

21. Leutnant Berg (inset) and the prize crew of the *Appam* (see p. 188).

22. *Möwe* coaling from the *St Theodore*, later the *Geier* (see p. 188).

23. The *St Theodore* was renamed SMS *Geier* -- the Vulture" (p. 192).

24. "A glance at her counter-stern would have revealed the name *Jupiter*. But that was a sham. In reality they had christened her *Wolf*." (p. 204).

25. "The buff-funnelled, 5,500-ton *Turritella*, owned by the Anglo-Saxon Petroleum Co., with a Chinese crew, British officers and a New Zealand captain" (p. 207) – captured by the *Wolf* and converted into the *Iltis*.

26. "They found her pilot, Fabecke... and his observer, Stein, ...but it was quite clear that the *Wölfchen* herself would not be taking to the skies for a while" (p. 218).

27. Karl Nerger (right), Captain of the *Wolf*, is welcomed by Admiral Scheer on his return to Keil (see p.242).

28. *Wolf*'s prisoners disembark at Keil (see pp. 242-3). Note the *Wölfchen* in the background.

29. "Soon she was to be famous under another name, SMS *Seeadler* – the Sea Eagle" (p. 247).

30. " A youthful sailor by the name of Schmidt was fitted out with a blonde wig and a dress to act as Luckner's spouse 'Josephine'" (p. 248).

31. Luckner, with his officers, sampling some of the *Horngarth's* champagne and cognac in the Pacific, June, 1917. Left to right, Dr Pietsch (physician), Luckner, Leutnant Kling, (first officer), Leutnant Pries, (prize officer), Chief Engineer Krause, Helmsman Luedemann (standing), Leutnant Kircheiss, (navigator and gunnery officer).

32. The *Seeadler* on the reef at Mopelia, having been set on fire on Luckner's orders (see pp. 256-7).

Assistant Steward Arthur Pennal, MMR723406.
Seaman Martin Connors, A8484.
Leading Seaman Alfred Kaye, A6439.
Seaman Frederick Dodd, A5985.
Stoker John Colenso, D/K28863.
Stoker Walter Crosbie, D/K28791
Leading Stoker John Davies, S8396.
Shipwright William Smart, P/M16854.
Wireman Stanley Woodison, P/M15547.
Chief Steward Alfred Townshend, Dis. A89681
Seaman Patrick Murphy, A8489.

Mentioned in Dispatches.
Chief Petty Officer George Truscott, D/140440.
Able Seaman Francis Hawkins, D/J29968.
Able Seaman Bruce Harris, D/S6495.
Able Seaman William Bethell, D/J20464.
Able Seaman John Dineen, D/J21305.
Able Seaman Harold Pearson, D/J28857.
Able Seaman John Parker, D/21521.
Able Seaman Thomas Lester, D/J25684.
Petty Officer George Warren, D/193430.
Leading Seaman Ernest Veale, D/181452.
Seaman Robert Pitt, B3250.
Seaman Alfonso Davies, C1514.
Stoker George Rees, C1536.

HMS *Dunraven*'s crew were paid off on 24 August, 1917. A service parade was held at the church in Devonport Barracks where the ship's ensign was dedicated, being carried down the aisle by the veteran Chief Petty Officer George Truscott, who had served with Campbell since the very beginning in the *Loderer*. Afterwards Campbell took his leave of them in a quiet corner. There was little emotion. "No applause," he wrote, "No cheers. When men have faced death together, this sort of thing is out of place."

As for Campbell himself, he carried on as Admiral Bayly's Flag Captain and later in the war commanded the cruiser HMS *Active*. Eventually he was promoted to Rear-Admiral in 1928, and found himself unceremoniously retired, 'axed', at the early age of forty-two under a programme of Government defence cuts, which aroused in him an acute bitterness. It is easy, perhaps, to imagine how this blow would have affected a man like Campbell, possessed as he was of the dogged 'never-let-go' nature of which his record as the most successful Q-ship captain was the result, and with which he, as a superb leader of men, was able to encourage his crews. It was a trait of character born in him. He carried it for the rest of his days.

Shortly before his death in 1953 he was in hospital. By now an epitome of the classic crusty old Admiral, he was engaged one day in an altercation with one of his nurses, who had become frustrated at his refusal to eat his custard. When the air had cleared a little, he explained to her that once, when he was a very small boy, his mother had tried to make him eat custard. He had refused, only to be told that he would be given no more food until he relented. It would have come as no surprise to the men who twenty-five years later served under him that he did not give in. Not only that, but the episode resulted in him going on a complete hunger strike for a whole week, after which his desperately worried mother was the one to give in. And furthermore, he had never, ever, eaten custard from that day onwards!

It would be remiss, however, to turn over the final page on Campbell without reference to a softer side to his nature, one which lurked behind the stiff upper lip. That he was devoted to his crews is beyond debate – and they to him. Those facts are transparently clear when one reads his references to Bonner, Orr, Truscott and the rest, and the angry letters that some of them wrote, ten years after the war, when they heard that the Skipper had been 'axed'!

It will be recalled that Martindale and Morrison were hurried to hospital in Brest after being wounded in *Dunraven*. Martindale recovered, but Morrison did not. His mother visited him in hospital in France shortly before he died. He was buried at Wallasey Cemetery on 3 October, 1917, being the fifteenth member of his large Wirral family to die on active service. Mrs Morrison wrote to Campbell thanking him for his kindness in arranging for her to travel to Brest. Campbell also arranged for Morrison's body to be returned to England and for the funeral bill to be sent to him. These facts are recorded in letters, but how he managed to arrange these things, at the height of the war, we will never know.

August, 1917, continued to be the blackest month of the war for the Q-ships. On the 13th the Flower-class Q-sloop HMS *Bergamot*, in commission less than a month, was torpedoed in the Atlantic by *U-84*. And the very next day another famous name met with disaster.

While HMS *Prize* was undergoing extensive repairs following her near-fatal scrap with *U-93* Sanders was ordered to report to the officer commanding submarines in the Western Approaches. It was suggested that the little schooner might work in co-operation with a British submarine. The submarine would not be connected by telephone to its 'parent', but would lurk close at hand, submerged, awaiting a signal from the Q-ship that a U-boat was in the offing.

A system of visual signals was devised, based on trivial detail. For example, a shirt hanging in the rigging for'ard meant that a U-boat was off the port bow. If it hung in the main rigging, it signified that the sub was on the starboard bow. And so on. All the British submarine captain had to do was to keep the schooner under non-stop observation and, when the signal was given, work his boat into an appropriate position to attack.

On 28 July *Prize*, freshly painted black with red trimmings, and posing as a Swede, sailed into the Atlantic, shadowed by the submarine *D-6*. For several days nothing was seen. Each night the submarine would surface and come alongside the schooner, and then dive before dawn to tag along astern. At last a man climbed up the rigging of the sailing ship and gave the arranged signal to indicate that a U-boat had been sighted. *D-6* closed with *Prize* so as to be able to read the next signal, which would tell her exactly where her prey was. But Sanders pre-empted the action, and it was to cost him his life. He considered that the U-boat was a sitting target for his gunners. (Chatterton says it was the *UB-48* on her way to the Adriatic via the north of Scotland.) In an uncharacteristically rash moment, the New Zealander gave orders to open fire, rather than adhere to the agreed plan, but *Prize*'s gun-crew failed to kill their quarry, who dived and disappeared. That night the British submarine came alongside as usual. As far as is known, the conversation between the two captains is not recorded, but one may imagine the disappointment of *D-6*'s commander.

Having disclosed his armament, and therefore blown his disguise, Sanders should have sailed for home. That would have been the classic Q-ship tactic. If the enemy has had a good look at you, and you have not sunk him, run away and change your identity. As it was, the German captain, being far from slow-witted, had an easy task in sinking the little schooner. All he had to do was to submerge, stay out of sight and bide his time. It was just before dawn on 14 August when the crew of *D-6* heard a mighty explosion. At full light they found that their companion had disappeared. They scanned the horizons in all directions for HMS *Prize*, Q21, or any of those who had sailed in her. No wreckage, no bodies, no lifeboats. Nothing.

Sanders did not live to wear the VC medal on his chest. It was presented to his father, Edward Sanders, by the Governor-General of New Zealand, the Earl of Liverpool, at Auckland Town Hall on 19 June, 1918.

The prickly William Garthwaite, Director of the Marine Navigation Co., now demanded to know from the Admiralty how much compensation he could expect for the loss of the *Prize*. Their Lordships replied, thanking him again for his generous patriotism, but their letter (which may be inspected at the Public Record Office) makes no attempt to answer his question!

The U-boats' attacks on the little fishing smacks had resulted in a surge of volunteers from among their number to sail as decoys, particularly on the East Coast. These had not been without success, as we saw when the Lowestoft boat *G & E* managed to damage *UB-6* as early as August, 1915. *G & E* sailed under many aliases, and on 15 August, 1917, she had become the *Nelson* and was working with one of her long-time partners, the *Ethel & Millie* (sometimes known as the *Boy Alfred*) off the Jim Howe Bank in the North Sea.

These two fighting midgets had sailed together on dozens of occasions. On 1 February, 1917, they had even claimed to have sunk *two* U-boats when fishing "back o' the Crossing". Although it seems that the sinkings were never confirmed, it is recorded that the Admiralty did pay a bounty to the crew of the *I'll Try*, which was the *G & E*'s alias that day. One of them, young Edward Fenn, a farm-boy from Lound, had earned five shillings (25p) a week on the farm. When the war came, he joined the Reservists and, having promised Skipper Tom Crisp that he knew how to make a good 'duff', (having watched his mother) found himself enlisted as the ship's cook at three shillings and sixpence (17.5p) per day. His share of the bounty was £17, which, as he recalled years later, resulted in a monumental celebration in the sand-floored taproom of the "Village Maid" when he got back to Lound.

On the afternoon of 15 August they were fishing peacefully when a shell splashed about hundred yards off *Nelson*'s port bow. It had been fired by a U-boat from about four miles' distance. The smack's forty-one-year-old skipper let go his nets and marked them with a buoy. "We'll have to let him have it!" he shouted. Edward Fenn dropped the fish he was cleaning for their dinner and he and the others ran for the ammunition. *Nelson*'s Royal Navy gunner, Leading Seaman Percival Ross, opened fire. But the little 6-pounder gun did not have the range and the submarine was able to savage them at will, without effective reply. Her fourth shell wrecked the bows of *Nelson*, and it was about the seventh that passed clean through the body of Tom Crisp, shattering both his legs and partially disembowelling him. The same shell then smashed its way through the deck and out through the side of the boat, which immediately started to sink.

Skipper Crisp's eighteen-year-old son, also called Tom, sent off a message by pigeon, calling for help, but *Nelson* was going down fast. The dying skipper refused to be lifted into the lifeboat and told his son to throw him into the sea. The younger Tom could not do this, (what son could?) and the crew watched in horror from the boat as the submarine continued to shell *Nelson* until she sank, carrying the body of their skipper with her. Only two months before, Tom's mother had died of hepatitis. Now he had lost his father too.

The German captain then turned his fire on to the *Ethel & Millie*. Soon he scored a direct hit and Skipper 'Johnsey' Manning and his crew took to their boat. What happened next was described by Tom Crisp junior at the Court of Inquiry on board HMS *Havelock* in Lowestoft. He said, "The submarine left off firing at the *Ethel & Millie* and picked her crew up. We saw the submarine's crew line the *Ethel & Millie*'s crew up on the submarine's foredeck. They tied the smack's boat up astern of the submarine and steamed to the smack. The wind being from the south-south-east was blowing the *Ethel & Millie* into the north-north-west until she was nearly out of sight. Just before the *Ethel & Millie* got out of sight a haze fell over her and we rowed into the south-east as hard as we could, the opposite direction in which the smack and the submarine were going. It was drawing in dusk then."

All the next day, Thursday the 16th, they rowed. Several times they caught sight of ships, but, despite trying to attract their attention with a piece of oilskin and a pair of trousers tied to an oar, none of these came to their rescue. During the day the pigeon with Crisp's message was picked up by another Lowestoft smack. It was not until the Friday morning that they found the Jim Howe Buoy. They tied up to it and Crisp climbed on top of it to wave his handkerchief at a passing ship. After forty-one hours adrift in their boat, their luck had turned at last. She saw them. It was the minesweeper *Dryad*.

The Court of Inquiry could come to no conclusion as to what had happened to the *Ethel & Millie* and her crew. Neither the smack nor the men were ever seen again. Nor were any of them; Skipper Manning, John Lewis, Edwin Barrett, Alfred Preece, Hugh Thomson, and the Royal Navy gunners, Able Seamen Spencer and Gibson, ever reported as being prisoners of war. The fact that they were lined up on the deck of the U-boat, with their hands up, as it made off, towing the *Ethel & Millie* astern, appears to be evidence laden with foreboding. Did the submarine (which was never identified) simply dive to let them drown? There are, of course, many other possibilities as to what may have happened. For example, once safely out of sight, the German captain may have taken the British sailors into the U-boat, planning to return to Germany with them as prisoners from one of the hated 'trap ships'. This would have made good propaganda. But what then happened to them? We know that the U-boat made off to the north-west and that five days later the *UC-41* blew herself to pieces on her own mines in the Tay Estuary. Was this the U-boat on whose outer casing Manning and his crew had been lined up? Were they still on board when she was laying her mines off Dundee? In all probability, these questions will never be answered.

The Victoria Cross was bestowed posthumously on Skipper Crisp, and his son earned the DSM for his bravery that day off the Jim Howe Bank. Young Tom collected his medal and his father's VC from the King at Buckingham Palace on 19 December, 1917, in company with Leading Seaman Ross, who had been awarded a Bar to his existing DSM. Then he went home to the house in Stanford Street, Lowestoft, which would be, from then on, a much lonelier place. It appears that he soon left the sea. The *Eastern Daily Press* reported in 1964 that he had retired after forty-two years' service as the operator of the Lowestoft Swingbridge.

The pigeon was not forgotten. It survived the war and was given a special place of honour at the 1921 East London Federation of Homing Pigeons Show. It even had its portrait painted, which can still be seen to this day on exhibition at the Maritime Museum, Lowestoft.

On 16 August the big ex-collier *Bradford City*, alias *Saros*, which had operated almost entirely in the Mediterranean ever since her introduction to Q-shipping in October, 1915, and had had at least one tussle with a U-boat, was torpedoed and sunk in the Straits of Messina, only ten days before she was due to be paid-off.

The facts surrounding the fight in which HMS *Acton*, a.k.a. *Gandy,
Harelda, Woffington*, or simply *Q-34*, was involved on the 20th are in
some dispute. According to Chatterton, who, as a serving officer closely
connected with the Queenstown 'set', and who therefore would doubtless have had access to much first-hand information, probably even
from Lieutenant-Commander Rolfe, the Q-ship's captain himself, what
happened was this.

The 1,300-ton freighter was attacked by a U-boat and Rolfe lit his
'smoke' boxes and turned on his fake 'escaping steam' pipes while the
panic crew abandoned ship. Still submerged, the submarine ventured so
close to the Q-ship that it actually collided with her side quite forcibly.
When it broke the surface it was met with a barrage of shells from the
Acton, which carried a four-inch gun, a 6-pounder, four 18" torpedo
tubes and four 200lb bomb throwers. However, the German, although
hit, was able to escape. That version we may take as being from as close
to the 'horse's mouth' as possible, and neither Campbell nor Ritchie
include the action as a Q-ship 'kill'.

However, Grant, who is often at odds with other historians, is
emphatic that Rolfe sank the submarine. According to him, it was the
Zeebrugge-based *UC-72*, commanded by Voigt. He says that it was this
boat which had damaged HMS *Penshurst* the previous day (which will
be dealt with later) and that she was destroyed by the *Acton*'s shells.
Furthermore, he insists, this was the last occasion in the war on which
a decoy sank a U-boat.

Commander Leopold Bernays, CMG, the rugged captain of HMS
Vala, Q8, was one of the Navy's most colourful officers. He had left the
Navy some years before the war to seek a new life in Canada, but had
returned at the outbreak of hostilities to serve the Old Country, as
had so many of his kind. Hard swearing and hard drinking (although
not a drop was allowed to be consumed on board his ships) were two
characteristics that he was famous for, and the stories that revolved
around him were legion, although many were probably apocryphal. He
was said to keep a bucket of coal on his bridge, and would hurl pieces
of it, accompanied by a stream of oaths that could only be matched by
the proverbial stoker, at any crew member who did not appear to be
working with the required gusto. But for all that, because he was so
much like one of themselves, and with no 'side', the lower deck understood him perfectly. They loved him and would follow him anywhere.
And the feeling was mutual. On one occasion, on being ordered on a

particularly dangerous mission, Bernays was heard to proclaim, "I'm not going without my old crew, they're the very best in the world."

Eventually he found himself in command of *Vala*, a 1,000-ton collier working out of Queenstown under Admiral Lewis Bayly. It appears from Admiralty records that they regarded the *Vala* as unsuitable for decoy work because of her slowness and small size, which seems strange considering that by August, 1917, she had given two years of unbroken service. And she had once been about to sink a U-boat at point-blank range when she was infuriatingly 'rescued' by a US destroyer which had scared the submarine into diving to escape.

What exactly happened to HMS *Vala* on 21 August, 1917, may never be known, except that she was sunk in the Atlantic with Bernays and all hands, probably by *UB-54*.

It had been a harrowing month for the Q-ships. No fewer than seven had been lost in the space of two weeks. They could count only one German submarine to their credit, plus an 'assist' if we allow *Chagford*'s part in the sinking of *U-44*, although another three U-boats, *UC-44*, *UC-41* and *U-50* had all been destroyed by mines. Two of them had been their own.

Chapter 8

1917
The Year's End

HMS *Stonecrop*, alias *Glenfoyle* or *Donlevon*, was a flush-decked 1,680-ton coaster, with her bridge well for'ard and her funnel right aft. She was not old, only having been built in 1913 for work on the Canadian Lakes, but she was painfully slow with a seven-knot maximum speed. For a Q-ship, speed was not of vital importance, but armament was, and in that she was not lacking. She boasted a 4-inch, a 12-pounder and a 6-pounder, plus four Stokes bomb throwers and four big 18-inch torpedo tubes.

The Royal Navy had taken her into service on 22 April, 1917, and appointed the wiry, and sometimes fiery, thirty-four-year-old Commander Maurice Blackwood to be her captain. He was born in Malta while his father, Captain Sir Francis Blackwood, was serving in the Mediterranean. The Blackwoods were a family who could trace their sailor ancestors far back into the mists of time. It was one of them, the First Baronet and Vice-Admiral of the Blue, who had hurried back to England bearing the despatches which told of Nelson's victory at Trafalgar. Maurice had entered Dartmouth at the age of fourteen and had spent much of his early career in destroyers on the China Station. Indeed, it had been at the race-track in Hong Kong that he had met Dorothea Edwards, who was to become his wife in 1915.

Three months had been spent in fitting out *Stonecrop* and on trials. A concrete lining had been added to her hull, which protected about two-thirds of it. Perhaps it was because of this that Blackwood found that she was nearly impossible to handle in any head wind or sea, but there was a war to fight and he took her on her first patrol out of Portsmouth on 22 August. Just before sailing, Lord Jellicoe himself had said to Blackwood, "Go where you like – but you must get results."

On 17 September she was cruising off the south-west of Ireland when her lookouts (two men in cloth-caps, pretending to chip the rust from the fo'c'sle), spotted a large U-boat on the surface some miles off. It was 4.43 p.m. when the German opened fire from long range. It was *U-88*. Although it was one of the Kaiser's bigger boats, this particular series presented but a slim target above the water-line. This meant that it was all the more important for such a submarine to be lured as close as possible to a waiting Q-ship. Blackwood turned and pretended to run away, sending out uncoded SOS wireless signals and occasionally firing his little stern-mounted defence-gun. For over half an hour this went on, and although the U-boat had not, so far, registered any damage on *Stonecrop*, the German shells were falling steadily closer as the submarine closed the range. Blackwood stopped and lit his 'smoke apparatus', which had been supplied by Brocks, the famous fireworks firm. As it happened, the intended display of pyrotechnics worked a little too well, because some of the phosphorus spilled out onto the deck and the port side of the after deck-house was soon in flames. There was a following wind and within seconds *Stonecrop* was engulfed in billows of thick smoke, looking for all the world as if she had taken a hit and was on fire. Her 'panic party' went through their particular version of the 'abandon ship' pantomime, which mainly involved making a bad job of lowering the lifeboat, which went down 'one end up' at a run. Then it seemed that some of the seamen had forgotten their coats and hurried back to fetch them before getting into the boat, exhorted by the shouts of their shipmates.

The German captain dived and came to within three hundred yards of the 'burning' coaster at periscope depth. Slowly he prowled around *Stonecrop*, with his two one-eyed periscopes inspecting it closely. And as he did so Blackwood, crouching on all fours, was watching him by squinting through the slits he had cut in the canvas bridge screen. Several times the U-boat presented an excellent target for the Q-ship's 18-inch torpedoes, but ironically the range for them was now too short! Eventually the German seemed satisfied that his victim was an honest merchantmen and nothing more, and the long grey U-boat with its rust-streaked conning-tower nosed its way to the surface. It was about six hundred yards off the *Stonecrop*'s starboard quarter. For a few long minutes nothing happened. Then it moved slowly towards the 'panic' party's boats, which were sitting on the Q-ship's beam. Blackwood had given the order to 'stand by' as soon as the U-boat surfaced. One may imagine the scene around the concealed guns, the men scarcely daring to breathe as they made silent signs to each other, their faces taut with suspense, but passing an occasional grim smile.

The U-boat was now only a few yards from the boats and broadside on to Blackwood's guns. He would not get a better target than this, and he knew that in Petty Officer George Lee he had one of the best gun-layers in the Navy. He whispered the range and bearing and then the words 'let go' into his voice-pipe. The flaps clattered down and the guns boomed. There was a mighty clang and a flash as Lee's third shot from the 4-inch caught the submarine at the base of the conning-tower, split-ting it in two. Great clouds of brown smoke poured from the gash. The next shell hit her on the water-line just below the for'ard gun, and the sixth in almost the same spot. It was plain that she had been holed in several for'ard compartments and was well down by the bows. The seventh shell hit her on the hull, well aft, and now a mist of either steam or spray caused by escaping compressed air surged from her. "Move up and down the waterline" were Lee's orders, and he certainly did that. All told, he landed between eight and twelve 4-inch shells on the sub-marine, including one which rolled back one of her plates like a sardine tin. Slowly her bows rose into the air and she slid backwards.

The 'panic' party, who were only a short distance away, could now see right under her keel as she hung in the water at an angle of forty-five degrees with the holes in her for'ard hull clearly visible. Her crew were unable to open the damaged conning-tower to make their escape as she sank by the stern. After a few seconds she reappeared. Her conning-tower was just visible above water, but she had a severe list to starboard and soon she sank again completely.

There was an element of vengeance in the sinking of *U-88*. Her captain was none other than Walther Schweiger, who, two years before, had commanded *U-20*. They did not know it, but HMS *Stonecrop*'s gunners had sunk the sinker of the *Lusitania*.

Many Q-ships, despite long and gruelling searches, survived to the end of the war without ever seeing a U-boat, let alone sinking one. The ocean is a big place. Others seemed to possess an uncanny knack of being in exactly the same spot as a German submarine. *Stonecrop* was one of these. Here she was, with only a couple of weeks' decoy service behind her, and not only had she sunk one U-boat, but she was about to go into battle against another one the following afternoon. But even as his crew celebrated their victory Blackwood had a strange feeling of loneliness. As he explained later, "Having come from crashing around the North Sea at 20 knots, in company with all the other members of a destroyer flotilla, it suddenly came to me that not a soul in England could have told you where the *Stonecrop* was at that moment, or even if she was afloat at all, not even the Commander-in-Chief, Portsmouth."

He had altered course to the north during the night and midday on 18 September found *Stonecrop* somewhat nearer the coast of Ireland. The watch had just changed and Blackwood was on his way to wash his hands before lunch when a torpedo was spotted racing towards their starboard bow. It was already upon them before the lookouts had seen it and was coming much too fast to allow for any evasive action to be taken. The explosion rocked the Q-ship, tearing into her forward plates, demolishing the wireless office and killing five sailors. The bridge and wheel-house were wrecked, leaving everything in a hopeless tangle. The spare lifeboat was shattered. Six of the eight howitzer hatches were smashed, some being blown completely overboard, and the steel ports of the 12-pounder gun-house were damaged. If only the torpedo had struck just six feet further aft it would have found the concrete lining and the story may have had a different ending. "If only they had been as lavish with the concrete as they had been with the guns," lamented Blackwood later.

Blackwood was knocked over in his bathroom by the force of the blast and by the time he had composed himself and hurried on to the bridge to put the telegraph to 'stop', *Stonecrop* was already well down by the bows. Discipline prevailed, despite the suddenness of the torpedo attack, and the usual routine swung into play.

But the U-boat did not show itself. Over half an hour went by. By now the waves were breaking over *Stonecrop*'s fo'c'sle. A periscope was sighted twice, once on the starboard bow and again on the port beam. But the range was three thousand yards, and in any case Blackwood, with a crippled ship, could not bring any of his guns or torpedoes to bear. By 2.20 p.m. she was so far down by the head that the for'ard 12-pounder gun crew found the sea breaking over them as they lay at their station. "It's pretty wet down here, Sir," called one sailor. Blackwood looked down and saw that Lieutenant Mash and his men were up to their knees in water and were each holding a couple of cartridges as high as they could to keep them dry, still hoping to get in a shot at the enemy. He ordered Mash to evacuate their position and reluctantly they came up onto the bridge. Then a huge sea carried away the bridge screen and Blackwood ordered all those men in the for'ard part of the ship to go over the side into the water, following himself when the bridge itself became submerged.

This left only the after part of the Q-ship above water, where the 4-inch gun crew were still closed up. Lieutenant Smiles had the Maxim and Lewis guns brought aft with their crews and stationed them in No.6 hatchway, from where, hopefully, they would get a chance to fire on the sub if it surfaced. Then, with every water-tight door closed against the ever-rising level within the doomed Q-ship, they waited for a glimpse of the U-boat while their shipmates from the for'ard stations swam around in the sea. *Stonecrop* was going down. At the last moment before she disappeared, with the sea lapping the after-deck, and growling and grinding noises coming from within as her engines and boilers broke free amid clouds of steam and smoke, Smiles ordered 'abandon ship'. He could not swim, himself, so just grabbed a nearby plank of the Oregon pine which was floating out of *Stonecrop*'s hold and jumped into the water with it, alongside the rafts and the other plank riders. Luckily for him, Blackwood, now in one of the lifeboats and in the process of gathering around him as many of his ninety-four remaining crew as he could find, soon spotted him and picked him up.

Stonecrop had gone, leaving a group of exhausted sailors, some in a couple of boats, some on a raft, and a few on planks, heaving about on the Atlantic swell. It was only then that the U-boat surfaced. It was *U-43*. She came up rapidly to the 'panic boat', covering it with her fore-gun. The captain, Juerst, leaned out of the conning-tower and hailed Lieutenant Booth, who was acting the role of the sinking steamer's captain. "What ship?" came the question.

"The *Winona*," Booth lied, "Baltimore to Queenstown for orders. 2,000 tons general cargo."

Apparently satisfied, the U-boat turned away with a surge of speed that almost swamped the raft and made off to the south-west. They were now completely alone on the ocean.

There had been no opportunity to send out any distress signals after the torpedo had smashed the wireless office and they had precious little food and water. Blackwood set them about making another raft from the planks and other floating wreckage. There was no time to be lost as the wind and sea were getting up. It was vital to get this done before darkness fell. They set to with a will and the hearty strains of 'Tipperary' floated across the water. The new raft had a freeboard of no more than a couple of feet, but it was the best that they could do, and Lieutenant Smiles clambered on to it, together with two other officers and twenty men.

Blackwood sent off one of the boats towards land to summon help. He hoisted a light in his boat, so that he and Smiles would not lose touch with each other, but, with a stiff wind blowing, somehow they drifted apart and in the morning there was no sign of the raft. They rowed about for several hours trying to find Smiles, but it was fruitless. There was nothing for it but to row towards land, and after some hard pulling they were not far from the coast of Ireland when they were picked up by a passing steamer, the SS *Ayleveree*, in the twilight of the following evening, which landed then at Queenstown at 3.30 a.m. on 20 September.

At about the same time the boat that Blackwood had sent away was also picked up by a patrol vessel. The search was now on for the missing raft. As many craft as could be spared were sent out, but it was no easy task. It was September, a typical time for gales in the Western Approaches, and 1917 was no exception. After two days the search was abandoned and the raft and its occupants given up as lost. But it was not lost.

When dawn had broken on the first morning and they found that they had become separated from Blackwood's boat, Smiles tried to rig up a sail, using an oar and a little scrap of canvas about four feet square. The raft stumbled along before a north-westerly all day, probably only making a mile or two. In the late evening a hefty sea broke over the raft, washing everybody into the water. There was a scramble to get back on board and when Smiles called the roll none of them were missing. What was missing, however, were two of their precious three gallons of fresh water, together with the single tin of biscuits which had been their only food. They had one gallon of water left for twenty-one men. Smiles took personal charge of the water and issued a stern warning to all of them against the dangers of drinking sea-water.

The following day brought much despair. They were all cold, wet and hungry as the raft drifted aimlessly, slipping and sliding from the peaks to the troughs in the swell. One man died in the forenoon and they put his body into the sea. Then they spied a destroyer. Everybody stood up and waved and shouted, but she did not see them and their hearts fell as they watched her slim shape disappear into the distance. Another man died in the evening.

They saw two ships on the fourth day. One was one of the searching destroyers, the other looked like a cruiser, but they were both far off – at least five miles – and neither saw the helpless seamen clinging to their pathetic island of planks. During that day another three men died. In spite of Smiles' warnings, two of them, crazy with thirst, had succumbed to the temptation of drinking sea-water. Water, water everywhere and not a drop to drink, as the famous poem goes. And it is true. For centuries sailors have known about the risks they take by consuming sea-water. It is said to drive them mad. That is not to say 'mad' in any violent sense. What actually happens is that the sudden large intake of alkaline salt disturbs the pH balance of the body, including the brain. Sufferers become confused and disorientated, maybe suffer from hallucinations, and are liable to commit acts of strange irrational behaviour. These two men had simply thrown themselves into the sea. Quite possibly they believed that they could walk on it.

The fifth day brought a mixture of hope and tragedy. The weather abated and the raft made several miles towards the Irish coast, aided by the little sail, to which they had added several coats and shirts. At about 10 p.m. that evening they spied a lighthouse, but were all too exhausted even to cheer. But seven more men had died during that day and an eighth was to go during the night. Smiles served out the last remaining drops of the gallon of fresh water. The sixth day, spent in sight of the coast, was soul-destroying. No rescuers came near all day. It was not until 4.00 p.m. that a patrol boat came along and pulled them on board.

They had been adrift for 123 hours, and only ten of the twenty-three men who had taken to the raft had survived. Out of an original crew of eleven officers and eighty-eight men that manned the *Stonecrop* four officers and forty men had perished.

The loss of his ship and half of his men weighed heavily on Blackwood's morale. As their captain, he felt personally responsible for every one of them. And sometime later, when some convoy ships sailing under the protection of the group of trawlers he commanded, working out of the Tyne, were lost in the North Sea he became even more despondent. His commanding officer, a Captain Wood, recorded on his Service History in April, 1918, that "the loss had affected him greatly" and that he was "not very stable in an emergency". Perhaps this was not so surprising, considering Blackwood's war experiences thus far.

At the end of the war Blackwood sailed off in the SS *Argyllshire* from Liverpool with his wife and family on a three-year loan to the Royal Australian Navy. By that time he seems to have recovered his natural *sangfroid* and a Captain Cayley remarked that he was "most capable". A born adventurer, he retired from the Navy in 1922 to go exploring in Papua-New Guinea, and later owned a gold-mine and a pearl-diving operation in Australia.

During the month of September, 1917, the Germans had lost another eleven boats, five in the minefields, two by ramming, one by suspected sabotage and one torpedoed by the British submarine *D-7*. A British seaplane bombed *UB-32* and the unfortunate *U-28* was too close to her victim, the ammunition ship *Olive Branch*, when it blew up off the North Cape. It is said that what actually happened was that a motor lorry being carried on the deck of the ammunition ship was blown into the air and landed on the U-boat, sinking it!

In October five more of the Kaiser's submarines were destroyed, all by mines, and one of Admiral Bayly's dwindling number of decoy ships, the Flower Class sloop, HMS *Begonia, Q-10*, was sunk in the Atlantic on the 6th. In fact, the remainder of 1917 was disastrous for the U-boats. No fewer than sixteen were lost in November and December, nearly all in the minefields or by depth-charging by the ever more successful convoy escorts.

Against that, the Germans torpedoed HMS *Peveril, Q-36*, off Gibraltar on 6 November. And there were two events which any story of the Q-ships would be gravely at fault to omit.

HMS *Candytuft*, another Flower Class Q-sloop, sailed from Devonport in early November to pick up a convoy bound for Gibraltar. She was disguised as a tramp steamer and was to perform the usual role of pretending to be a slow straggler at the rear of the convoy. It was to be a dramatic voyage. First of all, off Cape St. Vincent, at the far south-west point of Europe, she was fired on by an unidentified submarine, which wrecked her bridge. She managed to get in three shots in reply, but none of these scored hits, although the U-boat broke off the action. Captain W. Cochrane nursed *Candytuft* into Gibraltar for repairs, and when these had been carried out, he was ordered to escort the merchant ship *Tremayne* to Malta.

They sailed on the 16th and were only two days out when they were attacked again, this time off the North African coast. Quite suddenly a torpedo sizzled across the bows of the *Tremayne* and struck *Candytuft* aft. Such was the force of the explosion that her stern was blown completely off. All her officers were killed except Cochrane himself, Lieutenant Phillips and Lieutenant Errington, although the latter was severely wounded.

Cochrane ordered the *Tremayne*'s master to make for the nearest port, while he rigged a jury sail for'ard, with which he hoped to keep the rudderless, powerless *Candytuft* moving in the general direction of the shore. He sent most of the ship's company away in her boats, keeping only the guns' crews on board to man her two 4-inchers. After half an hour, which was spent in the classic Q-ship mode of suspense, Cochrane spied a periscope through his observation slit. Unwisely, he ordered his guns to open fire at it. All that earned him was another torpedo, this time catching the stricken *Candytuft* for'ard, completely wrecking the entire fo'c'sle. The effect was devastating. Besides the enormous amount of damage done to the hull itself, debris of all kinds rained down from the air; spars, lumps of coal and steel, bits of machinery, even a couple of hand-barrows, all plummeted onto the bridge and upperworks. Cochrane caught a nasty blow on the head, which left him dazed and staggering. One of the guns' crew was blown overboard and several men were injured.

The whole forepart of the ship was left hanging on by the proverbial thread, and presently it broke away altogether to drift for a few yards and then sink. And so the Q-ship was left without either stern or bows. Quickly gathering his wits, Cochrane ordered all watertight doors to be shut. This was no easy task, as he and his few men waded waist-deep into the eerie darkness of the various compartments, fumbling for hand-holds and door-clips, tripping over submerged objects and stumbling into floating debris. They managed to save her from sinking and, amazingly, the bowless, sternless, mangled derelict that had been *Candytuft* drifted onto the beach two days later. Cochrane and his men were rescued by a French trawler, although Errington died before they got him ashore.

Since severely damaging *U-84* in February, HMS *Penshurst* had had an eventful year. She was another of those Q-ships which seemed to attract U-boats like moths around a lamp, fighting altogether a record eleven actions during the course of the war. In March, 1917, came the last of these under Grenfell, who was shortly to be invalided ashore. Patrolling in mid-Channel, *Penshurst* was seriously damaged by a torpedo. She was able to be towed into Portsmouth, but it was to be many weeks before she was repaired and back on duty.

On 2 July, off the Scillies, with Lieutenant Cedric Naylor, Grenfell's First Lieutenant, now in command, her lookouts spotted a U-boat crossing their course about 6,000 yards ahead. The submarine was seen to dive. It was a classic manoeuvre. They knew that it was lying in wait for them to draw closer. With every eye keeping a sly lookout for the streak of a torpedo, Naylor plodded on innocently. When the attack came he was ready for it, and by a deft touch on the helm made the torpedo miss. When the U-boat finally surfaced *Penshurst*'s crew suffered a half an hour of shell-fire before revealing their own guns. They claimed over a dozen hits, but caused little damage, and the German disappeared when three British destroyers arrived.

On 19 August, not far from the same spot, a similar encounter occurred, but this time Naylor was unable to avoid the torpedo entirely. It caught *Penshurst* a glancing blow just below the bridge. The explosion caused a mountain of sea-water to be blown into the air, which then fell in a giant cascade, half-drowning the hidden guns' crews, flooding the well-deck and lower bridge and filling the starboard lifeboat to the gunwales. Holed in No. 2 hold, she took on a heavy list. The falling water had ripped away the screen concealing the 12-pounder on the starboard side of the lower bridge and also smashed the dummy lifeboat hiding another 12-pounder. Luckily, the U-boat, which Grant says was *UC-72*, was on the port side, out of sight of these guns.

Naylor sent out a general wireless signal saying he was under attack and opened fire. After three minutes the submarine dived and re-appeared on the horizon astern, where it stopped, watching developments, until the destroyer HMS *Leonidas* arrived, when it dived again. It was 7.26 p.m., nearly two and a half hours after the U-boat had first been seen. Most of the Q-ship's crew were transferred to the destroyer and the listing *Penshurst* wallowed towards Plymouth, where, aided by a tug, she tied up on 21 August and they repaired her yet again.

It was on Christmas Eve, 1917, that the gallant *Penshurst* met her end. At about midday she was in the Irish Sea. Naylor was shaping a course which he hoped would bring him into contact with a U-boat which had been reported off the Smalls. A submarine was seen submerging fine on the port bow about five miles distant. *Penshurst* tramped on doggedly, at her usual eight knots, but this time the torpedo struck a killer blow on a vital nerve centre, directly between the boiler and engine-rooms. She stopped dead in her tracks, paralysed, amidst clouds of smoke and steam. The 'panic crew' went away in the one boat that was undamaged and a couple of rafts. Again several of the guns were exposed by the force of the blast, but, strangely, the German captain seemed to ignore this, because he advanced to within 300 yards of the stricken ship at periscope depth. For over an hour he prowled round and round the Q-ship. Finally, he surfaced and started to strafe her with shellfire from his after gun. Naylor, with his ship now well down by the stern, could not depress any of his guns far enough to reply. All his gunners could do was to wait for a convenient roll which would bring their muzzles down for a moment, and in this way they did manage half-a-dozen shots at their adversary. But it was in vain. Although one shell hit the U-boat abaft the conning-tower, she was not critically damaged and left the scene when a fast patrol-boat appeared. Sadly for HMS *Penshurst*, help had come too late. All her crew were saved, but at five minutes past eight on that Christmas Eve she went to the bottom.

So ended the life of what was probably the most famous of all the Q-ships. She had served longer than most, seen far more actions than any of the others and been damaged repeatedly, only to re-emerge from the dockyard to fight again and again. Her crews, trained to a high level of skill by two superb seamen, Grenfell and Naylor, had always displayed wonderfully cool discipline. And yet for all that, to the uniformed observer she would have appeared as nothing better than any other insignificant, rusty old salt-caked tub.

But it *may* be that the Royal Navy wreaked vengeance on the killer of HMS *Penshurst* the following day. According to some Admiralty records, it had been the *U-110* which sank her. But Chatterton disagrees. He thought it was probably the *U-87*, which was itself sunk in the vicinity on Christmas Day. This U-boat, commanded by von Speth-Schulzburg, had just torpedoed a merchant ship in a convoy when one of the escort sloops, HMS *Buttercup*, managed to ram it, causing major damage. Shortly afterwards the Q-patrol-boat, *PC-56*, alias *Birdwood* or *Panache*, was picking up survivors from the merchant vessel when a periscope was seen. She dropped depth-charges, which literally blew the submarine to the surface, whereupon the patrol-boat swung round to ram it, firing 12-pounder shells as it came. *PC-56* was steaming at twenty knots as her sharp bows cut into the U-boat, completely slicing it in half. Both halves bobbed like anglers' floats in the water, and it took several more rounds of shell-fire from the British ships before these disappeared. There were no survivors.

Chapter 9

1918
The Final Curtain

As 1918 opened it could be said that the writing was on the wall for the U-boats. In the months of January and February the amount of British merchant shipping destroyed by them, both in terms of tonnage and in number of vessels, was only about half of what it had been the previous May and June. And the Germans were continuing to lose boats at an ever-increasing rate, nearly all by mines, depth-charges and ramming – nine in January, three in February, five in March, seven in April, fourteen in May.

The Q-ships had become largely redundant, thanks to the success of the minefields and the convoy escorts. At Queenstown Admiral Lewis Bayly had only three decoy ships left under his command at the beginning of February – *Wexford Coast*, which had been operating in Russian waters, the tiny 140-ton schooner *Eilian* and *Stockforce*.

HMS *Stockforce* was commanded by the twenty-six-year-old Lieutenant Harold Auten, RNR, who was one of Bayly's original band that had formed the nucleus of the Queenstown decoys back in 1915. In fact Auten served in Q-ships longer than any other officer. He had been First Lieutenant under McLeod in the ill-fated *Zylpha*, and when Hallwright had been killed on the bridge of HMS *Heather* in April, 1917, Auten had been appointed in command.

As an 'ideas' man, Auten had little time for Campbell. Privately, he claimed that it had been his own suggestion, at an early Queenstown conference, to cram the Q-ship holds with timber so as to make them difficult to sink. This may have been true, because Auten's superior,

McLeod, wrote a confidential report to Admiral Bayly putting forward the idea, which may well have emanated from Auten. Campbell had maintained that rocks would be better than timber or barrels, Auten alleged contemptuously. In turn, that may be half-true, because there was a need for *some* ballast, and it was better *not* to use coal for this in ships that were not built as colliers, because their holds did not have enough ventilation to disperse the build-up of dangerous gas. Campbell may well have made that point and Auten chose to distort his words.

Auten, tall, dashing and handsome, was what would have been described a decade or so later as a swashbuckler. (Indeed, he did spend much of his later life in the film industry in America.) In contrast, Campbell was a quieter, less flamboyant man, although he seems to have emerged as the most famous Q-ship personality after the war. One correspondent even saw fit to remind the *Daily Express* that there were other Q-ship heroes besides Campbell. It is easy to imagine that he and Auten may have had their differences.

Auten was never truly comfortable with *Heather* as a decoy. He made his feelings known to Bayly, who, after two and a half years of close working with him, had respect for the opinions of such a trusted subordinate. The Admiral concurred immediately and Auten soon found himself touring the docksides of Cardiff, Swansea and Newport in search of the ship which he already had in his mind's eye as an ideal replacement for the sloop. He found her at Cardiff. *Stockforce* was a little 370-ton steam collier, nearly new, with a twenty-nine-foot-wide beam which would enable her to pack a decent broadside. When they had finished fitting her out, her outward appearance had not changed, but tucked away out of sight was a surprising amount of armament for a ship so small. They had given her two 4-inch guns, two 12-pounders, one 3-pounder and two fourteen-inch torpedo tubes.

The Troubles in Ireland were, of course, an additional worry to the British at that time. There had been concern about spies around Haulbowline Dockyard, particularly as one of the Q-ships had been torpedoed recently, no more than four hours after sailing from Queenstown. Therefore, when *Stockforce* was due to depart on her first patrol, Auten persuaded Bayly to issue him with bogus orders as to sailing time and destination. Then, instead of sailing on a Tuesday as had been widely known on the dockside as being the intention, Auten suddenly weighed anchor on the Sunday night before and headed in a totally different direction from that shown in his 'orders'. And as a piece of double double-cross, he had added some *false* false pieces of disguise to his ship in the way of imitation wooden sides, a mizzen mast and a dummy boat, which were all dismantled and ditched as soon as he left harbour.

On 30 July, 1918, *Stockforce* met a U-boat. It was a calm morning, promising to blossom into a hot day, as she sailed up the Channel just off Guernsey, with the glass of its massed greenhouses already shimmering in the bright early sunlight. The lookouts were on keen alert as ever, including a black sailor whom Auten had recruited from a dockyard tug to give more realism to his 'merchant' ship. This man's lookout role was to loll on the rail as if deep in thought, smoking his pipe and occasionally spitting into the sea.

Just after eight o'clock a wireless signal was received saying that a U-boat had been seen working on a line between the Channel Islands and South Devon. Auten had been on many wild-goose chases. Indeed, it had been over a year since he had seen any real action, and that was when *Zylpha* had been sunk; after that the ineffective *Heather* had brought him only frustration. In fact she had almost led him to disaster, when he had charged flat out at eighteen knots at what appeared to be an impertinent U-boat periscope, only to realize at the last moment that it was the mast-tip of a sunken cargo ship. "Hard-a-port!!," Auten had bellowed just in time and the shuddering *Heather*, with her rails almost awash, did a near right-angled turn which seemed to defy the laws of physics. "Secure action stations, and hands to dinner," he had called down the voice-pipes flatly, but no doubt with his heart still pounding fast. And then, almost as an apology to the quartermaster, "Pipe 'Up Spirits'. Lay along for your rum."

But now, at last, perhaps they had a real chance for some action. He steered towards the Lizard so that the 'collier' would appear to be returning to Cardiff for more coal to take to France. In the middle of the forenoon two French sea-planes appeared overhead. They circled around *Stockforce*, their engines clattering fussily, and dropped a little red buoy with a message that there were German submarines about and advising Auten to steer away from danger. Nothing could have been further from his mind, of course, and he steamed on.

This only served to heighten the anxiety of the French pilots, who seemed to consider it their duty to act as escorts to this foolhardy British captain. They tagged along for a couple of hours, even zooming ahead on one occasion to drop bombs on what appeared to be nothing but an oil-slick. Auten and his crew were furious at the intrusion. The lower deck cursed and fumed about French sea-planes with salty vehemence. Auten wrote that they asked each other repeatedly, "Why don't they buzz off?" But then he was writing in 1919, in an age when it was considered indelicate to quote sailors verbatim in print.

In the end the sea-planes did turn back towards France and *Stockforce* was left to plod on her way. Nothing happened until the middle of the first dog-watch, when the officer-of-the-watch saw a disturbance in the water some way off to starboard. For a moment he thought it was a school of porpoises, but then realized that it was the track of a torpedo. He quickly ordered 'full astern' and put the helm hard over, at the same time sounding the alarm buzzer.

Auten was having tea in the saloon and raced on to the bridge just in time to see the torpedo about fifty yards away. It had almost stopped, nearly at the end of its run. It seemed as if it would pass ahead of *Stockforce*, but as it lost its forward thrust it turned, under nothing more than the force of the current, and struck the ship in No. 1 hold, square on a watertight bulkhead. The damage was immense. The whole of her forepart was wrecked, including the for'ard gun and bridge. Great showers of debris rained down from the air – baulks of timber, hatch-covers, bits of lifeboats, lengths of cable and rope, life-belts, unexploded ready-use shells, all to be followed by tons of falling sea-water.

Auten himself was blown up into the air and was fortunate to land under the chart-table which sheltered him from serious injury. Recovering his wits, he crawled out to assess the damage and saw a sight which caused him to roar with laughter. The black sailor, who was a natural comic by all accounts, had just emerged from the fo'c'sle when the torpedo struck. He was unhurt, but had walked into a solid deluge of white paint as it came down from the sky with the other debris, and was now a human snowman!

Miraculously, nobody had been killed, although one of the stewards, Starling, had become pinned under some heavy wreckage. Auten thought quickly. It would take some time to free the man and time was short, firstly because *Stockforce* was steadily going down, and secondly because they needed to deal with the U-boat. He went to Starling and explained the position. "Aye, aye sir," replied the steward cheerfully, "I'll lay quiet until you let me know."

Auten had the wounded sent below, where they were tended by

Surgeon-Probationer Strahan, working up to his thighs in the rising water. He knew that these men would drown like trapped rats if she went down now, but there was no alternative. Then he went aft, into the 4-inch gun house, which was the only place from which he could control the ship. The sheer weight of falling sea-water had stove in the roof of the shack, but the drenched guns' crew had quickly propped it up inside with oars so as not to reveal the gun to the Germans. With that, the 'panic party' did their performance, rowing away towards the port bow, and they all settled down to wait, with Auten peering through a convenient slit to watch developments.

The German captain, Viebeg, brought *UB-80* to the surface about half a mile away, after carefully checking the state of his victim through his periscope. The U-boat was one of a flotilla of six, operating out of Zeebrugge, which had wriggled their way through the Straits of Dover only a couple of days before on a concerted mission to attack the troop transports which were bringing more and more forces to Europe from the USA. It was strange, therefore, that he should have seen fit to torpedo a Q-ship. It was certainly unwise.

The 'panic party' pulled on their oars, moving slowly down the port side of *Stockforce*. Viebeg followed, but he was, as Auten put it, 'a very shy bird', and did not come too near the ship itself. Slowly approaching the boat, which had now stopped a short distance abaft the port beam, the submarine gradually came into the angle of fire of both the Q-ship's 4-inch guns. The 'panic boat' had done its job perfectly, drawing the U-boat to the exact spot where Auten wanted it. At last, Auten whispered down the voice-pipe connecting the two guns, "Submarine bearing red 90. Range 300 yards. Stand by. Let go."

The flaps fell down and the guns roared with a sudden violence which Auten confessed startled even him. The first two shells took away *UB-80*'s periscope and wireless, and wrecked the conning-tower, blowing one man into the air. The next shots hit the hull, causing volumes of white steam and blue smoke to pour out of the boat. She was now an immobile target as *Stockforce*'s guns continued to pound her. And as she received more and more hits she settled more and more by the stern. The men in the 'panic boat', seventy yards away, all stood up, waving their caps in the air and cheering, until eventually the U-boat lifted her bows fully clear of the water before sliding backwards to disappear.

But *Stockforce* was sinking herself. She had a 40-foot-wide hole in her side, and was already well down by the head. The recoil from the concerted blasts of her guns had altered her trim and suddenly she took a lurch which left her with a severe starboard list. It would not be long, surely, before she went down. There was not going to be room for everybody in the remaining boats, so Auten set a party to make a couple of rafts out of the timbers in the hold.

And there was still Steward Starling to be freed. He had lain quietly throughout the whole action, trapped under the wrecked 12-pounder gun, all alone in the for'ard part of the ship. When they got to him he was unconscious and the rising water was lapping around him. "Well, sir," he said to Auten later, "After you had gone, I lay there quiet. The last thing I remember was seeing the black cat." She too, it seems, had been blown into the air, to come down in the water, and as the pinioned Starling watched, she climbed onto a plank and shook herself dry, like a dog, before daintily picking her way to a drier spot.

With no wireless to call for help, Auten had a problem. His engines, set well aft, had been undamaged, however, and he was actually able to get *Stockforce* under way, pointed in the general direction of Plymouth. And as luck would have it two trawlers had heard the sound of gunfire and had hurried to the scene. Auten transferred the wounded and most of the crew to them and asked them to stand by. He had great affection for the ship that he had personally selected to be his own. He was going to save her if he could. But it was futile. Only eight miles from the beach, off Bolt Tail at the entrance to Bigbury Bay, the water entered her fireboxes and her stokers emerged from their flooded stokehold to clamber over the side. Reluctant to leave her even then, Auten and his First Lieutenant were still sitting on her port side rubbing strake as she went under, stepping into a waiting dinghy at the last moment.

Many awards were made for the bravery displayed in the first and last action of *Stockforce*, including a Conspicuous Gallantry Medal for the grim courage of Starling, who must have endured tremendous pain in absolute silence, and the VC to Auten himself.

A tragic incident occurred in the autumn of 1918. The Q-ship *Cymric*, an elderly 226-ton iron barquentine, was working off the coast of Yorkshire on 15 October. There had already been one near-disaster earlier in the day when *Cymric* had been on the verge of hurling a broadside of shells at a submarine which she had seen sitting on the surface, only to realize, just in time, that it was one of the Royal Navy's own ill-fated K-class boats.

But later the Q-ship's men could not believe their luck when they saw the German submarine, *U-6*, sliding towards them on the surface, bold as brass, obviously intent on attacking her with gun-fire. The sailing ship's gunners went to action stations. It appeared that their long months of frustrating boredom were about to end. *U-6* drew nearer, and when it came within point-blank range, up flew the White Ensign, down fell the shutters and *Cymric*'s 4-inch and 12-pounder guns belched forth. The submarine had no chance of survival, although she did not sink immediately, but drifted away into a thick bank of fog with her crew jumping into the water. The Q-ship followed and began picking up survivors. To their horror, they saw that these men were wearing cap tallies which read *H.M. Submarines*!

It had not been *U-6* at all, but the British *J-6*! *U-6* had been on the sea-bed off Norway for three years, ever since 15 September, 1915, to be precise, when she had been torpedoed by the British *E-16*. There had been a terrible mistake. British submarines carried their identification numbers in large white letters on the side of the conning-tower. Something had been hanging down on the left-hand side of the J – a piece of flotsam of some sort, or perhaps a strand of pale-coloured weed. In the gloomy light, the 'J' had thus became a 'U'. There were only fifteen survivors.

At the Court of Inquiry the Q-ship captain, who already wore the DSO and Bar and DSC and Bar, was exonerated from blame for the accident, which was found to have been a 'hazard of war'. *J-6*'s survivors stood and saluted him as he left the room.

But by this time any doubt as to the eventual outcome of the war against the U-boats had long since been dispelled. They had lost six boats in July, 1918, seven in August, nine in September and five in October, almost exclusively by mines, or depth-charging by escort ships.

And now, in the very last days of the conflict, with Austria-Hungary on the verge of collapse, the Germans abandoned their bases in the Adriatic, leaving their U-boats in the Mediterranean to attempt to reach Germany via the only available route, the Straits of Gibraltar. Some did manage to get home, against all the odds, which were very high, because the Royal Navy had crammed the narrow exit to the Atlantic with submarine hunters.

Among these was the now ex-decoy *Privet*, which we last saw in March, 1917, grounded on the beach at the entrance to Plymouth

Sound after she had sunk *U-85*. They had raised her and towed her in for extensive repairs, after which she had been sent to sea again to continue the fight, although no longer as a Q-ship, but as an out-and-out patrol vessel. On the night of 8 November, 1918, she was on station off Gibraltar when depth-charges from a couple of motor-launches flushed the *U-34* to the surface as its commander, Klasing, was trying to break out into the Atlantic. The U-boat came up near to *Privet*, which tried to ram it, unsuccessfully, although it damaged the conning-tower with shellfire. Klasing tried to crash-dive, but before he could do so, his boat had been hit three more times by *Privet*'s 12-pounder at point-blank range, and as a final *coup de grace* was plastered by a pattern of seven depth-charges. It was not seen again. Only three days later the Armistice was signed.

Chapter 10

Q-Ships – A Conclusion

Historians differ greatly as to the 'kills' credited to the British Q-ships. Perhaps that is not surprising, given the submarine's ability to make itself invisible at will, and also the undoubted skills that some of the German captains acquired in 'playing dead' in order to escape. Grant is adamant that *Stonecrop* did not sink *U-88* in the Bay of Biscay on 17 September, 1917. He insists that this boat had already been sunk twelve days earlier in the minefields off the coast of Holland, and that Blackwood's opponent that day was *U-151*, which was only slightly damaged and did in fact survive the war. It may well have been a case of mistaken identity, but from the vivid account given by the Q-ship's 'panic party', sitting in their boat only yards from the submarine as it received such a fierce onslaught, it would seem unlikely that it was only 'slightly' damaged, whichever U-boat it was. And it may be appropriate to take into account that both Campbell and Chatterton were serving officers at the time of these events, with close Q-ship fraternity connections, whereas the American Grant was working years later from archive material, mainly German.

On the other hand Grant credits *Acton* with the sinking of *UC-72*, which neither Campbell nor Chatterton see fit to include. Indeed, Chatterton describes that particular action as 'indecisive'. Nor does he agree that *Lady Olive* sank *UC-18*. According to him, this was a simple case of an exchange of shots which left the Q-ship sinking and the U-boat with two men killed and some superficial damage. The submarine then submerged and made off, leaving Lieutenant Frank and his crew to their ordeal, adrift in their open boats.

Chatterton includes the sinking of *UB-39* by the tiny Q-schooner

Glen off the Isle of Wight on 17 May, 1917, but again Grant challenges the identity of the U-boat, claiming that it was on this occasion *UB-18*, which sustained damage and was forced to return to Zeebrugge. The *UB-39*, he says, had *presumably* been the victim of a mine three nights before, but he offers no reason for making this presumption.

And of the three, only Chatterton alleges that *Stockforce* dispatched *UB-80* on 30 July, 1918. Campbell ignores it, and Grant denies it. He agrees that Viebeg was unwise to attack the Q-ship, but insists that *UB-80* returned safely to Zeebrugge after the encounter.

Then we have the problem of definition. When is a Q-ship action not a Q-ship action? Campbell, whose list comprises just eleven 'kills', seems to have only considered the 'classic' Q-ship decoy actions, where an unaided Q-ship has lured a U-boat to destruction by the various ruses at its disposal. But there were many other instances of U-boats being sunk by decoys. Grant mentions these sinkings, but he does not always acknowledge that they were carried out by decoy vessels, although Chatterton does include them in his narrative. We have already seen how the decoy trawlers *Inverlyon* and *Oceanic II* each sank a U-boat, and how two more trawlers, *Princess Louise* and *Taraniki*, did the same by working in partnership with a submarine. We have seen, too, how Godfrey Herbert's trawler *Sea King* depth-charged and destroyed a German submarine, and how the little 59-ton smacks *Telesia* and *Cheerio* blew up *UB-13* (or perhaps it was the *UC-3*) with their mined nets.

The Flower Class Q-sloops *Lychnis* and *Viola* sank *U-64* and *UB-30* respectively, both with depth-charges, and the drifter *Coreopsis* shelled *UB-85* into oblivion. Then there were the little *PQ* patrol boats, the PC class, which seem to have specialized in the ramming technique. *PC-56*, *PC-61* and *PC-62* all used this method to sink *U-87*, *UC-33* and *U-84*.

And they never did establish the identity of the U-boat which the Q-trawler *W.S.Bailey* depth-charged in the Firth of Forth on 24 January, 1918, although they found the wreck of it.

It has become commonplace, too, when thinking of the Q-ships, to consider them only for their fight against the U-boat menace. But that is to ignore another valuable contribution that some of them made. Their hunting down of the enemy's *merchant* shipping must not be forgotten. In this they played a similar role to that of the German decoy raiders, albeit closer to home.

Germany had traditionally obtained much of its vital supply of high-quality iron ore from Sweden. This was mined in the far north and was shipped by rail to the neutral Norwegian port of Narvik, where it could be loaded into ore-carriers, which would hug the long coast of Norway, keeping within territorial waters as far as possible, all the way south to Germany.

The Royal Navy's Tenth Cruiser Squadron, composed of armed merchant cruisers, was entrusted with the task of intercepting as much of this shipping as possible. But a glance at the map will show that the Norwegian coastline is spattered with a host of small islands and deep fjords, easy surroundings in which to hide, but hardly ideal in which to prowl with a 16,000-ton liner. It was here that the little Q-ships attached to the cruisers provided such crucial assistance and many thousands of tons of magnetic iron ore was prevented from reaching Germany thanks to them. It was a dour, dangerous and far from glamorous role which they played, and it has been largely unsung by the chroniclers of the war. To pay them at least some tribute, let us look at a handful of examples.

The steam trawler HMS *Tenby Castle* served as a Q-ship for over two years. On the morning of 7 July, 1915, in thick Arctic mist and drizzle, she stopped and captured the large fully laden Swedish ore-carrier *Malmland* and handed it over to the armed liner HMS *India* for safe-keeping. Later, patrolling off West Fjord, she met another steamer coming out of Narvik. It was the *Friedrich Arp* of Hamburg. Despite several warnings, the German captain refused to stop. This left Lieutenant Randall, the Q-ship's captain, no alternative but to sink her. He took her crew of thirteen prisoner and put them on board the waiting *India*. In one day HMS *Tenby Castle* had deprived Germany of 11,000 tons of ore and two ships.

The 550-ton *Tay & Tyne* was a passenger-coaster in peacetime, plying between Hull and Dundee. In February, 1917, the Navy requisitioned her and armed her with a four-inch gun, two 12-pounders, a 6-pounder, a 3-pounder and a 14 inch torpedo tube. One day, posing as an ordinary tramp, she came across the German flush-decked freighter *Düsseldorf* with 1,700 tons of ore. From 1,000 yards the Q-ship hoisted the signal to stop – 'M N'. The German ignored the signal, which brought a shell across his bows. He had had no idea that he was being decoyed until he found his own ship covered at close range by the muzzles of *Tay & Tyne*'s not inconsiderable array of guns. Despite protests from the captain and the Norwegian pilot that the ship was within territorial waters, a British prize crew was put on board and *Düsseldorf* was dispatched towards Scotland. It was only after a nightmare voyage of seven days across the North Sea that the ship and its valuable cargo reached the Firth of Forth. The weather was atrocious and the magnetic cargo created serious compass deviation, which meant that navigation around the known minefields could only be done by taking constant fixes from the stars whenever they were visible for a fleeting moment through the black clouds.

On another occasion *Tay & Tyne* was in company with HMS *Glendale*, Q-23, when they captured the German steamer *Valeria* with 2,200 tons of ore. They tried to reach Lerwick with their captive, but her coal ran out and they were forced to take her crew off and sink her.

The ex-Isle of Man packet-boat *King Orry* was sent to help with the iron ore blockade in the autumn of 1916. The breaks in her sides were covered with canvas to give her a flush-decked appearance. Derricks were fitted to her masts and her guns hidden under false deck-houses. She was painted black, with a yellow funnel and black boot-top, and, to provide a Scandinavian touch, the letters VI were added in front of her name to turn her into the *Viking Orry*. At nightfall she would sail inshore with all lights doused and move to within a very short distance of other vessels to inspect them. If she was satisfied, her black shape would simply melt away into the night. Often she was chased by Norwegian patrols, but was never caught.

One night a large cargo ship loomed out of the mist. She was heading back into the safety of neutral water, and to prevent her from doing this *King Orry* dropped a couple of 4-inch shells across her bows. Her captain said that as soon as he saw *King Orry*'s rakish lines he knew that the game was up. It turned out that one of his crew had worked on the Birkenhead Ferry before the war and recognized *King Orry* despite her disguise. It was a valuable capture of both ship and iron ore which sailed into Kirkwall with a prize crew on board.

It must be remembered that such vessels as *King Orry* were never constructed for long periods at sea in Arctic winter weather. They were made to ferry summertime holidaymakers, in her case from Liverpool to the Isle of Man. Some of the wartime conditions which their crews endured were almost beyond description. On many occasions it must have seemed to them that their ship would be smashed to pieces as the 90 m.p.h. winds churned up mountainous seas which battered and swamped them for days on end.

Such was the regard that Admiral Sir David Beatty held for *King Orry* that when the time came, at the end of the war, to receive the surrendered German fleet at Scapa Flow, he gave her the place of honour in the middle of the centre line of the waiting British ships.

So, although the ice-cool courage and the cast-iron tenacity of their crews, in conditions that were often scarcely believable, can only be marvelled at, how much did the Q-ships contribute, materially, to the winning of the war? A look at Campbell's meagre list of eleven U-boats, in isolation, would perhaps compel us to conclude that 'little' should be the answer. But that would be to take the narrowest view. And even if we take into account the sinkings made by *Inverlyon*, *Coreopsis* and all the rest, to bring the total up to a couple of dozen, we still would not balance the equation. We will never know how many U-boats, even though unsunk in their encounters with Q-ships, were damaged nonetheless, thus to occupy who knows how many man/hours of repair work in German dockyards. Judging by the number of 'probable' and 'possible' sinkings, it is likely that this hindrance was considerable. Who can ever say how many British merchant ships sailed safely into harbour, past a watching U-boat whose captain, well briefed to be cautious, was not *quite* sure that he was not taking on a Q-ship, and had decided that discretion was the better part of valour this time? And who can say by how much the pillaging of Germany's iron ore hastened her defeat?

In the care of the Public Record Office there is a document marked 'secret' and headed "Actions between Special Service Vessels and Submarines". Compiled by Naval Staff Intelligence in April 1919, it lists no fewer than sixty-two Q-ship actions with U-boats. It is prefaced by a memorandum to the effect that it is not a complete list of such actions. Indeed, that fact is immediately clear by the omission of both *Baralong* sinkings, as well as many other known incidents, and it often contradicts Campbell, Chatterton, Grant & Co. But what it does do is to emphasize the uncertainty of such statistics by its many 'probables' and 'possibles'.

Taking the broader view, therefore, it must be conceded that the Q-ships did their bit, at least until a better, and easier, way was adopted.

Chapter 11

The Germans Don Disguise

The newly commissioned British destroyer HMS *Lance* left the Thornycroft yard in Southampton on Saturday, 1st August, 1914, and steamed down to Gosport in the summer drizzle to take on fuel and ammunition. She sailed next morning at ten past six from Portsmouth's Excellent Steps Jetty, heading for Harwich where she was to join the Third Destroyer Flotilla. War was still three days away, but her captain, Commander Egerton, was in no doubt that it would come. In his log for that Sunday forenoon, as *Lance* steamed up the Channel, he entered, "Hands preparing torpedoes for war".

Egerton did not dawdle. The destroyer covered the last 109 sea miles from Sheerness to Harwich in four hours. By Tuesday the 4th the last hours of peace had almost ticked away and *Lance*'s afternoon watchmen were painting over her gleaming brightwork and topping-up more torpedoes. At 8.05 that evening Egerton darkened ship and she swung from her buoy throughout the night with one 4-inch gun crew closed up.

Lance sailed from Harwich at two minutes past six on the morning of Wednesday, 5 August, together with the rest of the Third Flotilla, led by the cruiser *Amphion*. The war, by then, was exactly seven hours and two minutes old.

The German excursion steamer *Königin Luise* had sailed from Emden the previous evening and headed into the North Sea. Her normal job was to ferry holidaymakers from Hamburg to Heligoland, but now she was on a different mission. She had been painted black, with brown superstructure, and a yellow funnel with a black 'boot-top', which just happened to coincide with the colours of the steamers belonging to the

Great Eastern Railway Company. And instead of being packed with happy excursion-trippers, she was now crammed with mines.

Lance, accompanied by one of her sisters, HMS *Landrail*, was in the course of her North Sea patrol when she was approached by a fishing smack. The skipper reported that he had seen a ship behaving suspiciously off the Outer Gabbard. She was throwing things overboard. The two destroyers hurried to investigate. Sure enough, there was a steamer, and things were being thrown overboard. One of the destroyer's officers, Edwards, said later that at first sight they looked like grand pianos. *Lance*'s log reads "10.30. *Saw suspicious ship*. 11.25. *Opened fire*. 11.35. *Enemy observed to be sinking*". They picked up some survivors, and landed them as prisoners at Shotley Pier that evening.

Lance had fired the very first shots of the war at sea. And, as we will see, the *Königin Luise* was the first of several German ships which would sail in disguise.

The *Vienna* was a North Sea ferry, owned by the Leith, Hull & Hamburg Steam Packet Co. She had the misfortune to find herself in Hamburg on the day war was declared and was seized by Germany. The *Admiralstab* fitted her out as a mine-layer, mounted two 4-inch guns hidden behind her gunwales and renamed her SMS *Meteor*. Then they sent her, disguised as a Russian, commanded by thirty-four-year-old Korvettenkapitän Wolfram von Knorr, to lay mines off the Kola Peninsula and in the White Sea. It was a very successful cruise.

The authorities were impressed and decided to send her on a second expedition in August, 1915, this time to lay mines in Scottish waters, in the Moray Firth. Throughout the night of 7/8 August, in hazy summer-time moonlight, von Knorr laid 374 deadly eggs. Unbeknown to the Germans, no less a personage than the British Prime Minister Herbert Asquith was in secret conference at that very moment with Admiral Jellicoe on board the flagship HMS *Iron Duke* just a few miles away at Invergordon. Needless to say, British security was particularly tight, and in fact two patrol boats had already reported some strange lights which they were unable to identify. Orders were radioed to all vessels to keep a sharp lookout.

One of these, an armed boarding steamer the ex-Manx packet *Ramsey*, spied smoke at 0500 on the morning of the 8th. Her captain, Lieutenant-Commander Raby, rang down for Full Speed and in half an hour they caught up with the stranger. She was a Russian tramp.

Ramsey blew her whistle for her to stop for inspection. Suddenly the Russian flag came down, the German Ensign was raised and a broadside spat forth from the intruder. At the same time a deluge of machine-gun fire played like a hose along the decks of the boarding steamer, killing Raby and the other officers on the bridge, and a torpedo sped across the short distance separating the two ships to explode in *Ramsey*'s after mess-deck, completely shattering her stern.

One of the forty-six British survivors of the crew of ninety-eight said later, "Very many lives were lost as most of the crew were below decks. We had no time to return the fire. She went down in less than four minutes. As soon as we were put on board the German ship, the Commander sent us below to get some dry clothes and medical comforts. He said he was sorry that we had lost so many brave men and asked if we would like to have a Church Service in their memory, which we gladly accepted. They were very good to us, and gave us plenty of cigars and cigarettes. They gave each of us a mattress and a blanket and sent us down into the hold. We had tea, and then lay down for the night. All was quiet until about midnight when we heard gunfire. They had sunk a small Norwegian schooner which was bound for England with pit-props. Her crew were sent below with us.

"The delay caused by this sinking was our salvation, as we were only an hour or so from Zeebrugge and internment. We learned afterwards that our fast cruisers at Harwich received orders at 6 p.m. on Sunday to proceed at full speed after the *Meteor* and that she was making for Zeebrugge. About midday on the Monday we were summoned up on deck, and learned from the Germans that British cruisers were in chase. Their smoke was just visible on the horizon. The Germans had been warned by a Zeppelin, which was scouting for them. They decided to abandon their ship. There were a lot of Danish fishing luggers about. One of these was commandeered and into her we were packed, along with their own crew and the Norwegians.

"The Commander and two officers remained on board to place a time fuse bomb in her, after which they joined us in the lugger. When the cruisers hove in sight, they were just in time to see the *Meteor* blow up and sink.

"The first cruiser was HMS *Cleopatra* and one of our survivors, a signalman, signalled to her that we were on board the lugger. She replied for us to take charge of the lugger and follow her, but the German captain would not allow this, as we were now under a neutral flag. The cruiser made off to report this to Commodore Tyrwhitt, who was some way off in the *Arethusa*. While she was gone, the Germans transferred us to another lugger, a Norwegian, while they made off in the Danish one. Then the *Arethusa* came up and sent over a large boat to take us off. Thus we had had the unique experience of sailing under four different flags in one day – German, Danish, Norwegian and British."

Chapter 12

The Black Seagull

Korvettenkapitän Graf Nikolaus zu Dohna-Schlodien was a Silesian aristocrat with a goatee beard, a classic example of one of the Kaiser's Navy's wealthy officer class. And he was bored. He was a navigation specialist, but there had been precious little navigating for him to do so far. All his efforts to find some action had met with disappointment. For over a year Germany had been at war, yet all Dohna-Schlodien had done was to pace the decks of the heavy cruiser *Posen* as she did her rounds of duty with the other Wilhelmshaven guardships, with three days shore leave every three weeks.

He was having a snooze in his rooms on Wilhelmshaven's Prinz Heinrich Strasse during one of these breaks when a courier delivered a message. It was a 'tip-off' from a friendly senior officer who had been charged with appointing a captain for a new raider to follow the *Meteor*. If Dohna wanted the job, he must act quickly. Needing no second bidding, he dressed hurriedly, hailed a taxi and sped to Fleet Headquarters.

His sheer enthusiasm landed him the appointment and he left the interview with orders to find a suitable merchant ship. She needed to be roomy enough to carry many prisoners and coal for thousands of miles' steaming. She needed to be strong enough to withstand the recoil of the 6-inch naval guns which she would carry. She needed to be faster than the average freighter. Above all she needed to look harmlessly ordinary. Dohna went to Kiel and Emden and Rostock, but it was in Bremen that he found her. She was nearly new, having just been built for the Afrikanische Fruchtkompagnie to hump bananas to Germany from the Cameroons. Therefore, she had big refrigerators for fresh food supplies. She weighed-in at 4,790 tons and was 100 metres long. She was dazzling white with a gold funnel. Her name was *Pungo*.

In his keenness, the slowness of officialdom in commandeering the *Pungo* drove Dohna to despair. A month went by and he heard nothing. Then the *Posen* was ordered to proceed through the Kaiser Wilhelm Canal to counter the threat of the Russian Fleet in the Baltic. Still he had heard nothing more about the *Pungo*. Perhaps they had forgotten about her. But, no. He had just completed the task of navigating the *Posen*'s 18,800 tons through the tricky canal when a wireless message came through. He was to return to Bremen and await orders.

At Bremen he found a skeleton crew already assembled and waiting, and his orders were to board *Pungo*, take possession of her in the name of the Kaiser and take her to Wilhelmshaven for refitting. The *Admiralstab* had in mind for her to be a disguised mine-layer, nothing more, but Dohna nursed more exciting ambitions. For him the furtive work of a *minenleger* held little glory. He did not want *Pungo* to be just another *Königin Luise*, but another *Emden*! When her mines had all been laid, Dohna was intent on going raiding.

The *Admiralstab*, in their stuffy innocence, knew nothing of this. And Dohna did not intend them to know – not until he had already fitted her out as a marauder. He took the Dockyard Engineer, Brodersen, into his confidence, and things got underway. All through October and November, 1915, workmen swarmed over *Pungo*, with clanging hammers, buzzing drills and glowing blow-torches, as they transformed her from a banana-boat into a bandit.

Dohna ordered five guns – four 150 mm (6") quick-firing SK L/45s, which he mounted for'ard, two on each side, and a single 105 mm (4.7") SK L/45 aft. The larger guns were to be hidden behind hinged screens cut into the sides of the ship and the stern gun was camouflaged as a piece of steering gear, with a big ship's wheel around its barrel. Then came the mines. Five hundred were lined up on her upper cargo deck, on special pallets, ready to be rolled into the sea through her stern chute. Her magazines were placed for'ard, under the crew's mess-deck, with stacks of dry provisions around them as a measure of safety. As an after-thought, they gave her four torpedo tubes, two on each side on the main-deck, amidships.

Dohna had been 'softening up' the authorities with his ideas for a while by now, although he had not, as yet, revealed all that he had done in anticipation of their approval. As it happened, they had become concerned at the worldwide condemnation that their Unrestricted Submarine Warfare policy was receiving, and when Dohna finally put it to them that he should be allowed to fight a 'cleaner' war, as a surface raider, reminding them of the spectacular early successes of the *Emden* and the *Kronprinz Wilhelm*, they concurred. So that was it, they were going raiding! And it was with the blessing of the Kaiser!

And *Pungo*, or rather the HD 10 as she had become known in the Dockyard, was given a far more noble name. They commissioned her as SMS *Möwe*, the Seagull, a fitting name for one who would fly, free, with the ocean as her pasture. Dohna had picked his officers and crew very carefully. But he had not yet told them exactly what their true mission was to be. As far as they knew they were preparing to go mine-laying in the Baltic. Nevertheless, it was with great enthusiasm that they took *Möwe* out on trials, testing her for speed, practising their gunnery and all the other skills that a crack crew would be expected to display. And with the hard driving of their captain, Count Nikolaus zu Dohna-Schlodien, that is what they became – a crack crew.

It was a white Christmas in 1915, and it was celebrated with beer and champagne and with much jollity on board the *Möwe* as she sat alongside in Kiel. And the next day, at ten o'clock in the forenoon, Admiral Bachmann came on board to carry out his official inspection. He went away satisfied. The Seagull was ready to fly the nest.

At 1700 hours on 26 December, 1915, *Möwe* left her moorings to slide down the canal towards Cuxhaven, and the North Sea. But first she paused at the entrance to the canal to pick up the last mail her crew would be receiving for a while. Already they had realized that they were not going mine-laying in the Baltic at all. Westwards down the *Nord-Ost See Kanal* was not the way to the *Ost See*. They scrambled to send off last letters to their loved ones, but their fond words never even left the ship. Dohna, needing the utmost secrecy, confiscated the letters and kept them in his office.

There was one last job to do before *Möwe*'s disguise was complete. The next day Dohna anchored in a quiet cove near the mouth of the Elbe, out of sight of prying eyes, and all hands were set to painting out her white and gold Afrikanische Fruchtkompagnie livery. By the end of the day she was a dull black Swedish tramp, with the words SAGOLAND – GOTEBORG painted on her stern. And she had been joined by a companion. It was a slim grey U-boat, which had been assigned to act as her scout, to travel a few miles ahead of her, keeping a look-out for British patrols, as she ran the gauntlet of the Royal Navy's blockade.

The submarine was none other than *U-68* commanded by none other than Kapitänleutnant Ludwig Guntzel, the very same U-boat commanded by the very same captain which, eighty-six days later, in the Atlantic, would be blasted into pieces by the shells and depth-charges of Gordon Campbell's *Farnborough, Q-5*.

As it was, their departure was set back a day. Storm-force conditions during the night had sent huge seas into the secluded anchorage. The Seagull rode it out, but in the morning Dohna saw that all the previous day's painting work had been in vain. The battering waves had washed most of it off. There was nothing for it but to get out the black paint and the brushes and the ladders and the slings, and paint her all over again. It was not until just before dawn on the morning of 30 December, 1915, that the capstans rumbled and the chains clanked as *Möwe* lifted her anchors and headed out into the gale-tossed grey waters of the *Deutsche Bucht*, the Heligoland Bight.

Dohna kept each duty watch closed up at action stations throughout this dangerous passage. He was thankful for the rough squally weather, which shortened visibility, and by nightfall they had parted from *U-68* and were running northwards, tight to the coast of Norway. It was not until this point that Dohna mustered his crew and dispelled the rumours that had been percolating around the ship. At last everybody knew the true nature of their mission.

New Year's Eve found *Möwe* north of the Shetlands, having turned to battle her way westwards against an inhospitable wintry blast from the Atlantic. Dohna's orders were to lay mines in as many as possible of several key areas pinpointed by the authorities. One of these was along the far north coast of the Scottish mainland, between Cape Wrath and the Pentland Firth. This was a busy thoroughfare, carrying traffic between the east and west of the northern British Isles, plus of course many Royal Navy ships in and out of Scapa Flow. But this was no weather for minelaying close-in to an enemy shore and he decided to wait for the storms to abate, north of the Faeroes, before making his first run. The next day was calmer, and he turned south-east to ride over a dark-green swell towards his target zone. But his charts were woefully inaccurate. The water here was deeper – ten times deeper – than the place they were seeking and it was early evening before the leadsman sang out the right figure, "Fifty-five metres!" Dohna was relieved, but he badly needed to rest before starting to lay his mines. He turned back to the north-west and, ordering the Officer of the Watch to turn away at full speed from *any* craft that were seen, he went to his cabin to sleep.

The sun was high on a bright clear winter's day when he returned to the bridge. Now to some serious work. The black ship turned towards the coast, with all eyes on the lookout for British patrols. So far there had been no sign of them whatsoever. In fact Dohna had become somewhat uneasy about the absence of any ships guarding what was, after all, a main domestic seaway near a major naval anchorage in wartime. Could it be that he was sailing into a trap?

Two hundred and fifty-two of the Seagull's mines had been prepared under the watchful eye of Oberleutnant Kühl, the specialist mine and torpedo officer, and now they sat in straight lines on the after upper-deck, waiting to slide, one by one, down the special tracked runway which had been rigged over the stern. By 1600 the few hours of winter daylight had passed and Dohna was able to take a 'fix' from the Sule Skerry Light on his port bow, as he steered *Möwe* towards Dunnet Head in the Pentland Firth. And with the darkness came the rain, sleet and snow. It was going to be a filthy night.

Kühl clutched his stop-watch as he stood on the after-deck, swathed in heavy weather clothing, and looked up at the bridge with eyes screwed against the driving sleet. He was proud of his specialist skills and now was the time for him to demonstrate them. Careful timing of the intervals between each drop was essential if the correct patterns were to be laid, and he would be responsible for telling the bridge when to change course, so as to stitch those precise patterns into the sea as per the drawings Berlin had prepared. *Möwe*'s engines throbbed as she picked up speed. Kühl was ready. He waved his arm, rapped out a sharp order and the first mine trundled down the chute. It was 1800 hours exactly on 2 January, 1916.

The steady rhythm of the loud splashes that the mines made was drowned by the howling of the wind, which rose steadily to Force 12 – hurricane. And snow came with it, so thick that it seemed as if a white curtain had been drawn around the ship's rail, while down below, in the stifling heat of the boiler-room, the stokers sweated at their shovels to keep her engines at full tilt. If any British patrols were out in those conditions, they did not catch sight of the black Seagull laying her eggs. And by midnight, when the duty watch went below, frozen and drenched, they had laid all 252; 130 in the Pentland Firth, around the approaches to Scapa Flow itself, and the rest sprinkled all the way westwards to the tip of Cape Wrath.

Now was the time to run away, to disappear into the Atlantic. Dohna ran on through the still raging storm, anxious to put as many sea miles as possible behind him. He had hardly slept for several days, but it was not until nearly dawn the next morning, when they were well clear of land and the weather had eased, that he left the bridge and went to his cabin. His ship had taken a fearful battering from the weather. She was letting in water through her damaged hatch-covers, soaking everything and everybody on the for'ard mess-deck. But it could not be helped. She ploughed on into the grey ocean wastes, while her captain slept soundly.

Dohna had done a good job for the Kaiser off the north of Scotland, but where to strike next? Wisely, he elected to ignore other targets around the British Isles. The *Admiralstab* had given him a free hand to lay his mines wherever he chose, but had suggested some preferred areas. One was the Atlantic coast of France, where the big ports of Bordeaux, Nantes and La Rochelle were important to the Allies on the western front. Refreshed by sleep, he turned to the south. To keep the enemy guessing by being highly mobile was astute strategy. He mustered his crew, congratulated them on their fine performance and told them they were off to the Bay of Biscay. And they all gave three cheers for SMS *Möwe*.

They did not know it, but they had more reason to be pleased with themselves than they realized. The incessant foul weather throughout December and early January had prevented the British Grand Fleet from carrying out its routine manoeuvres. For all that time it had been cooped up in Scapa Flow, unable to flex its muscles. By 6 January conditions had improved sufficiently for some of the great ships to stir and they came out to exercise. One of them, the old 17,500-ton 12" battleship *King Edward VII*, one of the famous 'Wobbly Eight', had come charging towards Cape Wrath with her sixteen Babcock & Wilcox boilers at full steam and the din of her 18,000 Indicated Horse Power, vertical triple-expansion engines roaring in the ears of her 780 sailors. She had run straight on to one of Kühl's mines. It took her several hours to sink. *Möwe* had opened her account.

Chapter 13

The Gull Goes Fishing

There was time to relax as *Möwe* steamed southwards through the Atlantic. The lower deck hummed to the chatter of easy gossip, the card-players gathered around the mess-deck tables and the rest sat reading or smoking or simply dozing. In his cabin Dohna read more of the Sherlock Holmes stories to which he was addicted – then it was time for more work.

They found the Bay of Biscay smooth as satin and the French Navy apparently as insouciant as their British allies had been in the Pentland Firth. There was no sign of *les matelots*, except when the Germans were followed for a while, with their hearts in their mouths, by what appeared in the darkness to be a patrolling cruiser. It turned away after a while, obviously satisfied as to their innocence. And there was a rush to action stations a couple of times when the lookouts thought that they were being attacked by a swarm of torpedo boats which turned out to be a harmless fleet of fishing smacks. Apart from those two incidents, their nighttime excursion was uneventful. In bright moonlight Kühl embroidered the 100-mile stretch between the mouths of the Loire and the Gironde with the last 248 of his mines. The final one fell into the Gulf of Gascony with a ten-foot high phosphorescent splash at one minute short of 0400 hours on 10 January, 1916, and the ship ran away again into the Atlantic. (The French authorities got wind of Dohna's exploits the very next day, and by 21 January, only eleven days later, Allied minesweepers had cleared all the mines. But it was too late to save the steamer *Belgica* and the Spanish ship *Bayo* which both struck mines and sank.)

Möwe was now free to roam, and, what was more, she was free of

The First Cruise of the *Möwe*

1. *Farringford*, 11 January, 1916
2. *Corbridge*, (captured) 11 January, 1916
3. *Dromonby*, 13 January, 1916
4. *Author*, 13 January, 1916
5. *Trader*, 13 January, 1916
6. *Ariadne*, 15 January, 1916
7. *Appam*, (captured) 15 January, 1916
8. *Clan McTavish*, 16 January, 1916
9. *Edinburgh*, 22 January, 1916
10. *Corbridge*, (sunk) -
11. *Luxembourg*, 4 February 1916
12. *Flamenco*, 6 February, 1916
13. *Westburn*, (captured) 8 February, 1916
14. *Horace*, 8 February, 1916
15. *Westburn*, (scuttled) 23 February, 1916
16. *Maroni*, 23 February, 1916
17. *Saxon Prince*, 25 February, 1916

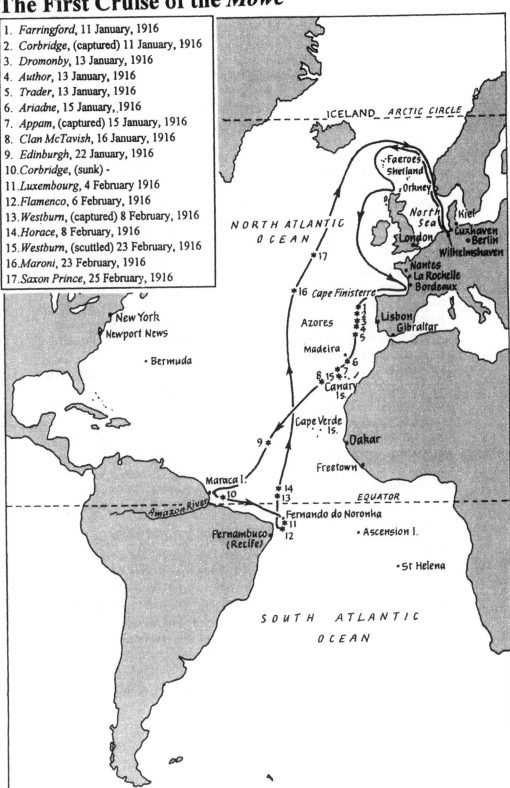

the awesome nightmare of having a British shell burst among those hundreds of highly explosive mines on her cargo deck, blowing the ship and everybody in her to smithereens. Dohna had fulfilled the main mission with which Berlin had charged him and now he could embark on the adventure which was his own true aim. The Seagull was about to become a bird of prey.

Dohna turned to the south-west. He gave a wide berth to Cape Finisterre on the north-west tip of Spain, so as to keep well to the west of the Gibraltar – UK shipping lane. They were now into much warmer waters. The storms and blizzards off the north of Scotland were a million miles away. Here it was spring already and the loungers and gossippers could enjoy the sunshine on the upper deck. Two hundred miles away on their port bow the almond blossom of Portugal was bursting forth.

They were about 150 miles west-nor'west of Oporto when a shout went up "Rauch!" The lookout had spied smoke. Dohna hoisted the Red Ensign and the crew shook themselves alert as they went to their action stations. Möwe's engines steadily picked up and soon they were churning out fifteen knots towards the smudge on the horizon. It was the British steamer Farringford, a tall-funnelled tramp, lumbering along under a full load. The bandit was about to overtake her when more smoke was seen, this time away to port. Dohna knew that he could easily catch the slow Farringford and turned away to check the newcomer. It seemed that she too was a British merchantman. He over-hauled the Farringford again, ran up the German flag, dropped the screens to reveal the muzzles of his guns and fired a shot across her bows. She stopped immediately. Bringing Möwe in close so that the bridges of the two ships were no more than fifty yards apart, Dohna yelled, "Evacuate ship!"

There was no time to be lost if the second ship were not to escape and report what she had seen at the nearest Allied port. That would mean an early end to the flight of the Seagull. There was a heavy swell running and to transfer the merchant crew by boat would be a slow process. It would have to be done hull to hull, and so, with the plates of the two ships grinding together as they heaved over the mounds of green water, the British seamen stepped aboard the raider and their ship was quickly sunk with a couple of well-aimed shells at her water-line.

Dohna crammed on speed again, and in a couple of hours he had the second ship in sight. But this one was not going to be quite so easy. She was the Cardiff collier *Corbridge*, with 4,000 tons of coal for Brazil. Despite the German's shot across her bows, she tried to out-run him, spouting sparks and smoke high into the twilight as her firemen heaved on coal as fast as their arms could go. But she was well within range of *Möwe*'s guns, and when more shells began to splash uncomfortably close, her master, David Barton, could see that there was no escape. He hove-to and turned on all his lights.

This was a valuable catch for Dohna. Before long the time would come when he would need more coal and Germany had no friendly coaling stations in the Atlantic. The only way that he could lay his hands on fuel was to steal it from his victims. He put a prize crew on board the *Corbridge*, a dozen men under Leutnant Badewitz, and the two ships turned back on their tracks. Dohna wanted to check that the *Farringford* had indeed finally sunk, and without trace. He wanted no telltale clues left in his wake. It would be several days before she was reported overdue, and as yet the Allies had no inkling that another German raider was at large in the Atlantic. It was important to keep it that way as long as possible. He had no need to fear. There was no sign of the *Farringford*. In the morning, leaving the nine 'neutral' members of the crew of the *Corbridge* to help the prize crew, he took Barton and all his British sailors on board the *Möwe*. Badewitz was dispatched with the collier to wander around in mid-ocean, well away from the shipping lanes, with orders to rendezvous at a specified time and spot. And the bandit steamed on south. It was 12 January, 1916.

The next day was a lucky thirteenth of the month for the *Möwe*. First, the collier *Dromonby*, which was on her way from London to South America, with coal for HMS *Glasgow* and the other Royal Navy cruisers there (which soon would be hunting the *Möwe* herself) went to the sea-bed with all 5,000 tons of it in her blown-out bottom about 200 miles due west of Lisbon. And at half-past three that afternoon along came another English steamer, the trim little *Author*, bound for South Africa. Dohna shot the thoroughbred racehorses she was carrying – he had no way of accommodating them – and she too was soon beneath the waves with her sea-cocks open. The 3,600-ton freighter *Trader*, up from Peru with 5,000 tons of sugar for the British Admiralty, came hurrying over to offer any help that may be needed. For this act of decency she was rewarded with some explosive charges in her hull and an Atlantic grave. All three ships had been sunk within a radius of five miles. And it was still only twenty to six.

The German sailors enjoyed a day of rest on the fourteenth. Not a single plume of smoke, nor a sail, was seen all day. But the fifteenth was different. By now *Möwe* had reached the latitude of Madeira. It was a beautiful sub-tropical morning, fresh and calm. The off-duty watch were still at breakfast when the lookouts sighted the 3,000-ton steamer *Ariadne*, bound for Nantes with her cargo of cereals. Dohna had sunk all his victims so far with explosive charges placed in their bottoms. His gunners had had no target practice since their exercises in the Heligoland Bight. He decided to let them sink the *Ariadne* with shell-fire. It was a good idea that went wrong. As they began to find their mark, so their target began to burn. And as she burned, she produced a great mountain of smoke, which hung high in the cornflower-blue sky like a giant parasol.

Dohna did not know that the British cruisers *Essex* and *King Alfred* were patrolling the coast of North West Africa, supported by the armed merchant cruisers *Carmania* and *Ophir*. What he did know was that the smoke from the burning *Ariadne* would be visible many miles away. He expended one of his valuable torpedoes into her and she sank quickly, but even after she had gone there was still that huge pall of smoke in the sky. He hurried away.

But as he did so he found himself faced with a dilemma. There, coming out of the haze, was the biggest British ship they had yet seen. It was the Elder-Dempster Line's passenger liner *Appam*, 7,781 tons, bound for Southampton. She was not likely to be carrying much in the way of cargo, but her roomy frame would solve one of Dohna's most pressing problems. He now had 150-odd prisoners on board the *Möwe*. They were becoming a hindrance. Taking a final look at the *Appam* through his big Zeiss telescope, he decided to take her and use her to house his 'guests'. He noted that she sported a wireless. He would have to get in very close before any alarm calls went out. The raider was now less than 1000 yards from the liner, flying one of Dohna's latest 'inventions'; a tattered German Navy Ensign, well blackened by smoke and weighted down to stop it flying in the wind. Nobody could accuse Graf Nikolaus zu Dohna-Schlodien of flying a false flag. Indeed, nobody could tell exactly what it was at all.

Up fluttered an international flag signal on *Möwe*'s halyards: M.N. "Stop Immediately". The liner's master, Captain Harrison, did not hesitate to obey. He stopped. Instantly his wireless call-sign JBQV, began to cackle a distress signal, but as soon as the operator saw the bandit's guns trained on his office he closed down. Dohna moved in closer. He had hoisted a clean ensign to flap at his stern. There was no mistaking his identity now. But as the *Möwe* came round the stern of the *Appam* the German was surprised by two things. Firstly, he found himself facing a gun. It was only a small defensive stern gun, it was true, but it was being manned by men in Royal Navy uniforms. Dohna was taking no chances. His gunners put two or three shells close over the heads of the British sailors, who were sensible enough to see that to try to fight with a 3-pounder against a ship armed like a light cruiser was suicidal. The second surprise was a small group of people on the upper deck of the liner. Unlike most of the other passengers, who were struggling into life-belts with worried looks on their faces, these people were cheering and waving their handkerchiefs at him. *Möwe* had netted a beautiful catch. The *Appam* did, after all, have a valuable cargo of rubber, palm-oil and other commodities which Germany craved. And among her 160 passengers were some very important colonial officials, and a number of British Army officers and troops. As for the people who had been cheering on the upper deck, these were German nationals from Cameroon (a German colony), who had been on their way to intern-ment until their surprise rescue.

Dohna did not want to send the captured liner off to a neutral port with his prisoners right away. The minute she made port the word would be out and the hunt for him would be on, with all the Royal Navy's many ships in the Atlantic on the scent. As yet he had only been raiding for less than a week, and in all probability none of his victims had yet been listed as overdue. As for the unfortunate *King Edward VII*, it was assumed by the British that she had struck a mine laid by a U-boat, not a black-painted tramp steamer. There was still time for some more banditry and the *Appam* had plenty of room for more prisoners.

He took the German ex-internees on board the *Möwe*, plied them with champagne to celebrate their unexpected freedom, gave all the able-bodied men white arm-bands and revolvers and recruited them to assist Leutnant Berg, a thirty-nine-year-old from Schleswig-Holstein, who was to command the prize crew on the *Appam*. Then they all toasted the Kaiser.

With the exception of some of the Lascar seamen, who were willing to work as crew for the Germans, the prisoners were all transferred to the liner. Before they left, each man of military age was required to give his parole that he would not take up arms or sail again in a ship carrying contraband of war for enemies of Germany for the duration of the war. Later, this promise would worry the master of the *Corbridge*, David Barton, as will be seen.

The two ships set off, sailing southwards, with the big liner following her captor. But the surprises were not yet over for the prize crew. Idly poking around in the holds of the ship in which they had once been prisoners, but now controlled, they came across sixteen small boxes containing gold bars and bags of gold-dust. One and a half million marks worth of gold!

They were well to the south of Madeira the next evening when they met a 5,800-ton freighter with two red bands round her black funnel. *Möwe's* lamps blinked Morse into the gathering dusk, "What ship?" Instead of an answer, Dohna received the same question, "Who are you?"

"*Author*," he lied cleverly, "Liverpool to Durban." The other captain seemed satisfied and replied, "I am *Clan MacTavish*." That was enough for Dohna. He made, "German cruiser here. Stop your engines." The British captain flashed back, "I have stopped." But the German could see that this was a lie by the tongue of creamy lather that boiled under the stern of the British ship. He was going Full Ahead! He was going to try to escape! And at that instant the *Möwe's* wireless operator reported that the *Clan MacTavish*, call sign JBQH, was babbling out wireless messages as fast as she could go!

Dohna grabbed his megaphone and shouted down at his gunners to fire at and destroy the other's wireless office. The 6-inch guns of the raider opened up, but this did not stop the signals from streaming out. Not only that, but *Möwe* herself came under fire from a little 3-pounder gun mounted aft on the upper deck of the merchant ship. Dohna looked at the muzzle flashes from this puny weapon in disbelief. They were actually going to fight him! He ordered Rapid Fire. This fighting had to be stopped. He had no time to waste in fighting when at any time a British cruiser might appear on the scene. The range was only 300 yards and the heavy shells from the raider were soon punching holes along the freighter's waterline and causing serious damage to her bridge and boiler-room. One of them burst among a crowd of seamen trying to lower one of their lifeboats, killing sixteen of them and wounding several more. Her main boiler had been holed and great fountains of steam were hissing from deep inside her. Her captain, seeing his position was hopeless, finally stopped. Dohna lost no time in sending over a boarding party under Leutnant Pohlmann, who reported that she was carrying rubber, wool and leather. Regrettable as it was, she had to be sunk, cargo and all, after he had put her survivors on board the *Appam*. She went down nose first.

Dohna did not know it, but at that moment he was actually sandwiched between the cruisers *Essex* and *King Alfred* which lay to the north and south of him respectively. And the former had just received one of the *Clan MacTavish*'s distress signals. He was relatively safe, however, because not only were they each well over a hundred miles away, but for some reason which has become lost in the pages of history, *Essex*'s telegraphist did not report reception of the signal for some hours. As it was, Dohna made an unwittingly lucky decision as to the course which he and the faithful *Appam* would steer after bidding farewell to the doomed *Clan MacTavish*. It was due west. Out of danger.

They parted company during the night and *Möwe* swung south in mid-Atlantic, leaving Leutnant Berg to sail straight on in the *Appam*, heading for internment in the USA. He was in no hurry. The more he loitered, so much more time for *Möwe* to do her secret work. A fortnight passed before she arrived off Newport News, Virginia, on 1 February, 1916. It was only then that the British learned that *Möwe* even existed.

Insurance underwriters in London had had the jitters for over a week. On 25 January *The Times* reported, "A reinsurance rate of sixty per cent was quoted on the British steamer *Trader* of 3,608 tons, overdue from Balbao, and 30 per cent on the *Appam* of 7,781 tons, belonging to the British and African Steam Navigation Company, which is overdue from West Africa. On the British steamer *Ariadne*, 3,035 tons, from Rosario for France, 20 per cent was quoted."

The *Appam*'s arrival in the USA sparked off a diplomatic wrangle. *The Times* special correspondent wired from Norfolk, Virginia, dateline 3 February: "Three of *Appam*'s passengers – Sir Edward Merewether, former Governor of Sierra Leone, Mr Frederick Seton James, CMG, Administrator of Lagos (Nigeria), and Mr F.C. Fuller, CMG, Chief Commissioner of Ashanti – were invited by the American authorities to land last night, and in spite of a raging gale, they came ashore. They were accompanied by the captains of six of the vessels sunk by the German raider which captured the *Appam* – Mr Evan Jones

(*Trader*), Mr David Barton (*Corbridge*), Mr Robert Reid (*Ariadne*), Mr John Brackett (*Dromonby*), Mr Ralph Yeates (*Author*), and Mr John P. Jones (*Farringford*). Lieutenant Berg objected that the prisoners were on German territory, but the American official replied, 'Perhaps so, but in American waters, and having asylum in these waters, they are entitled to and will receive American protection.' He assured the remainder of the British subjects detained on board by Lieutenant Berg's objections, of similar protection."

Safely ashore, and surrounded by reporters, David Barton described how the main armament of the raider was "masked by a collapsible steel forecastle which falls away when the ship gets within range of her prey". He said that she seemed to have several names. One of them was, or had been, the *Ponga* (sic) and her sailors wore different names on their cap-ribbons. Some were SMS *Möwe*, while others were SMS *Paw*.

Evan Jones explained how he lost his ship. "I had no chance whatsoever, and even if I had wanted to scrap for it I could not have made good. You see she was right on top of us before I knew what kind of ship she was. Of course, I was not looking for German raiders, for I knew they had all been swept from the seas months before. She was just an ordinary looking old tramp. She came limping along, and the first thing I knew was that she was alongside and I was looking down into the muzzles of half a dozen mighty nasty-looking guns. They ordered us to abandon ship and twenty minutes later we saw the last of the *Trader* as she plunged down."

Sir Edward Merewether gave a long and detailed account of the capture of the *Appam* herself: "The way in which she managed to catch us was artful in the extreme. When we picked her up on the horizon she hove-to, flying the Red Ensign on the fore-peak – a distress signal, which meant she was out of control. Captain Harrison believed she was a British tramp, and changed course to bear down on her. . . . Almost simultaneously with the magical transformation of the supposed tramp into an armed cruiser, one of the forward guns spoke sharply and a shell shrieked over our bridge. . . . We were whipped and we knew it. . . . The Germans began to parley with us through a megaphone. Captain Harrison frankly admitted that he had a number of German prisoners aboard. . . . When the prize crew came aboard, the first thing they did was to free the German prisoners, and gave them revolvers and rifles and put them as guards over us. . . . I had no idea that Germans could be so courteous as these Germans proved to be. . . . This spirit of decency, in my opinion, was largely owing to the fine example set by Lieutenant Berg himself. . . .

"During that time, we had an opportunity of seeing Germans in action. . . . She was about three miles away when we picked up the *Clan MacTavish* on the horizon. . . . The cruiser made straight for the British ship. To all appearances, the cruiser was quite the inoffensive lumbering freighter that we had mistaken her to be. But some sharp-eyed sailorman aboard the *Clan MacTavish* must have read her real identity aright, for suddenly a gun belched forth and the shell went screaming across the water and buried itself a scant fifty feet abaft of the cruiser. Then the railings and the deck-houses fell away and the German let go a broadside. It was a fine fight, for half an hour or so. . . . Finally the *Clan MacTavish* heeled over as if some giant had struck her a sudden blow, and in a very short time she had disappeared. . . . It was during the night that the cruiser left us. Where we were at the time, where the cruiser headed for, cannot even be guessed by any of us. All we know is that next day, we found ourselves all alone, without a ship in sight."

The answer to the question was that Dohna was off to find the *Corbridge*. He needed coal. There she was, at the exact spot he had ordered, well to the west of the Cape Verde Islands. The two ships lay together on the calm ocean, barely nodding on the swell. In sweltering heat the Lascars hauled the bags of coal over the gang-planks, creating clouds of choking gritty dust which settled over everything and everybody. Dohna did not want to linger in these parts, and after he had taken enough coal for another few days steaming, the collier and the bandit parted.

One of the secrets of success of a sea highwayman is to be a phantom of the oceans. Dohna had waylaid a cluster of ships off north-west Africa, and now he intended to pop up again on the other side of the Atlantic, off the northern coast of Brazil. But one more victim was to meet her doom before he reached his next hunting ground. She was the little barque *Edinburgh*, of 1473 tons, who had sailed before the wind all the way from Rangoon, homeward bound for Liverpool via Cape Horn with a cargo of flaked rice. She was sitting becalmed about 700 miles south-west of Cape Verde, when *Möwe* came over the horizon. Dohna dispatched her to the bottom with some explosives. It was 22 January, 1916.

Badewitz had been ordered by Dohna to take the *Corbridge* to Maraca, a remote swampy island of inhospitable jungle just to the north of the Amazon delta, and await him there. It was an ideal place for a pirate's rendezvous. With its dangerous sandbanks and treacherous swirling currents, ships did not venture there often. Indeed, the only chart available to the Germans had been made by an English survey vessel half a century before. The coaling of the *Möwe* could be finished there in relative safety.

The black-hulled bandit nudged her way through the narrow channels, churning up the silt with her propeller, to join the collier a couple of days later and complete her coaling. After three days of continual toil, they had taken on over 1,000 tons and *Möwe*'s bunkers were brimful. The empty *Corbridge* was of no further use to Dohna. He took her out to sea and sank her.

Dohna headed south-east, to cruise along the approaches to Pernambuco. This was a track where one would expect to meet plenty of traffic. But not a single ship was seen for five days. And then, off Fernando do Noronha, the lookouts saw smoke and the raider gave chase. It was the Belgian collier *Luxembourg*, bound for Buenos Aires. She had nothing in her cargo of any use to the German; it was composed purely of 6,000 tons of coal which soon found its way to the Atlantic seabed. Her crew were nearly all neutral Greeks and Spaniards, who insisted on bringing their pets on board the raider, and *Möwe* became a floating zoo, with chattering monkeys and squawking parrots and dogs of all descriptions wandering the decks.

The next day, 5 February, brought some sobering, if not unexpected, news. Intercepting a wireless message, *Möwe*'s operator learned that the Pacific Steam Navigation Co's *Flamenco*, a steamer of 4,629 tons, could be expected in these very waters the following morning. It was a simple matter to lay in wait for her. Dawn had not long broken when they sighted her yellow funnel. Dohna signalled her to stop, but the British captain ignored him and started to send out distress signals – call sign HJKC. The steel gun screens on the fo'c'sle of the raider came down with a clatter and a broadside of 150 mm shells wrecked the *Flamenco*'s wireless office and started several fires. The merchant ship carried a crew of fifty-two and they immediately hastened to take to their boats. In the general chaos, one boat overturned in its davits, spilling twenty men into the shark-infested sea. It was exactly the scene which the British Q-ship panic crews rehearsed and acted so well. But here it was the real thing. The Germans picked up nineteen of them, but of the twentieth there was no sign. Almost certainly he had been taken by the sharks. The *Flamenco* herself went down with her bottom blown out.

As was his practice after every capture, Dohna pumped the newcomers for helpful information. The *Flamenco*'s crew included several neutrals. Edwin Hoyt says that they told Dohna that only a day or so before, the *Flamenco* had been stopped by the British cruiser HMS *Glasgow* and warned that there was a German raider at large. The neutrals did not want to be aboard any ship when it was being blasted by six-inch shells from a twenty-five knot cruiser. They were more than happy to tell Dohna what they knew. Once more he could not afford to loiter for a moment. The *Möwe* was headline news. The cat was well and truly out of the bag.

(HMS *Glasgow*, on patrol from the Cape Verde Islands to Pernambuco, had actually sighted what her log says was 'a Belgian vessel' at 9.00 a.m. on Wednesday, 2 February. This was almost certainly the *Luxembourg*. The log makes no mention of any sight of the *Flamenco*. It seems that Hoyt's information was confused.)

A change of *Möwe*'s appearance was the first priority. Out came the paint-pots and the raider acquired a different coloured funnel. The shipwrights and carpenters got to work and some of her upper-works took on a changed profile. Where to go next? It would be logical for the British to think that she was heading for southern waters, towards either the Indian or Pacific Oceans. Indeed, German agents in San Francisco had already "leaked" an opinion that she was expected in the Pacific. If ever Captain Graf Nikolaus zu Dohna-Schlodien needed to be a Phantom of the Ocean, it was now. He sailed north. And he was in a hurry.

The stokers heaved on the coal. The important thing now was to vacate the South Atlantic. A day or so later they passed a neutral steamer, the Norwegian *Estrella*, whose wireless started to pip with a description of the 'black-hulled freighter' she had just met. In the middle of the ocean Dohna could do little about the colour of his hull. The best he could do was to paint his funnel again. Was the net closing in?

It may have been wiser, in the circumstances, for Dohna to have let pass the next British steamer he met and to have played it quietly for a while. But a raider is a raider and the collier *Westburn* was still many days from her destination of Buenos Aires. She would not be reported overdue for a long time to come. The usual shot across the bows brought her to a stop and, while Dohna was in the process of deciding what to do with her, more smoke was sighted on the horizon. It was the British freighter *Horace*, 3,335 tons, with general cargo.

With the crews of the *Edinburgh, Luxembourg, Flamenco*, and now the *Westburn* and the *Horace* on board the raider, the old problem of over-crowding recurred. Dohna came to a decision. He quickly sank the *Horace* and transferred all 180 prisoners to the *Westburn*, which was to be taken to Santa Cruz, Tenerife, (a neutral port) under a prize crew commanded by the trusty Leutnant Badewitz, just as his colleague Berg had done with the now famous *Appam* in the USA. It was 8 February, 1916.

For two whole weeks, as she steamed north, *Möwe* saw not a single ship, although, unknowingly, she came within a hair's breadth of meeting the cruiser HMS *Highflyer* which was on patrol to St Paul's Rocks, and which had sunk the raider *Kaiser Wilhelm der Grosse* off Rio de Oro on 26 August, 1914.

The *Westburn* arrived at Santa Cruz on 22 February. The prisoners were allowed ashore, but the Spanish authorities refused to allow Badewitz to remain in port for more than twenty-four hours without being interned. When the *Westburn* put to sea again the British armoured cruiser HMS *Sutlej*, which had been in Santa Cruz harbour, was waiting for her outside the three-mile limit. Most historians agree that Badewitz scuttled the collier under the guns of the *Sutlej*, although Hoyt, in his book *The Elusive Seagull*, says that the cruiser sank her, and that "it was as simple as that". In *Sutlej*'s log Captain Basil Fanshawe entered: "Tuesday 22nd February 1916, off Santa Cruz. 5.15 p.m. Observed cargo s.s. hoist German Naval Ensign. About two miles from shore. Action stations. Weighed anchor. 6.15 p.m. Same vessel, s.s. *Westburn* (Sunderland) anchored half mile off-shore. 6.30 p.m. proceeded to return to harbour and took on cutter. 7.45 p.m. proceeded from harbour, outside territorial waters. Wednesday 23rd February. 9.30 a.m. Proceeded into Santa Cruz to communicate. 11.50 a.m. stood out to sea, outside territorial waters. 3.10 p.m. s.s. *Westburn* weighed and proceeded eastern direction, close to shore. 3.40 p.m. s.s. *Westburn* anchored. Stood out to intercept steamer. 3.50 p.m. Action Stations. 4.05 p.m. Spoke s.s. *Tarahina*. 4.10 p.m. Secured. 4.43 p.m. Observed s.s. *Westburn* to sink at her anchorage." It would seem that Hoyt was wrongly informed again.

As for Badewitz, this intrepid officer eventually escaped imprisonment in the Canaries dressed as a priest and reached the Spanish mainland port of Cadiz, where the German *U-35* was in harbour to carry out emergency repairs. He persuaded the captain to land him at Pola, the Austro-Hungarian naval base in the Adriatic, from whence he made his way back to Germany.

It was not until 23 February, when *Möwe* had passed to the north of Cape Finisterre, that Dohna made another catch. There, in the eye of his telescope, was the red and black funnel of the 3,100-ton French freighter *Maroni*, bound for New York out of Bordeaux. He was reluctant to sink her; she was carrying 50,000 bottles of Pommery champagne, but these were dangerous waters in which to tarry, and down to the bottom she went. The German boarding party returned from the *Maroni* with a bundle of recent newspapers which were soon being avidly digested by Dohna and his officers. They had acquired quite a name for themselves, it appeared. According to the French Press *Möwe*'s crew lived on a diet of little babies, and the raider could make twenty-five knots, and was faster than a British battleship. The English papers were demanding that these pirates should be hung from the nearest tree.

On her outward voyage the long dark nights and winter weather had helped Dohna to smuggle his ship past the British blockade. But now, in late February, each day meant more minutes of daylight, and no time was to be lost if he was to make a home run. He kept well to the west as he bisected the trans-Atlantic shipping tracks, hoping to outflank the British patrols.

25 February was an eventful day. Firstly, at 6.00 a.m., 600 miles west of the Fastnet Rock, *Möwe* claimed the final victim of her cruise, bringing the total to fifteen. She was the Prince Line's 3,471-ton *Saxon Prince*, coming home from the USA with a cargo largely composed of gun-cotton. Captain William Jameson and his crew joined the other captives on board the raider and the *Saxon Prince* was soon no more.

Secondly, a wireless message was received to inform Dohna that the Kaiser had awarded him the Iron Cross, First Class, and fifty Iron Crosses, Second Class, for him to distribute among his crew as he saw fit.

So far it had been a tremendously successful venture, but there were anxious moments ahead. There was that irksome blockade to evade again. It would have been safer to go to the north of Iceland, but by now *Möwe*'s engines were not in good shape. She badly needed a refit. The northern route would give her an extra 750 miles to travel back to

Wilhemshaven and there was not much left of the *Corbridge*'s coal in her bunkers. It would mean, too, several more days at sea, days which would enjoy less of the comforting cover of winter darkness. The choice had to be the shorter, but much more dangerous route, to the south of Iceland.

Thanks to the high-quality of the stolen Welsh coal, and the careful expertise of the Chief Engineer, the amount of smoke emitted from the tall funnel of the raider was kept to a mere wisp. A posse of Royal Navy ships could be lurking over every horizon. Dohna did not wish to invite them to investigate any tell-tale smudges. As they passed north of the Faroes and approached the coast of Norway, their nerves were as tight as violin strings. Every shadow in the dusk, every patch of mist, every distant squall hid a grey cruiser in the imaginations of the lookouts. It came as a welcome relief when, on 28 February, the weather worsened and the banks of icy fog and swirling blizzards made them invisible to any enemy eyes. And when the snow stopped the sky remained heavily clouded so that there was no moon as *Möwe* slid stealthily south-east-wards.

There was one last hurdle to cross. The western approaches to the Skaggerak were being closely patrolled by the British. To make it into the Heligoland Bight, and home to Wilhelmshaven, Dohna had to get past these vigilant eyes. And at 1550 hours on 3 March, it seemed as if he was not going to make it. Mountainous clouds of smoke ahead were reported by the lookouts. It was nothing less than a squadron of six cruisers of the Royal Navy, with a swarm of escort destroyers fussing around them! But it seemed that a shabby salt-caked tramp was beneath their dignity to investigate, because the majestic grey armada simply steamed past her as if she did not exist. They vanished into the distance, and the hearts of the crew of the *Möwe* were still pounding when another similar squadron appeared! But they, too, were uninterested in the insignificant rust-streaked tub flying a Norwegian flag at her stern.

Darkness fell. Dohna was almost home. He called Wilhelmshaven to say that he would be off Horn's Riff at 0600 in the morning. An enormous greeting awaited the return home of the black Seagull. Ships of the High Seas Fleet came out to escort her into harbour and she steamed down the sand-duned coast of the North Frisian Islands flanked by the battle-cruisers *Derfflinger* and *Moltke*. It seemed as if the whole German Navy was there in harbour, bedecked with flags and blowing their hooters as the thousands of sailors roared a welcome and waved their caps in the air. It was 4 March, 1916.

And for Korvettenkapitän Graf Burggraf Nikolaus zu Dohna-Schlodien there was a summons to present himself before the Kaiser at Imperial Headquarters in France. He was given a two-hour audience, at which he related the adventures and successes of SMS *Möwe* to a delighted Emperor. When he emerged, he had been presented with Germany's highest decoration, Pour le Mérite, otherwise known as the Blue Max. Then he took a little time to visit his soldier-brother, who was with a company of infantry at nearby Verdun, after which he went off to do a bit of deer-stalking and to see his mother in Silesia.

Chapter 14

The Flight of the Condor

The *Guben* had only been launched at Rostock the week before war broke out. She was a two-funnelled tramp, 4,962 tons, owned by Deutsch-Australische Dampfschiffs-Gesellschaft, and was intended for work on the Hamburg-Australia run. The German Admiralty requisitioned her during 1915 and fitted her out for war. The first thing they did was to remove her over-conspicuous second funnel. Then they gave her four 15 cm guns, two on each side, concealed by hinged gunwales, and a single 10.5 cm gun, mounted aft, hidden in a false deck-house. In addition, two 50 cm torpedo tubes were installed, also behind hinged flaps, one each side of the forecastle. They re-named her S.M.S. *Greif* – the Condor. Come early 1916, and no doubt encouraged by the successes of the *Möwe*, which was still at large in the Atlantic, the German Admiralty decided that she was ready for service, and she was commissioned at Kiel on 23 January.

In mid-February her commander, forty-one-year-old Fregattenkapitän Rudolf Tietze, was proud to have his new ship inspected by the Kaiser's brother, Rear-Admiral Prince Henry of Prussia, no less, together with the Commander-in-Chief, Baltic, Admiral Bachmann, before he took her through the *kanal* to Hamburg. With two large Norwegian flags painted on her sides, flanking the word NORGE, and the legend *Rena – Tonsberg* around her stern, the Condor sailed on 27 February, into a comforting curtain of grey North Sea mist and flurries of snow. In fact it was the same damp curtain through which, at that very moment, the *Möwe* was making a stealthy homeward run in the opposite direction.

For once the Germans had been careless. At the gala inspection ceremony in Kiel, the usual official speeches had been made in the presence of His Royal Highness. One of them, however, had been unbelievably indiscreet. It was almost as if the speaker had forgotten that his country was at war. The plan for the *Greif*, he announced, was to sail down the Atlantic and round the Cape of Good Hope to assist von Lettow-Vorbeck in his East African campaign. This may have been an intentional 'red herring', but nevertheless it alerted British espionage to the imminent emergence of a raider. And on this occasion British espionage worked well.

At 11.38 a.m. on 28 February the Admiralty telegraphed Admiral Jellicoe, who ordered out the light cruisers *Inconstant* and *Cordelia* from Rosyth, and *Calliope, Comus* and *Blanche* from Scapa Flow, together with destroyer escorts, to form a double patrol line across the northern part of the North Sea.

Rear-Admiral Dudley de Chair's Tenth Cruiser Squadron formed the outer screen of the British North Sea blockade, patrolling north of Iceland in the Denmark Strait, south of Iceland, and between Scotland and Norway. It consisted of armed merchant liners, and by the spring of 1915 these numbered twenty-nine. They were all at least 7,000-tonners, requisitioned from the major shipping lines, fitted with several six-inch guns, as well as smaller calibre armament, and manned mainly by reservists with a smattering of regular Navy specialists. Their thin hulls gave them no protection against shellfire, it was true, but they were fast enough, at about seventeen knots, to overhaul most tramp-steamers. And they consumed vast quantities of coal.

One of them, the 15,800 ton *Alcantara*, belonging to the Royal Mail Steam Packet Line, was flying the White Ensign under Captain Tom Wardle, R.N. She was about to leave her patrol on the Faeroes – Norway beat to steam south to take on yet another feast of coal on 29 February. But at five past eight in the morning her wireless bleeped out a command:

"Alcantara not to leave patrol pending further orders. Armed disguised enemy merchant auxiliary may pass patrol line today."

It was only forty minutes later that her lookouts saw smoke on the port beam, and about ten minutes after that the *Alcantara*'s sister ship, the *Andes*, which was out of sight over the northern horizon, signalled, *"Enemy in sight. Steering NE. 15 knots"*. A little later she added, *"Vessel steering north. . . . Painted black, black funnel, two masts. . . . 15 knots"*.

Wardle rang down for Full Speed and steered a course to place his ship between the stranger and the *Andes*, which made another signal, "*This is the suspicious ship*".

Approaching her from astern, Wardle noted that she wore Norwegian colours and was the *Rena* of Tonsberg. A quick reference to Lloyds' Register revealed that such a ship did indeed exist, but all the same Wardle hoisted the International Code flag signal, M.N: "Stop instantly." For good measure, he fired two blank rounds to warn her. She hove-to obediently and claimed to be bound for Rio de Janeiro from Trondheim for a cargo of coffee.

Wardle ordered a boarding-party to prepare to inspect the Norwegian. In his report later he described what happened next; "At 9.40 the boat was being swung out and I was closing stranger on her port quarter when I noticed her ensign staff drop over the stern, and men clearing away a gun on the poop. At the same moment stranger fired a shell at our bridge, which put the telemotor steering gear, engine-room telegraph, and all telephones on the bridge out of action, besides killing and wounding men."

With her steering gear pipes severed, but still underway and at speed, the liner wallowed out of control, although still closing the other ship. Wardle despatched a messenger from the bridge to order the after steering gear to be re-connected, but by now there was a deluge of machine-gun fire sweeping the decks of the *Alcantara* and the man was cut down as he ran. It took a vital ten minutes to bring the big ship under control. *Greif* turned and tried to make a run for the safety of neutral Norwegian waters, but the British ship was fast, even though she was damaged, and started to overhaul her.

The British 6-inch guns now opened up and, with their first round, knocked out the stern gun of the raider, killing most of the gun's crew and setting fire to its 'ready-use' ammunition. In reply, German shells were holing the unarmoured skin of the liner repeatedly, close to the waterline and in her coal bunkers. Then Tietze tried a torpedo shot. This struck the *Alcantara* amidships, but it entered deep into her fuel bunkers and the force of the explosion was well muffled by the coal. By now the range was down to well under 800 yards. A British shell burst on the port-side 6-inch gun of the German, another burst in her engine-room and her oil-fuel tanks were seen to be aflame.

Both ships, neither of which was ever designed to withstand a blow from a naval shell, were inflicting terrible damage on each other. The

Alcantara was listing heavily to port and the "*Rena*" was seriously on fire. The *Andes* was now five miles away. Her captain, Commander C.B. Young, RN, who had taken command only a few weeks previously, seeing that the *Alcantara* was nearest to the stranger, had turned away to continue his patrol, leaving the other liner to apprehend and inspect her. But as soon as he heard gunfire he turned back and the *Andes* sped to the aid of her sister.

Opening up at a range of 6,500 yards, the *Andes*' shells devastated the bridge and upper-works of the raider. *Greif* was now under heavy fire from both British liners. The *Andes* alone fired ninety-eight six-inch shells at her in the course of the action. At 10.18 Tietze, seeing his position was beyond hope, ordered 'cease firing' and 'abandon ship'. The German sailors were seen pouring over the sides of their flaming ship and at 10.22 boats began pulling away from her sides. The unfortunate Tietze, the last to leave, had his head taken off by one of the *Alcantara*'s shells as he was sliding down a rope.

But the *Alcantara*, too, was doomed. At 10.45 Wardle ordered 'abandon ship' and a quarter of an hour later she rolled over on her beam ends. Seventy-two sailors had lost their lives in her, with many more wounded. Among the latter was one who, by the end of the war, could be said to have had a charmed life. He was John Priest, a twenty-nine-year-old fireman who was a survivor of the sinking of the *Titanic*. Since then he had been in her sister ship, the *Olympic*, when she collided with the cruiser HMS *Hawke*. Now it was his bad luck to be aboard the *Alcantara* when she went into action, and he was wounded. Later he was to be in the ambulance transport *Brittanic* when she was sunk, and finally received head injuries when serving in the hospital ship *Donegal* when she was torpedoed in the Channel with 639 wounded British soldiers on board.

Meantime the light cruiser HMS *Comus*, Captain Alan Hotham in command, together with her destroyer escort HMS *Munster*, part of Jellicoe's emergency patrol, had turned north at speed to assist. Hotham's log reads, "Tuesday 29th February 1916. At Sea. 6.35 a.m. increased speed to 20 knots. Zig-zag 20 degrees. 10.33 Sighted smoke. 10.37 Action Stations. 10.50 Sighted three vessels in action ahead. 10.57 Observed *Alcantara* listing heavily and enemy burning fiercely. 11.06 *Alcantara* overturned and sank. Closed her boats. 11.25 Closed *Alcantara*'s wreckage. *Munster* standing by survivors. 11.39 Opened fire on *Greif* in German colours. 7,400 yards. Carried out four

Battle Practice runs, *Greif* having abandoned ship. 12.12. Ceased firing. 12.15 Stopped. Picked up 40 survivors and Captain Wardle R.N. from *Alcantara*. 12.52 Proceeded past *Grief*'s wreckage. 1.08. Stopped. Picked up five officers, 112 ratings, ex-*S.M.S. Greif*."

Comus turned away. Her log goes on: "6.20 p.m. Ceased zig-zagging. Reduced to 15 knots. Departed this life two German seamen from exposure. 9.17. Sighted Outer Skerries, Shetland. Committed to the deep the bodies of two Germans. Increased to 20 knots. 11.00. Increased to 23 knots." And on the following day "Wednesday 1st March 1916. 10.45 a.m. Anchored in Leith Roads. Discharged 115 prisoners into HMS *St. Elves*."

The grave of SMS *Greif* is at 61.45N, 1.10E, not far from that of her opponent. Under a dank shroud of mist, she had ghosted herself through the lines of the Royal Navy's patrols all the way up the North Sea. She had been on the verge of a successful break-out. Her crew were probably already silently congratulating themselves. But the vigilance of the very last sentry the 'long-stop' *Andes*, had foiled them. With the sole consolation that she had sunk the *Alcantara*, the flight of the Condor had lasted a mere fifty-six hours.

Chapter 15

The Seagull Flies Again

Dohna-Schlodien had taken himself just about as far away from the sea as it was possible for him to go for his deer-stalking holiday in Silesia and Hungary. Meanwhile in the dockyard the tired *Möwe* was also enjoying a well-earned rest and having a face-lift. Engineers and workmen toiled all over her. Tall dockside cranes swung to and fro over her decks dangling new machinery and equipment. Wagons and carts rumbled up to her gangways laden with supplies of every description and then clattered away empty. By the time her captain returned, duly refreshed from his sojourn in the countryside, the Seagull's refit was complete and her old appearance, which had become too well-known by far, had vanished. Now, instead of a tall skinny funnel, she had a shorter stumpier one. Her masts were no longer raked, but stood bolt upright. The positioning of her derrick posts and ventilators had been re-arranged and her lines had been altered to give her an almost flush-decked profile.

Dohna-Schlodien was, of course, a national hero already. The German propaganda machine had made sure of that. The spring of 1916 had been a bit of a flat spot in the war for Germany, and the return of *Möwe* had given the nation a much-needed boost in morale. Newspapers and magazines had been full of articles about her exploits and Dohna's face had become almost as well-known as the Kaiser's. He shunned all this publicity as far as possible, but took advantage of the increased influence with the *Admiralstab* that his reputation brought with it. The next time *Möwe* went ocean cruising, he persuaded his Admirals, she would not be hampered by any tedious *minenleger* duties. Next time she would carry no mines. She would sail as an out-and-out raider.

By now it was midsummer, 1916, no time, with its clear moonlit nights and good weather, for an out-and-out raider to attempt to run the blockade. To keep his crew at peak efficiency while awaiting orders to sail again for the Atlantic, Dohna took to making short exercise cruises out of Wilhelmshaven or Kiel. It was on one of these, towards the end of July, that the *Vineta*, under which name the Seagull sailed, caught the British steamer *Eskimo*, 3,225 tons, with cargo and passengers, just outside Norwegian territorial waters. Dohna fired shots across her bows and she stopped. The indignant British captain protested that he was within Norwegian waters, but nevertheless his ship was quickly boarded and taken to Swinemunde as a prize. She had given Dohna's boarding-party and prize crew some valuable practice. It had been over five months since they had sunk the *Saxon Prince*.

Winter was the classic season for raiders to sail from German ports, with its dark, windy, rainswept nights, or, better still, some fog and a decent blizzard. By late November Dohna was champing at the bit, anxious to be off. Guided by information gleaned by his observant colleagues in the U-boat service, which gave him a rough picture of the British patrol movements in the North Sea, he decided to go on the 22nd if the weather was favourable.

Indeed the morning of the 22nd indicated that some particularly foul conditions were in the offing. At 0900 he gave orders for full steam to be raised and by early afternoon the crew were all aboard and the ship was ready to leave harbour. As far as they were concerned it was going to be just another practice jaunt up the Kieler Bucht and out into the Baltic and back in a couple of days. As for the name *Vineta*, the Admirals could call their ship by whatever name they chose. For her crew she would only ever have one name – SMS *Möwe*.

It was four o'clock in the damp afternoon dusk when the tugs eased her away from her comfortable berth in Kiel. The black Seagull was ocean-bound again. Soon she slipped out of German water, past the silent Danish islands and was close to the coast of Norway. And all the time, to Dohna's delight, the weather worsened. They ran north, through seas piled high by the storm which now raged, but which mercifully screened them from the enemy. Tossed and bucked as if their 4,788-ton steel ship were a weightless rider in some hellish maritime rodeo, it was impossible for normal life to proceed. Stores were hurled around in the holds, breaking open boxes and cases and spilling their contents. Cursing cooks could not cook as their pots tumbled from the red-hot stoves in the heaving galley. Crockery smashed as it fell from lockers and hooks on the mess-decks. Vomiting men stumbled from hand-hold to hand-hold as they tried to make their way from one place to another. It was the kind of weather which prompts God-fearing folk in sea-ports the world over to pray for their sailors. For four days this ordeal continued, but it was an ordeal which they knew was worth running. Better this than a six-inch shell from a British cruiser.

Then came the last and most dangerous hurdle, the one at which *Greif* had fallen as she had been about to turn west for the Atlantic, the outer screen of the blockade, between Iceland and Scotland. Dohna was in luck. His wireless operators, alert as they were at all times, were never more so than when they were blockade-running. Here, as the wind howled, sending cascades of spindrift flying around the aerials and swaying masts of the lurching *Möwe*, their ears were glued to their apparatus, eavesdropping across the wavelengths, eager to snatch even the smallest scrap of useful information. What was that? It was two British warships talking to each other! It was in code, of course, but they were able to untangle enough of it to learn the ships' positions, and the fact that they planned to rendezvous at 0800 the next morning at a point 100 miles due west of the Faroes. In *Möwe*'s chart-room the navigator's dividers danced a stiff-legged polka across the chart to plot a course which would neatly bisect the two enemy ships, which were still 160 miles apart. Dohna pointed her bows between them and listened with satisfaction as the engines picked up their revolutions to Full Speed in response to the swinging shovels of the sweating firemen. At a furious twelve knots which set her steel frame throbbing and jingling she bull-dozed through the gap, ploughing aside the racing white-capped hillocks to surge into the open Atlantic. They were free again.

Dohna steered south-west in weather that was still foul, to hunt along the busy trans-Atlantic tracks. The winter afternoon light had almost gone on 1 December when the shape of a large steamer was seen through the murk. She was too far off and it was too late in the day for him to catch and board her. Indeed, he did not even know at that stage whether she was an enemy or a neutral. He sent his gun-crews to Action Stations, where they remained all through the night, soaked and chilled, comforted only by a pre-dawn breakfast of bread and coffee, while the

The Second Cruise of the *Möwe*

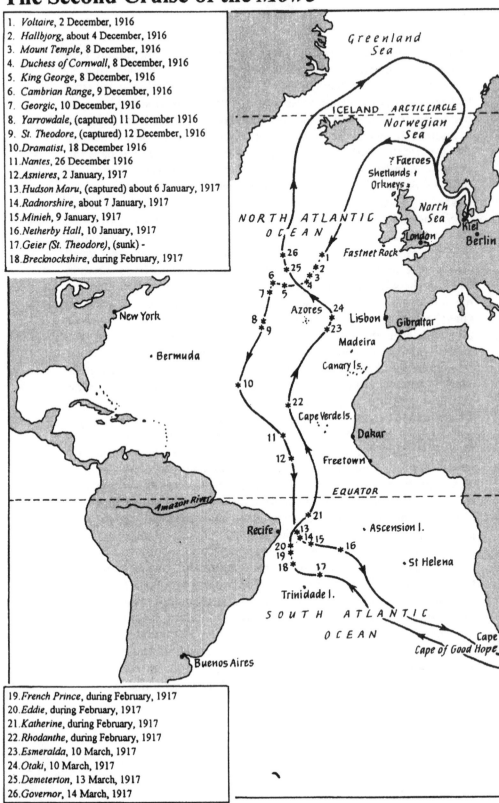

1. *Voltaire*, 2 December, 1916
2. *Hallbjorg*, about 4 December, 1916
3. *Mount Temple*, 8 December, 1916
4. *Duchess of Cornwall*, 8 December, 1916
5. *King George*, 8 December, 1916
6. *Cambrian Range*, 9 December, 1916
7. *Georgic*, 10 December, 1916
8. *Yarrowdale*, (captured) 11 December 1916
9. *St. Theodore*, (captured) 12 December, 1916
10. *Dramatist*, 18 December 1916
11. *Nantes*, 26 December 1916
12. *Asnieres*, 2 January, 1917
13. *Hudson Maru*, (captured) about 6 January, 1917
14. *Radnorshire*, about 7 January, 1917
15. *Minieh*, 9 January, 1917
16. *Netherby Hall*, 10 January, 1917
17. *Geier (St. Theodore)*, (sunk) -
18. *Brecknockshire*, during February, 1917

19. *French Prince*, during February, 1917
20. *Eddie*, during February, 1917
21. *Katherine*, during February, 1917
22. *Rhodanthe*, during February, 1917
23. *Esmeralda*, 10 March, 1917
24. *Otaki*, 10 March, 1917
25. *Demeterton*, 13 March, 1917
26. *Governor*, 14 March, 1917

Möwe followed the steamer, slowly closing the distance between them.

She was the Lamport & Holt *Voltaire*, 8,618 tons, in ballast from Liverpool to New York. Her master, Mr R. A. Knight, had listened well to the advice of the Naval Intelligence Officer in Liverpool and was following the recommended track across the ocean. He may have reflected on this when at 7.30 a.m. on 2 December his ship was overtaken by *Möwe* about 650 miles west of the Fastnet and ordered to stop. Knight did not stop immediately, but turned to show his stern to the intruder and began sending out wireless distress calls. This brought an instant reply in the form of a salvo of shells, one of which crashed into the *Voltaire*'s wireless office. At this Knight did stop and ordered his crew of ninety-four to abandon ship. They sat in their boats, watching the German boarding-party go to work and, minutes later, heard three loud explosions from the bowels of their ship. She settled quickly, but for once Dohna had not been quite as lucky as usual. There had been a witness to the event. A neutral Dutch merchantman, passing by on his lawful occasion, had seen all, just before the black, white and blue funnel of the *Voltaire* disappeared for ever.

The Dutchman radioed, "Did you pick up the crew of that sinking ship?" Dohna had indeed done so, but he made no reply. Perhaps he was preoccupied with the thought that the presence of another German raider would be broadcast to all stations before the day was out. It would have been prudent to vanish and reappear far away, but for the next week it seemed as if enemy merchantmen were hovering around *Möwe* like moths around a candle, more or less right on that very spot. It was a sumptuous feast that no raider could refuse.

The *Samland* was the first to show. She was a big refrigerated freighter, carrying 9,000 tons of meat from the USA to Belgium for the Red Cross. She also carried the words 'Belgian War Relief' on large boards hanging from her sides and a certificate signed by the German Ambassador granting her safe passage. Dohna fumed. All he could do was to destroy her wireless and let her go. But she knew his secret and she would make port in five days.

Then came the Norwegian *Hallbjorg*, 2,586 tons, from New York for Bordeaux with rubber, machine parts and motor vehicles. She was neutral, but her cargo was contraband of war. Down she went.

Next came the buff-funnelled 9,792-ton *Mount Temple*, owned by the Canadian Pacific Railway. *Möwe*'s gun crews went to Action Stations behind their screens, and the usual charade was played with a few men in civilian clothes making themselves seen on deck. The *Mount Temple* was not alarmed to be meeting such a tramp on this busy ocean track. The two ships were now beam to beam, passing each other at a combined speed of over twenty knots, some 300 yards apart. Dohna had ordered two boarding-parties to stand by for this one. She was a really big catch. Down clanged the raider's gun screens to reveal her portside muzzles trained on the freighter. Up shot the *kriegsflagge* over *Möwe*'s stern. But the British crew did not intend to submit easily. They ran to their little stern gun and opened fire. But it was a hopeless cause. They managed to fire only once or twice before *Möwe*'s six-inch broadsides destroyed their gun, killing three of its crew and wounding several others. The boarding-parties came alongside and Leutnant Pohlmann scrambled up the ropeladder which was begrudgingly thrown over the side of the big ship only after he had demanded such a courtesy at the point of his revolver. He walked up to her master, Captain Sergeant, bade him good morning and fired a stream of questions. Sergeant replied that he was bound for Brest, from Quebec, with an 8,000-ton cargo of assorted foodstuffs and a consignment of 700 horses for the French Government. Pohlmann's signaller semaphored this information across the water to the watching Dohna. "*Versenken*," came the command. "Sink her".

Within minutes the evacuation of the 111 merchant crew and their bags and trappings was underway and the boarding parties had placed their time charges and explosives. "Hurry!" came the order from Dohna. His lookouts had spotted more smoke in the distance.

The last boatload of men were still crossing between the two ships when the bottom blew out of the *Mount Temple* with a deafening explosion. But the task had taken too long and the smoke from the distant ship had disappeared. Whoever she was, she had gone. Dohna was furious, not only because he had lost his prey. Men had been killed on the *Mount Temple* and one of the wounded died in the night, despite the efforts of Dr Winkel, the raider's surgeon, to save him. Unnecessary slaughter was not Dohna's style. His business was the destruction of ships and their cargo, not human beings. He summoned Captain Sergeant before him and harangued him for stupidly and recklessly risking men's lives by resisting his heavily armed ship with a gun that was little more than a toy. But for that, he stormed, he himself would not have needed to fire his own guns and nobody would have been hurt. Sergeant stood his ground, however, and replied that he was entitled to defend his ship. After that exchange, it seems, both men had a great deal of respect for each other.

[It was not the first time that the *Mount Temple* had been involved in major drama in this corner of the North Atlantic. Four and a half years before, on a chilly starlit night, she had ploughed her way towards a sinking ship in answer to her distress call. But she had been given an inaccurate position – twenty miles out – and of course she had found no sign of her. That ship, in the form of two gigantic pieces of twisted scrap metal, now lay 13,000 feet down on the sea-bed to the south-east of Cape Race. She was the *Titanic*.]

Möwe had hardly turned a screw when the 152-ton bark *Duchess of Cornwall* hove in sight, with a cargo of salt meat from Canada to Gibraltar. She was never to reach her destination, or ever see St John's again.

The rest of the day, 8 December, was quiet until four o'clock in the afternoon when the *King George*, a 3,852-ton Clyde-based steamer came into view. Her master, John Burnett, was not likely to risk a shell busting through her side, because among the cargo she was carrying from Philadelphia to Manchester was 600 tons of gunpowder! Dohna blew her up anyway.

Just before midnight another steamer was sighted. *Möwe* tagged along behind her all night and sank her in the morning. She was the Furness Withy freighter *Cambrian Range*, 4,234 tons, master W.E.J. Moore, nine days out of Baltimore, with wheat for Liverpool. It was 9 December, 1916, 620 miles due east of Cape Race, Newfoundland. One week had passed since the Seagull had made the first kill of her second ocean foray. In that week she had sunk six ships, totalling 29,234 tons.

Dohna had every reason to feel satisfied with his progress so far, but the following evening brought some sobering news. Evidently, the *Samland* had reached port, because the German wireless operator intercepted a message sent out from Bermuda, *en clair*, to all British ships: "*Government war warning begins . . . Enemy raider sighted 7 a.m. 4th December . . . Probably high speed . . . Take all precautions.*"

No doubt Dohna spent much of the night reflecting on his position, and planning his next move. But whatever his thoughts had been, they were hastily cast aside at 7 o'clock the following morning, only a little more than thirty miles from where the *Cambrian Range* was now resting on the bottom. The shout went up, "Rauch !" (smoke) and the raider gave chase. It was the biggest ship that she had yet encountered, more than double her own size. She was the White Star Line's four-masted freighter *Georgic*, 10,077 of the finest tons that Harland & Wolff ever sent down the Belfast slipways. When a warning shot splashed across her bows she turned away from the Germans. With billows of smoke and sparks spouting furiously from her buff and black funnel, and her red and white-starred swallow-tailed pennant fluttering defiantly at her mast-head, she crammed on full speed. Her master, A.H. Summers, ordered his stern gun to be manned, while his wireless room babbled out a torrent of distress signals.

This time Dohna was in no mood for old-fashioned niceties. Seeing the *Georgic*'s gunners preparing to fire, he snapped out an order and seconds later *Möwe*'s own guns spoke. At a range of only 300 yards, it took but a few salvoes to wreck the merchantman's wireless office, knock the little stern gun out of commission, scattering its crew in all directions, punch holes in her funnel and ventilators and completely destroy three of her lifeboats. Such was the fury of the firing that it was fortunate that only one British sailor was killed. At this, Summers saw that he had no real chance of saving his ship. He stopped his engines.

Aboard the *Georgic* panic took hold as crew members fell over each other in their haste to lower the remaining lifeboats. One overcrowded boat capsized as it came down, hurling its occupants into the water, leaving them to struggle on to its rounded wooden bottom as it rose and fell on the swell, and cling there desperately waiting to be picked up.

The boarding party, led as usual by the well-practised Leutnant Pohlmann, went across and presently the signaller's flags were giving Dohna details of the captured ship and her cargo. She was bound for Brest from Philadelphia with thirty-six armoured cars, several thousand tons of cotton, 1,250 horses for the British Army in France and a crew of 142.

Dohna and his crew were deeply distressed by the fact that in order to do their duty they would be faced with the task of killing 1,250 horses. But it had to be done. These animals were enemy animals. They were intended to carry food, ammunition and supplies on the Western Front against the Germans' own countrymen. By 10 o'clock that morning all 142 of the British crew had been transferred to the waiting raider and the explosive charges were in place along her water-line, ready to tear her bottom open. These exploded, sending huge towers of water into the air, but she did not sink. Anxious to get away from the vicinity, Dohna expended one of his valuable torpedoes into her, but still she did not sink, owing to the vast amount of buoyant cotton that was stacked in her holds.

She teased him until about three o'clock that afternoon; settling slowly, listing first to port, then righting herself and then listing to starboard, but floating all the while. Then, when she finally started to sink, the neighing of the panic-stricken horses was so pitiful that Dohna ordered as many of them as could still be seen to be shot. And after she had gone, great bubbles of air rumbled to the surface from her innards, with bodies of horses and bits of other wreckage. It was a harrowing scene.

Including the ships sunk on her first cruise, the *Georgic* had boosted the tally of the Seagull past the 100,000-ton total, which called for some celebration. Nikolaus zu Dohna-Schlodien was not a mean man. In recognition of their achievement, he awarded each of his officers two marks and the lower-deck men one mark apiece. That night, in the officers' mess, they dined on champagne and chicken. But his success had created another problem. He now had 446 prisoners on board, in addition to his own crew of 250. Apart from the question of sheer breathing space (plus the constant worry that such a mass of men could quite easily overwhelm their captors), how was he going to feed such a crowd?

He resolved to put his next victim, whoever she was, to the same use as he had put the *Westburn* on his first cruise. (It will be recalled that Dohna had transferred his prisoners to her and dispatched her to Santa Cruz, where she now rested on the bottom, having been scuttled by Leutnant Badewitz). He did not have long to wait. On the morning of 11 December along came the *Yarrowdale*, 4,652 tons, plodding her way homeward from the USA, laden with a treasure chest of 117 brand-new trucks, 3,000 tons of steel ingots and 30,000 rolls of barbed wire, not to mention the fact that her coal bunkers were almost full.

This threw a new light on the situation. Because of the low volume to weight ratio of her cargo, she had ample room in her holds for all of Dohna's prisoners. And the value of that cargo to a hard-pressed Germany was immense. This was no ship to use as a worthless *lumpensammler* (literally – a rag collector), fit only to be sent into a neutral port at the risk of internment. Furthermore, the dauntless Reinhold Badewitz, having made his way back to Germany from the Canaries via Spain and Austria-Hungary to rejoin Dohna in Berlin on his return from

Möwe's first cruise, and having pleaded with his Captain to be included in the next adventure of the Seagull, was there on board. Dohna had, at his right hand, the very man for the job of taking the *Yarrowdale*, with all her cargo, crew, and 442 prisoners, through the blockade and back to Germany. She already carried enough coal for the voyage. She was even painted in the same colours as *Möwe* - black with grey upperworks. He summoned the young officer and put the idea to him. It was a dangerous mission. Would Badewitz be prepared to attempt it? "Of course," was the reply, "It is done."

It blew a storm for the rest of the day and all through the night. Next morning the waves were still crashing against the sides and over the decks of the two ships. The horizon rose and fell by a mile and the rain continued to fall in a solid driving deluge. Any transfer of prisoners and prize crew to the British freighter across such a sea by the ships' boats would be suicidal. And to complicate matters, the German lookouts had caught a glimpse of another passing vessel between the heaving mountains of water. Bidding the *Yarrowdale* to follow, Dohna set off after the newcomer. It took an hour to catch her. They were 520 miles west of the Azores.

She was the *St Theodore*, a 4,992-ton 'three island tramp' from Liverpool, sporting a natty red funnel with a black boot-top and a red, white and blue collar. And she carried in her holds the very thing that Dohna was hoping to find – coal – 7,000 tons of it. She offered no resistance.

By early afternoon the weather had abated, but not by much, and Dohna was anxious to put prize crews aboard the two captives before night fell, lest they escaped in the darkness. The seas were still as high as a yard-arm, but it had to be done. The boat looked as frail and tiny as a pea-pod as it rode the huge swell, disappearing from time to time behind a wall of water, as it carried Leutnant Kohler and his boarding-party across to the other ship. It came as a relief to see them standing on her bridge, with the signalman tossing his flags to say that all was well.

The whole day was spent in transhipping men and provisions to the *Yarrowdale*. There was a worrying occurrence about midday when another steamer passed by at some distance. Dohna was preoccupied with the task in hand and did not attempt to chase her. All the same, she must have wondered what the little flotilla of three ships was doing, sitting clustered together like ducks on a village pond in the middle of the Atlantic. The *Möwe*'s wireless operator listened intently for any signals coming from her, but there was a comforting silence.

Evening came and it was time for the *Yarrowdale* to depart. Dohna watched her go with a heavy heart as he reflected on the fearsome task that Badewitz had undertaken. His prize crew consisted of a quartermaster's mate, two petty officers, nine seamen, four firemen and an engineer's mate. These few men had been charged with the control of 298 enemy seamen, 104 neutral seamen and seventy-five officers, including seven captains. In addition, they were faced with the ordeal of taking the ship and this mass of humanity through the blockade. As a safety measure, Dohna had addressed the prisoners himself a few hours before. Working himself into a towering rage in true Prussian manner (his own words), the Silesian Captain warned the prisoners that if they made the slightest trouble Badewitz had *orders* to sink the *Yarrowdale* immediately. The prize crew would take to the boats and leave them all to perish. It was the best that he could do to help the loyal Leutnant. He hoped that it would work. The *Yarrowdale* drew away. She melted into the darkness, with her signal lamps flickering – *auf wiedersehen*. She had gone. *Möwe* turned south. It was 13 December, 1916.

To be seen in company with the *St Theodore* would have aroused suspicion, so Dohna sent her away, ordering Kohler to rendezvous with him about 21 December at a point west of the Cape Verde Islands, exactly where he had met up with the *Corbridge* to take on coal eleven months before. In the meantime *Möwe* would carry on hunting. But hunt as she might, it seemed as if the entire British Mercantile Fleet had fled from the ocean. Not one came along. Plenty of other traffic was seen as the days rolled by, but they were all neutrals. It was not until 18 December that the German sailors were stirred from their leisure on deck in the warm sun.

The *Dramatist* had sailed from San Francisco and through the Panama Canal, homeward bound for Liverpool. Her arrival brought several good things for Dohna-Schlodien, as well as another 5,400 tons to add to his score. Before sinking her, he stripped her of her wireless equipment. This would eventually be installed in *St Theodore*, which he intended to convert into another raider. He had persuaded the *Admiralstab* to allow him some spare guns for this purpose and several of the little two-inchers were resting in his hold ready to go to work. Then there was her cargo. She had thousands of tons of the succulent fruits of California, salmon and poultry, wine and vegetables. All day *Möwe*'s crew pulled cheerfully at their oars as the boats carried this bounty back to the raider. For the engine-room gang there was help in the form of fifty-five Indian firemen. These, being fully acclimatized to the heat, would be a boon for taking over much of the hot work in the stokehold in the tropics.

Besides all these good things, the *Dramatist* brought information. Her wireless had picked up signals from several stations over the past few days. Radio Jamaica and Radio Bermuda were repeating messages to All British Merchant Vessels – ABMV, ABMV, ABMV. A German raider was out, they warned. Ports were closed after dark and light-houses were blacked out. All merchant ships and troop transports had been ordered urgently into the nearest port.

So this was why they had seen no British ships for days. Freetown, Dakar, St Helena, Bermuda, Georgetown and the eastern seaboard ports of the USA were all crammed with Allied freighters, colliers and transports waiting for the 'all clear' from the Admiralty. But why had the *Dramatist* herself rashly ignored the warning? Probably, we will never know.

Naturally the radio stations made no mention of British plans to trap the *Möwe*. In fact, the presence of the Royal Navy in the Atlantic was awesome. The Fourth Cruiser Squadron, under Vice-Admiral Browning, was on the North America – West Indies Station with seven armoured cruisers, two armed merchant cruisers and the old battleship *Caesar*. Off the west coast of Africa there were the Fifth and Ninth Cruiser Squadrons, with five armoured cruisers, three armed merchant cruisers and some sloops. Off the east coast of South America was the cruiser HMS *Amethyst*, with two armed merchant cruisers, while her companion HMS *Glasgow* was under refit in Simonstown. Also at the Cape was the cruiser *Kent* with some destroyers. All these were supported by units of the Royal Canadian Navy off Newfoundland and the French West Indies Fleet under Admiral Taures. In addition, it will be remembered, there was Gordon Campbell in the *Farnborough*, Q-5, who had sailed in breach of orders from Cape Breton in the forlorn hope that he would meet the German on the way home.

For all that, the Atlantic held a lot of water in which to find one small ship. The Admirals divided the huge expanse of ocean into zones which each would search. Taures was asked to keep a special watch in the vicinity of the Maraca Islands, in the Amazon delta, where *Möwe* had coaled from the *Corbridge* on her first cruise. But Dohna was far too cagey to be caught like that. He had always been convinced that the coaling job had been reported by British spies. He would not venture there again.

He sank the hapless *Dramatist* and steered south. And here was where a vital factor came into play, one which can mean success or failure for a sea raider, despite whatever skills he may, or may not, possess as a seaman. It was that fickle thing called Luck. Without knowing it, Dohna had steered down an invisible corridor in mid-ocean. He had sailed into the only chink in the pattern of search zones that the Admirals had arranged among themselves!

Möwe was two days late for her rendezvous with the *St Theodore*, rejoining her in the late afternoon of 23 December. Next day, well to the west of the Cape Verde – St Helena track, the business of creating another raider got underway. Out came the screwdrivers and the soldering irons, the spanners and the wrenches, the crowbars and the lifting gear, and they toiled all day in the warm sun. When they had finished, the *St Theodore* sported the *Dramatist*'s wireless plus two 52mm guns, one for'ard, one aft. Now it was Christmas Eve.

Dohna-Schlodien proved many times that he was a decent man. Before leaving Kiel, he knew that, with luck, they would spend Christmas in some remote part of the ocean. He had packed away two Christmas trees and some paper decorations ready for the festivities. He had even obtained enough parcels from the Red Cross for every man to receive a present. Even the prisoners were not forgotten. Each of them had a present too. First of all, there was a divine service, presided over by Leutnant Wolf, after which they sat down to feast on the good things provided by the *Dramatist*. Later in the evening the officers went down to the lower deck to distribute the presents. Somebody had an accordion and the singing went on into the night. And all the while the black-hulled bandit slid quietly over the calm dark water, leaving just a gentle wash of phosphorescence behind her.

Doubtless Christmas had been happily celebrated, too, on board the 2,670-ton four-masted French square-rigger *Nantes*. But it was the last Noël that she would see, because on 26 December, 1916, on her way to London with 3,250 tons of Chilean saltpetre, she ran across the *Möwe*. She was most unfortunate, because her captain had moved well away from the usual shipping lane so as to avoid the raider! It was a pity they had to sink her. She was beautiful.

At last, on 28 December, the *St Theodore* was ready to go raiding. With some skilful tweaking, *Möwe*'s technicians had boosted her wireless range from fifty to a hundred miles. The guns had been tested and found to be satisfactory. Dohna appointed Wolf to command her. Kohler was to go with him as prize officer, taking his trusty nineteen-man crew. At Wolf's request she was renamed SMS *Geier* – the Vulture.

But the ocean still seemed bereft of British merchant ships as the raiders resumed the hunt, while the Royal Navy continued to scour the vast tracts of water in their own vain hunt for the hunter. They were not of course aware that there were now two of them.

St Sylvester's Day arrived – New Year's Eve. Dohna had taken to his bunk with an attack of acute rheumatism, no doubt brought on by the humid weather. The rain had been incessant and a warm gale had blown with a ferocity which carried particles of sand in the air all the way from the Sahara to encroach into eyes, clothes, food and machinery. Everybody seemed miserable, but none more than Dohna. Even his favourite Sherlock Holmes stories could not take from his mind the exruciating pain of the rheumatism as he tossed and turned in his cabin. The rules of courtesy demanded that he joined his officers for dinner on such a festive night and he struggled into some clean whites and forced himself to go down to the mess. But he was in agony, now shivering with fever as well as tortured by the rheumatism, and soon he retired to his bunk. Just before midnight he felt obliged at least to drink a New Year's toast with the lower deck. He stumbled down the passage and met his radio officer, Bethke, coming the other way. Bethke's face was beaming as he handed Dohna a signal. The captain propped himself against a door as he read it.

> "To MÖWE. Badewitz detachment arrived safely Swinemunde . . . Best Wishes and Happy New Year. ADMIRALSTAB."

So the *Yarrowdale* had made it! And she had presented the Kaiser with a seasonal gift in the form of a whole fleet of American trucks, steel for thousands of bullets and shells and guns, and enough barbed wire to protect several miles of the Flanders trenches. The news came as a welcome tonic for everybody. It was also an omen of future success. (Evidently, Dohna frequently changed his 'identity'. On 13 February, 1917, *The Times* announced that the fifty-nine neutral American sailors who had been taken to Germany in the *Yarrowdale* had arrived in

Switzerland. According to them, the raider which had sunk their ships was the *Ritz* of Bremen. They said she had a dummy removable funnel, seven concealed quick-firing guns, four torpedo tubes and could make eighteen knots).

On 2 January the 3,000-ton French sailing vessel *Asnières* yielded twenty-nine prisoners, a couple of fat porkers, a coop of hens and several brace of pigeons before they sank her with the cargo of Argentine wheat she had been carrying home to France. But she was only the second ship that Dohna had sunk since 19 December. It looked as if the British tactic of keeping close to coastal waters was working well. There was only one thing for it. If they refused to come out, he would have to go in and get them. He headed south. Perhaps the coast of South America would pay better dividends.

He was right. Off Pernambuco he captured the Japanese *Hudson Maru*, a 3,800-ton painfully slow and ancient tub on her way to New York. She would make a perfect *lumpensammler*. Then along came the Royal Mail Steam Packet Co's *Radnorshire*, up from Santos with 6,500 tons of real coffee, which was enough to make any German's mouth water, having only tasted *ersatz* acorn coffee for months. He took 100 tons of it before he sank her.

Möwe cruised slowly up the coast, with every eye intent on the clear horizon for signs of smoke. Or worse, the grey upperworks of a Royal Navy cruiser. A strange looking vessel approached. The strangeness was that she was riding very high in the water, which meant that she was empty. She drew nearer. Dohna could see from her lines that she was a collier. An empty collier? That could only mean that she had recently coaled a ship. And the only ships to coal at sea were warships. He was right again. She was the Admiralty collier *Minieh*. She was captured with all speed. Dohna ordered the boarding-party to stand on no ceremony, but to charge straight for her chart-room and confiscate all the charts, papers and other documents they could find, before they could be destroyed. It was a wise move. But the information obtained by it must have made Dohna's spine run cold. *Möwe* had been hunting right in the centre of one of the main search zones! The fox had been catching rabbits while sitting plumb in the middle of a pack of hounds! And within the last couple of days the *Minieh* had coaled both the cruiser HMS *Amethyst* and the armed merchant cruiser *Macedonia*, either of which could easily have blown the Seagull to Kingdom Come. Despite being plied with Dohna's whisky, Captain Williams insisted that he did not know where *Amethyst* was, although she can hardly have been much more than twenty miles away over the horizon. Even without this knowledge, it was clear to Dohna that the time had come to vacate the area. And quickly. The collier was sunk without further ado and the raider and her Japanese captive steamed away from the Brazilian coast, due east, back into the wide South Atlantic, as fast as the rickety old *Hudson Maru* could chug. It was 9 January, 1917.

The Ellerman Line's *Netherby Hall* was a real tramp. Her ports of call over the past five weeks had been Calcutta, Lourenço Marques and Cape Town, and now she was on her way to Trinidad and Havana. She crossed the path of another tramp with a black hull and the Red Ensign at her stern, south of the equator at thirty degrees west, on 10 January, 1917, and this brought her tramping to an abrupt end. Captain Jenks and his crew were taken aboard the raider and most of her 6,000 tons of general cargo, mainly rice, went to the floor of the Atlantic still inside their 4,400-ton ship.

This brought the number of prisoners in the hold of the raider to over 300 and it was time for Dohna to play his *lumpensammler* card. Most of them were transferred to the *Hudson Maru* and after another two days' steaming away from the nearest port, Pernambuco, she was released to make her way back there. Meantime, after pretending to sail north, and making much smoke in evidence of this, Dohna turned back on his tracks in the night and headed for his rendezvous with *Geier*, west of St Helena. Three green lights winked cautiously in the darkness. It was the Vulture's identity signal. She was already there, waiting, but she had only one conquest to report, and that was the Nova Scotian schooner *Jean*, a puny 215-tonner.

To take on coal at sea was a hazard which faced the German raiders repeatedly. Two steel ships, tied side by side, even in the gentlest of mid-ocean swells, grate and grind together with alarming force, causing much mutual damage. And here was no exception. The *Möwe* and the *Geier* had a combined registered tonnage of nearly 10,000 tons, and, although the German sailors had spent the past week industriously plaiting heavy rope fenders in readiness for the task, the ships rolled so heavily that they were of little use. And as the coal came out of *Geier*, so she rose in the water, just as the *Minieh* had done when coaling *Amethyst*. This increased the arc of her roll and she smashed several of *Möwe*'s for'ard plates. For three days the crews toiled, black-faced and ankle deep in coal dust. And all the time the weather was worsening, making the job well nigh impossible. Dohna had taken 1,000 tons. That would suffice for now. He sent *Geier* away to resume raiding, with orders to meet up again at Trinidade Island, off the Brazilian coast, around 10 February.

By now, *Möwe* had been at sea for two months and was beginning to show signs of wear and tear. In the normal course of events she would have been due to go into the dockyard for refit. But the best that Dohna could do for her, 8,000 miles from home in the wilds of the South Atlantic, was to let his worried Chief Engineer, Bruns, spend a day or two attending to his lengthy List of Defects as far as was possible. With her engines stopped and all power shut off, *Möwe*'s engineers set about the mysterious skills of their trade under Bruns' watchful eye. It was not until 21 January that he declared that she was ready to raise steam.

They sailed south-east. Dohna had decided to try his luck off the Cape of Good Hope. But it was a fruitless venture. They saw no British ships at all. This was not surprising because the wireless had been humming incessantly with messages and warnings from station after station about the raiders. Yes, raiders, because they knew that there was a second one at large, now that the *Hudson Maru* had spilled the beans in Pernambuco. Most British shipping had been diverted up the east coast of Africa and homeward via the Suez Canal. For the men of the *Möwe* it was a time of enforced indolence and sleep. And for Dohna, doubtless, some more of the adventures of Sherlock Holmes. On 3 February he turned back north-westwards to keep his appointment with *Geier*. The Atlantic was still so deserted that she was the first ship they saw. Together they headed for Trinidade Island.

This may be thought to have been a dangerous move, because the anchorage at Trinidade was a known favourite coaling-place for German raiders. Graf Spee's ships had used it and the *Cap Trafalgar* had actually been caught there by *Carmania*. But the South Atlantic was not over-endowed with friendly havens for a lonely raider on a secret mission. It was a chance that Dohna simply had to take. In pitch darkness he charged into the anchorage at full steam with his guns and torpedoes already unmasked and at action stations, just in case there was a British warship there to be caught off-guard. But there was nothing.

In the morning the coaling began again. Here the weather was fine, the sea as smooth as a bowl of cream and the work proceeded apace.

By four o'clock in the afternoon they had taken on 600 tons, which filled *Möwe*'s bunkers to the top.

The Vulture had sunk another ship while the Seagull had been cruising off South Africa. Some historians say it was the 1,227-ton Norwegian sailing vessel *Staut*. But *Geier* had come to the end of her usefulness. For one thing she had steamed many thousands of miles and was in very poor repair, but, more importantly, Dohna now needed every lump of her coal for *Möwe*. That evening they steamed away from Trinidade and, as soon as they reached deep water, the empty *Geier* was sunk. As she went down the men of the *Möwe* lined the rails to cheer her. The Vulture had worked well for the Kaiser.

It was the start of a busy time as they headed westwards towards the South American coast. The next day they sank the 8,423-ton *Brecknockshire*, another Royal Mail Line casualty, and the day after that the *French Prince* of the Prince Line, 4,766 tons. And the black funnel of their latest victim, with its white Prince of Wales feathers proudly emblazoned on the side, had hardly disappeared beneath the waves when the 2,652-ton Whitby steamer *Eddie* was sent to the bottom with her 5,000 tons of good Cardiff coal.

Then came a game of cat and mouse with a British auxiliary cruiser and *Möwe* was almost caught. Dohna had started to chase after a distant feather of smoke. Then, peering through his trusty Zeiss telescope, he saw that there were, in fact, two feathers. Two ships together! His instincts, sharpened by experience, told him to be suspicious. Yet again he was right. It was HMS *Edinburgh Castle*, 13,000 tons, with twice the armament of his own and a much faster turn of speed. She was in the process of taking coal from the collier *Headcliffe*, but, having seen *Möwe*, set off to chase her.

But Dohna's luck held good. The *Edinburgh Castle*'s boilers were in sore need of a clean and she could barely make fourteen knots herself. Dohna dodged into a convenient squall and altered course. And when the squall cleared there was no smoke astern of the raider. She had escaped.

Superb tactician that he was, Dohna needed to be constantly weighing up the odds for and against him in every given situation. He had just had an uncomfortably close shave with the *Edinburgh Castle* and his wireless operators were intercepting more and more coded signals between ships which were clearly not far away. It seemed as if the British were cramming the South Atlantic with ships in their hunt for him. He could not be sure of capturing more coal (and transferring it safely to his ship) once that which he had taken from the *Geier* had been consumed. Without coal, the Seagull would simply drift, like the Flying Dutchman, around the ocean until one of those ferocious grey cruisers found her and killed her. Surely the sensible thing to do now was to head for home.

As the *Möwe* crossed the Rio–Dakar transatlantic track, she met the *Katherine*, 2,926 tons, with Argentine grain, and a week later, 330 miles north-west of Cape Verde, the *Rhodanthe* of London, 3,061 tons. Both these ships were dispatched without ceremony.

10 March, 1917, was to be a day which would stay in the memory of Dohna for the rest of his life. By now *Möwe* had left the tropics behind her and was well into the latitudes where she would be crossing the main Europe–USA shipping lanes. It was a busy part of the ocean. And the weather had changed rapidly from a serene blue-skied warmth to a grey-skied gale-lashed cold. The sailors shivered.

It was before dawn, about 420 miles west of Lisbon, when *Möwe*'s lookouts reported a ghostly shape some way off through the pre-daylight murk. It drew nearer. It appeared to be a steamer with a yellow funnel. All her lights were dowsed. Dohna was unable to identify her in the darkness, but to move closer may have sent a stream of Morse pouring from her wireless office. Instead, he snapped on his searchlight, trapping her instantly in a pool of incandescence, and signalled her to stop immediately. She was the Pacific Steam Navigation Company's *Esmeralda*, 4,678 tons, master F.W. Malin, in ballast from Liverpool for the USA to collect a consignment of mules and horses for the British Army. There were 120 men on board, which included fifty-two American 'muleteers'. Malin was in no position to offer resistance and the *Esmeralda* was sunk, but the number of prisoners transferred from her to the raider made for serious overcrowding. There were now over 400 crammed in the after-hold.

Dohna sailed on north. The wind had dropped and it was now broad daylight between the heavy squalls and the thick banks of spring fog which had descended over the mid-Atlantic. The lookouts, as vigilant as ever, were now straining their eyes to sight other ships, be they foe to fear or victim to kill. Even neutrals posed the danger of collision in these conditions. One thing was certain – the *Möwe* would find no friends.

She was about 350 miles east of the Azores when the shout went up.

They had caught a glimpse of a large ship seconds before the swirling fog had closed in front of them like a pair of hastily drawn curtains. Dohna steered cautiously towards the now invisible stranger. Now the fog lifted again, just long enough for him to catch sight of her. She was big, and something told him that she would be fast. He sent for Engineer Bruns and ordered him to be ready for a sustained period of top speed, and to assign his strongest firemen to the task of feeding the furnaces. But Bruns had been carefully conserving their limited supply of coal. He replied that it would take over half an hour to raise his fires and boilers to full pitch. The thing now was not to lose contact with the stranger while the engine-room gang, with the sweat trickling through the soot on their blackened bodies, heaved on the coal. But as the speed of *Möwe* increased, so did that of their quarry. She was making a run for it.

Dohna had been right – she was certainly fast. In fact, with her two triple-expansion engines and a Parsons exhaust steam-turbine driving three shafts, she was the fastest ship that the Seagull had met in all her travels, able to push her 9,575 tons along at a spanking fourteen knots. And with a long-chased 4.7 inch gun mounted on her stern, crewed by Royal Navy gunners, she was the most heavily armed. She was the *Otaki*, owned by the New Zealand Shipping Company and commanded by a thirty-eight-year-old Aberdonian, Archibald Bisset Smith, bound for New York in ballast.

Below, in *Möwe*'s engine-room, anxious eyes watched pressure gauges as the captain called for more and more speed. She ploughed through the heavy swell, sometimes with her single propeller clearing the water as she put her bows down to plunge into the next trough, causing her frame to shudder and her wildly spinning shaft to sing alarmingly. Still the firemen sweated, until the pressure gauge needles were hovering on the danger point and *Möwe* was actually gaining a knot on the *Otaki*. After two hours only a mile and a half separated them.

By this time, of course, there was no question of decoying the British ship. The dour Bisset Smith knew he was being chased and he had no doubt as to the identity of his pursuer. And when he saw the *kriegs-flagge* raised at her stern and a shot screamed over his bows, his reaction was predictable. His 4.7 inch spoke back, just missing the bridge of the raider. A fight was on. In the packed after-hold of the *Möwe*, four hundred hearts beat a little quicker. For two hours they had listened to the furiously churning pistons and the whine of the shaft beneath them. They had felt all the shudders of the speeding ship. Now they were deafened by the guns above them. And they had heard another ship fire back. Had they been chasing, or were they being chased? Had the Germans caught another victim, or had the Royal Navy caught them? Perhaps it was HMS *King Alfred* or HMS *Sutlej*. If it were, their steel prison would be blown to bits. And them with it.

They had no cause for undue alarm. Although the *Otaki* sported a 4.7, she was no real match for the raider's four 5.9 inch guns, one 4.1 inch and a couple of 22-pounders. In a broadside to broadside duel, the merchant ship would have been quickly deafeated. But this was a stern chase fight. Only the *Möwe*'s two starboard 5.9s, trained fully forward, would bear on the *Otaki*. That evened the odds a little, but it was only a question of time. One German shell burst next to the British gun, scattering the crew, but they were soon back in action. A British shot crashed through *Möwe*'s bows, another smashed into the bridge, wrecking much of her signal equipment. But all the time a continual hail of 5.9 inch shells was crashing into the stern-part of the *Otaki*. Another salvo from the merchantman's bluejacket gun-crew exploded into *Möwe*'s starboard coal bunker, blowing fragments of burning material in every direction, causing several fires to break out. These spread rapidly to other compartments, including the firemens' mess-deck. The helpless prisoners, battened down in the after-hold, were threatened with asphyxiation from the smoke and fumes. For twenty minutes the firing was hectic from both ships as they tore flat out across the water.

But now the British ship's after-part was little but a tangle of metal. Flickering tongues of flame could be seen through the smoke which poured from her poop and she was clearly going down by the stern. She had almost come to a stop and her gun was silent. Dohna saw boats being lowered and men going over the side. He ordered his gunners to cease firing.

Both sides had taken a severe mauling. No fewer than thirty-seven German shells had hammered their way into the *Otaki*'s stern. Her Third Engineer, two apprentices and a deck-boy had been killed and nine others wounded. Chief Steward Willis had been drowned as he jumped over the side. Captain Bisset Smith, Chief Officer Roland McNish and the ship's carpenter stayed on board after the boats had left. McNish and the carpenter jumped into the water at the last moment

199

before the *Otaki* slipped out of sight with her Red Ensign still proudly flying. Nobody saw what happened to Captain Bisset Smith. He was never seen again.

On 7 June, 1917, at Buckingham Palace, King George V presented Bisset Smith's widow with the VC. It had been awarded to him posthumously for his gallantry against overwhelming odds. As a Merchant Navy Officer, it had been necessary to appoint him as a Temporary Lieutenant RNR, backdated to 26 February, 1917, to make him eligible for it. McNish was awarded the DSO and the *Otaki*'s bluejacket gun crew, Leading Seaman Worth and Able Seaman Jackson, the DSM. The apprentices, one of whom, Basil Kilner, was killed, were mentioned in dispatches.

Möwe was still afloat, but several fires still raged within her and she was taking in water through holes along her for'ard waterline. Nearly every one of her engine-room gang had been wounded, or worse. Dohmke and Lenz lay dead in the stokehold, one disembowelled and the other almost decapitated by flying shards of steel. Sturm died in agony before Doctor Winkel could operate to save him. Pungs and Gratz died that night and Oppermann the next. Such was their reward for the hard stoking which had caught the *Otaki*.

The Seagull was in no shape to tackle the blockade. It took them three days to extinguish all the fires, although the ship still reeked of smoke long afterwards, despite all their scrubbing and painting. She had sustained some damage to her boilers; two of them were down completely, meaning that she would only be able to make half-speed until the engineers had attended to them. But the main problem was her leaking hull. A party of volunteers undertook the task of going down on ropes, outside the ship, to try to plug the holes with some of the cotton bales they had taken from the *Netherby Hall*. It was a difficult and dangerous business. The sea had got up, causing the ship to roll badly. They were working underwater for much of the time, and only able to snatch hurried gasps of air before the next wave crashed against her side. Eventually, on the third day, all was ready to resume the run for home.

Suddenly there was smoke! It was a 6,000-ton freighter, the *Demeterton*, on charter to the British Admiralty and bound for Newcastle laden with Canadian timber. And she had a stern gun. Surely Dohna would not push his luck any further? The *Demeterton*'s master, Captain A. Spencer, had seen no reason to suspect the intentions of the scruffy little tramp until she suddenly altered course and bore down upon him with a German Naval Ensign flying over her stern. His gun was not even manned when the flaps in the gunwales of the stranger dropped down to reveal her gun muzzles and a shell screamed over his bows. As the British Q-ship captains had already proved, a ship loaded with timber is difficult to sink. They left the *Demeterton* floating upside down, about 730 miles east of Cape Race.

They would soon be needing to worry about running the blockade. Comfortingly, the North Atlantic weather was filthy. With black clouds racing across the grey sky and dark, surging hills of water tumbling around them, all under an incessant deluge of driving rain, visibility was down to no more than a few yards. Against such scenery their own black and grey ship was nigh-on invisible. But before they reached the danger zone there was more drama.

The following day they caught sight of a ship. She was a 5,500-ton freighter with a red and white-collared black funnel. Dohna could never resist a sinking and, to the dismay of his crew, whose minds were now set on home, he set off after her. But this time the expert deceiver was almost decoyed himself. *Möwe* had chased her prey for an hour, but was gaining on her so painfully slowly that Dohna had sent the hands to dinner early in case there was a fight. When he did get within range, and fired the usual shell across the bows, the other captain ignored it and kept running. At this Dohna shouted, "Open fire!".

It was one of their very first 5.9 inch shells which was lucky for the Germans. It burst on the after-upperworks of the freighter, blowing a deck-house to pieces, under which was revealed – a gun. She had a gun! Or rather she had had a gun. The gun's crew had been in the act of preparing to fire when *Möwe*'s shot blew their cover away. One of them was hurled straight into the sea. Another had his hand torn off. Flying splinters zipped through the air, damaging the funnel and the bridge. All told, four British seamen were killed and nine others wounded, including both the First and Second Mates.

She was the *Governor*, another ship on charter to the Admiralty. For her to have successfully decoyed the *Möwe* would have been sweet revenge. It had been exactly fourteen months earlier that her little sister, the *Author*, had been sent to the bottom by this same bandit, 1,000 miles south of this spot, with her cargo of racehorses.

But Fate had not favoured her. Here she was, 950 miles west of the Fastnet Rock, on 14 March, 1917, now at the mercy of the same guns. Her master, Captain Packe, had no option but to surrender. As he had done with other captains who had resisted him, Dohna lambasted Packe for causing unnecessary deaths and injuries in the face of hopeless odds. By all accounts, Packe, a fierce little man, informed the German that if he had not been so unlucky in having his gun exposed, he would have taught him some English manners.

The *Governor* was sunk by torpedo and *Möwe* headed towards Iceland and the blockade. And as she went, Doctor zum Winkel and the doctor of the *Brecknockshire* toiled in the lurching ship's sick bay, operating and amputating among the wounded. By now conditions in the prisoners' hold were scarcely bearable. With the latest captives, there were now 593 men cooped up there. Tempers frayed easily and there were several times when it looked as if there would be a riot.

Dohna ran north as far as 69.0 N 11.0 W, well inside the Arctic Circle, before turning sharply to the south-east to run down the coast of Norway. They were not likely to meet any more merchant ships in these latitudes. Nor did they.

Indeed, the blockade run was astonishingly uneventful. Lookouts' eyes remained peeled and wireless operators' heads stayed glued inside their headphones. Plenty of wireless traffic was overheard, but nothing to concern them. And plenty of smoke was seen over the horizons as British patrols quartered the North Sea, but no ships came near. Dohna was not to know it, but one particular cloud of smoke they sighted, north of the Shetlands, was that from the death throes of a German raider known as SMS *Leopard*, or rather, as she had been disguised that day, of a Norwegian vessel named the *Rena* – the same unlucky bogus name and nationality that had been worn by SMS *Greif*, which now lay on the seabed not many miles away.

Leopard was even more heavily armed than *Möwe*. Behind the hinged flaps in her gunwales she had no less than five 5.9 inch guns, four 3.4 inch and two 21-inch torpedo tubes. But she had failed to break through the blockade. Her commander, Korvettenkapitän Hans von Laffert, had chosen to make a fight of it when challenged by the cruiser HMS *Achilles* and the armed boarding steamer *Dundee*. It was a brave action, but after an hour's furious battle, the would-be raider was enveloped in smoke and masses of flames from the explosions of literally dozens of shells from the British ships. Her forward plates were glowing red-hot when she sank, almost horizontally, at 4.35 a.m. It was 17 March, 1917.

Why should the sinking of the *Leopard* be of any particular interest to Dohna? Because, in fact, she was none other than the *Yarrowdale*, which he had last seen when her lamps had winked goodbye away in the Atlantic three months ago, and whose arrival in Swinemünde had been radioed to him on New Year's Eve. The Germans had fitted her out for raiding, re-named her and sent her out to emulate her captor. Her career had lasted six days.

Möwe passed through the Skagerrak. With Sweden to port and Denmark to starboard, they had made it home, barring accidents. Shepherded by an ice-breaker through the frozen Kieler Bucht (the ice was late in breaking up in the spring of 1917) the Seagull arrived home to a second hero's welcome and the Kaiser appointed Graf Nicolaus zu Dohna-Schlodien to be his royal naval aide. It was 22 March, 1917.

That same day Reuters cabled from Amsterdam, "An official telegram from Berlin states that the auxiliary cruiser *Möwe*, under Commander Count Dohna-Schlodien, has returned to a home port from her second cruise in the Atlantic." On this the naval correspondent of *The Times* commented, "No complete account of the 'armed and disguised vessel of mercantile type' which the Admiralty announced had been sighted in the North Atlantic on December 4th has appeared, but people who were taken on board her as prisoners gave a very different description of the vessel from that which was issued concerning the *Möwe*. Some of them even went so far as to say that she was the old German cruiser *Vineta*. It is also curious that at the beginning of October last the death was announced of Captain Count von und zu Dohna-Schlodien who commanded the *Möwe* on her first raid, and who was said to have been killed by a shell on the German front in France while commanding a battalion of the 35th Infantry Regiment. In these circumstances it seems likely that the new German story must remain, at least for the present, one of the war's mysteries." Clearly, British Intelligence was unaware that the captain of the *Möwe* had a brother in the Army.

As for the ship herself, she was handed over to the British after the war to make some small compensation for the 188,984 tons of their shipping that she had sunk. She was passed into the ownership of Elders & Fyffes to resume her original purpose of carrying bananas. A little while later it was announced that she had stubbornly refused to answer to her helm and had been involved in a collision in the Manchester Ship Canal.

Chapter 16

The Black Wolf

In early 1916 the German Navy took over the nearly new 6,000-ton Hansa Line freighter *Wachtfels* and set to work on converting her to a marauder. They armed her with seven six-inch guns and four twenty-two inch torpedo tubes on swivel mountings, all of which were concealed behind side-screens which could be lowered when she came into action. Hidden in a special compartment in her stern, which was fitted with extendable rails to allow them to drop well clear, were 465 mines. In addition, she was equipped with a Friedrichshafen seaplane, taken aboard in parts, to be assembled later. This aeroplane would give her eyes to see far across the ocean. She had room in her bunkers for 6,500 tons of coal, which gave her a range of 42,000 miles at nine knots.

On 30 November, 1916, her hot-headed but chivalrous captain, Karl Nerger, sailed her out of Kiel and up the Kattegat to begin what was to be one of the most remarkable voyages in the history of seafaring. Although she carried armament almost equivalent to that of a light cruiser, there was nothing warlike about her appearance. With her black hull, white superstructure and one tall, thin funnel, she looked just like any other harmless tramp.

A glance at her counter-stern would have revealed the name *Jupiter*. But that was a sham. In reality they had christened her *Wolf*.

Nerger sailed north, hugging the Norwegian coast, just as Dohna-Schlodien had done only a week before in the *Möwe*. *Wolf*'s departure had been delayed by a fire on board in the dockyard, which proved to be a blessing in disguise because now it was late November and the weather was likely to worsen and provide poor visibility to screen him from the prying eyes of the Royal Navy. His prayers were answered as he passed between Bergen and the Shetlands near the point where he would need to leave the coast and beat westwards towards the Atlantic. Blizzard after howling blizzard came down in a heavy white curtain as *Wolf* lurched and rolled her way blindly through the raging storms, with freezing spray driving across her decks, coating her in layers of ice inches thick. One towering wave washed a life-raft overboard. Instantly the contact with the water set off the calcium flare attached to the raft, bathing the scene in an icy blue light. It was a moment of tension. If the flare's brilliance were to attract the attention of a British cruiser the adventure would be over almost as soon as it had started. Fortunately for the Germans, the atrocious conditions allowed them to remain unseen. Nerger ploughed around the north of Iceland, through the Denmark Strait and, doubtless with much relief, turned south to seek the comparatively warm hospitality of the heaving swells of the mid-winter North Atlantic.

SMS *Wolf* was free, but she did not go hunting immediately. Nerger's brief had been to "interfere with enemy shipping in distant seas, especially the Indian Ocean" and he took her due south through the middle of the Atlantic, taking pains to avoid contact with any other vessels, especially when bisecting the main east/west shipping lanes. Her crew were able to relax and enjoy the sunshine as they sailed towards a southern hemisphere summer. By the middle of January, 1917, they were approaching the Cape of Good Hope. On the other side of the South Atlantic *Möwe* was having a feast. She had already sunk sixteen ships. (As a matter of interest, we know that Dohna-Schlodien, too, was in the vicinity of the Cape of Good Hope for a short time towards the end of January. Could it be that he and Nerger had arranged to rendezvous there, for whatever reason, but missed each other?).

Off the Cape and in the Indian Ocean there were patrols of British, Australian, French and Japanese cruisers and destroyers, well over fifty ships, plus a host of smaller vessels. These meant constant vigilance. The pleasure cruise was over. It was time to go to work. First, now in sight of the South African coast near Cape Town, at a convergence of shipping lanes, Nerger decided to drop some of his mines. At dusk on the evening of 16 January, 1917, as he prepared to go to work, his lookouts reported columns of smoke on the seaward horizon. It was the cruiser HMS *Cornwall*, with a convoy of troop transports. They passed on, unaware of the presence of the raider.

Under cover of darkness *Wolf* laid a field of fifty mines, each with two hundredweights of high explosive packed into its metal shell, off Saldanha Bay about 100 miles north of Cape Town. By the following day they had steamed round the Cape of Good Hope to lay another similar field off Cape Agulhas (Needles) at the very southernmost tip of Africa.

The mines were set to float just beneath the surface of the water, anchored to the seabed, gently swaying with the current and nodding to each other as they waited for their first victim. They had a surprisingly long wait – over a week – before the first innocent freighter sailed to her doom. In fact *Wolf* opened her score with a double. On 25 January the British ships *Matheran* and *Portugal* both struck mines in the Saldanha Bay field, although the latter was saved and towed into port. But by that time Nerger was long gone and far away.

The British, by an unfortunate coincidence from their point of view, had reduced their Indian Ocean patrols only the previous day, when Admiral Grant had re-deployed the ships covering Colombo and Penang. The news of the loss of the two merchant ships off South Africa soon brought them back to reality, however, and when the Bibby Line's 7,000-ton passenger ship *Worcestershire* and the Blue Funnel Line's 6,700-ton *Perseus* both hit mines and sank off Colombo, thousands of miles away, and the German's work off South Africa produced yet two more victims, the 11,000-ton *Tyndareus* and the 3,500-ton *Cilicia*, all within a few days of each other in mid-February, a full scale 'red alert' was called.

For Nerger there was nothing for it but to be nimble and keep continually on the move if he was to stay ahead of the pack that would now surely be in hot pursuit of him. Leaving the Cape, he rounded the south of Africa and hurried north towards the coast of India. At the very time that the *Matheran* and the *Portugal* were meeting with disaster off South Africa, *Wolf* was steaming towards the Maldives, eager to put as many sea miles as possible between herself and the further minefields that she had just laid south of Bombay and near Colombo where the unfortunate *Worcestershire* and *Perseus* were to meet their fates.

Nerger enjoyed some more extraordinary luck when laying his mines off Colombo. The contours of the seabed form a narrow shelf here, about ten miles wide, around the coast. Outside this radius, the water is too deep to allow for an effective field of mines. The job had to be done close inshore, and this was a particularly dangerous spot in which to attempt such a task. Colombo was a big and important port, and a major factor in its wartime defences was the two very powerful shore searchlights which continually swept the seaward approaches at night. A distance of ten miles was well within the range of their beams. On the face of it, it was impossible for Nerger to do his work undetected, but his brief had been to operate "especially in the Indian Ocean", and this was one of the most important spots in that ocean. That is why the Royal Navy's presence was usually very evident, in the shape of at least a couple of cruisers tied up in Colombo Harbour at any one time. Nevertheless on a black, moonless night, the *Wolf* slunk to within about six miles of the breakwater. It had to be done.

But as she was busy at her task the inevitable happened. Two blinding rays converged upon her and held her in their glare. The mines stopped splashing over the stern and Nerger cleared his ship for action. It looked as if the game was up. The searchlights remained steadily fixed on the motionless shape of the raider. Her guns' crews crouched behind their screens, hearts in their mouths. Would one of the cruisers in harbour slide away from its berth and simply steam down the beam towards them? If she made a run for it, would her ten knots carry her beyond the range of those lights before they could catch her?

These questions were never put to the test because the searchlights moved on! The *Wolf* had not been sighted at all! Or at least, if she had been seen, she had been mistaken for a shadow or a trick of the light. Nerger finished laying his thirty-nine mines, two of which were to do for the unlucky *Worcestershire* and *Perseus* a few nights later, and quietly slipped away.

There was an ironic twist to the meeting with the British freighter that Nerger encountered, just north of the Maldives. She was the buff-funnelled, 5,500-ton *Turritella*, owned by the Anglo-Saxon Petroleum Co., with a Chinese crew, British officers and a New Zealand captain. He stopped her with a shot across the bows. She turned out to be none other than *Wolf*'s very own Hansa Line sister, the former *Gutenfels*, which had been seized by the British in Alexandria early in the war. Understandably reluctant to sink her, Nerger decided to use her as an auxiliary. Taking her officers as prisoners on board *Wolf*, he transferred one of his small guns and some mines to the captured ship, put some of his officers aboard, with Kapitänleutnant Brandes in command of the Chinese crew, renamed her *Iltis* and sent her westwards across the Arabian Sea with instructions to lay a minefield off the port of Aden.

Nerger did not have to wait long to meet his next victim, because the *Iltis* had only just gone when he ran across the Calcutta-bound 4,500-ton steamer, *Jumna* at about 5.30 a.m. on the morning of 1 March. Her master, Captain Wickham, was in his bath when he heard gunfire. He had been told by British naval authorities at Suez that there were no German ships in the Indian Ocean and assumed that the firing was from a Royal Navy patrol ordering the *Jumna* to heave-to for her papers to be examined. Happy to leave his Chief Officer to attend to such things, Wickham took his time in going up to the bridge. But the *Jumna* had not stopped, and furthermore, there were shells whistling over her bridge from the black ship that was passing from port to starboard across her bows and flying the German Ensign. Wickham's first instinct was to try to ram it and he rang down for Full Speed, but the German was too fast for him. When he gathered his wits, however, Wickham realized that it would have been suicide to resist the well-armed raider and signalled to her that he had stopped. Nerger circled the *Jumna* cautiously for about an hour before sending over a boarding-party which took Wickham and his officers on board *Wolf*. The merchant crew were put to shovelling her coal for transfer to the raider. The ships lay alongside each other, their plates scraping together as they rode the ocean swell while the coal was hastily loaded into *Wolf*'s bunkers. Then an explosive charge ripped out the *Jumna*'s bottom and she went to the depths with her cargo of Spanish salt. It was 4 March, 1917.

On board the bandit, Wickham and his crew were bundled down into the 'tween decks, aft, which was littered with bits of scrap iron, bags of lime, odd pieces of timber, coal dust and all kinds of rubbish. If this was to be their home, it was certainly not going to be a luxurious one.

The unfortunate *Iltis*, meanwhile, was to have but a short career in the German Navy. Brandes had just finished laying his mines off Aden when he was challenged by the sloop HMS *Odin*, which was on a routine nightly patrol offshore to check that the port's lights had been effectively blacked out. The bulk of the 6,000-ton intruder was clearly visible in the bright moonlight, but the fact that she was showing no lights at all aroused the suspicions of the sloop's captain, Lieutenant-Commander Palmer. Palmer signalled the routine questions regarding identification and destination, but Brandes' answers, although he gave his name as Meadows, the actual name of the *Turritella*'s master, did not satisfy him at all.

Palmer decided that he would make a fuller investigation in the morning and for the rest of the night the *Iltis* found herself held firmly in the glare of *Odin*'s searchlight. Escape was impossible. The sloop's potential speed alone was enough to prevent this, besides which his one small gun was no match for her fire-power. As the first rays of the sun were cracking the eastern horizon and Palmer was preparing to send across a blue-jacket boarding party, he saw boats being lowered from the suspicious ship. Their oarsmen were pulling hard away from her sides as two enormous explosions erupted within her and she slowly sank. Brandes had scuttled her.

(There were accusations of atrocity against the Germans following this episode. Almost exactly a year later, on 7 March, 1918, in an announcement no doubt delayed by the stifling cloak of wartime security, the Exchange Telegraph Company cabled from Melbourne, "Captain Pearse, Red Cross Commissioner, states that while the *Turritella* was minelaying off Perim [in the Red Sea], a British gunboat appeared. The Germans got into the boats and blew up the *Turritella* with Chinese in the stokehold and engine-room. The gunboat captured the Germans, who were recently tried for murder in Bombay.")

Ashore in Aden, the Chinese survivors from the *Iltis*/*Turritella* were only too pleased to tell the British authorities about their recent experiences, including of course a full description of *Wolf*. Nerger had learned of the fate of the *Iltis* from intercepted British wireless messages and was only too well aware that his cover was now blown. The need to lose himself in the expanses of the ocean was urgent, so he pointed *Wolf*'s bows to the south-east and headed towards Australia.

Nerger now made good use of his seaplane, the little *Wölfchen*. From high in the sky she would not only be able to guide him towards any likely prey but would give early warning of any Allied warships in the vicinity. As it happened, on 11 March, to the east of Diego Garcia, she spotted the 4,000-ton *Wordsworth* bound for London with a cargo of rice. It was bad luck on the freighter. She would normally have been well clear of the vicinity but for the very poor quality of the coal she had taken on in Colombo, which refused to produce a good head of steam. Taking her crew and passengers on board the raider, Nerger sank the freighter and sailed on.

The *Wordsworth*'s master, J.W. Shields, of South Shields, had not seen his cousin and fellow 'Geordie', Wickham, of the *Jumna* for two years. Strangely, it did not seem all that surprising that they should meet again in the dirty hold of a German raider in the middle of the Indian

The Cruise of the *Wolf*

1. *Turritella*, (captured) 26 February, 1917
2. *Jumna*, 4 March, 1917
3. *Wordsworth*, 11 March, 1917
4. *Dee*, 30 March, 1917
5. *Wairuna*, 22 June, 1917
6. *Winslow*, late June, 1917
7. *Beluga*, 10 July, 1917
8. *Encore*, 15 July, 1917
9. *Matunga*, captured 6 August, sunk 26 August, 1917
10. *Hitachi Maru*, captured 26 September, sunk 7 November, 1917
11. *Igotz Mendi*, captured 10 November, 1917
12. *John H. Kirby*, 30 November, 1917
13. *Marechal Davout*, 14 December, 1917
14. *Store Brore*, 4 January, 1918
15. *Turritella*, (scuttled)

Ocean! They were to be only too pleased of each other's company in the months to come.

For over a fortnight all was quiet. Although the Germans were constantly vigilant, they were well away from the main shipping lanes and it was not until 30 March, off the coast of Western Australia, that they met up with the three-masted barque *Dee*. The sailing-ship offered nothing in the way of lootable cargo, being in ballast bound for Fremantle from Mauritius. Nevertheless, she was quickly sunk and her crew joined the growing number of prisoners locked below decks on the *Wolf*.

It is difficult to understand Nerger's next moves. For two whole months his ship was buffeted and tossed as she heaved her way over the gigantic waves of some of the most hostile seas on the planet, on the verges of the Southern Ocean, well to the south of the Great Australian Bight. Here, in the Roaring Forties, it rains and blows incessantly for eleven months of the year with unrelenting violence. If he was hoping to meet merchant ships out of any of the Australian or New Zealand ports, surely he was far too far south. Whatever his reasons were for staying there so long, putting himself and his men and their prisoners through such a seemingly pointless ordeal, that is what he did. All without sinking a ton of Allied shipping.

By now, it had been over five months since *Wolf* had left Kiel. Her battered crew badly needed a rest and her boilers and machinery needed attention. Nerger had to find somewhere safe to hide up for a while. He headed up the east coast of New Zealand towards an uninhabited volcanic speck of a mere 7,000 acres in the Pacific known as Sunday Island.

Sunday Island (or Raoul), is in the Kermadec Group, which nudges longitude 180 about six hundred miles nor'-nor'-east of New Zealand. It had been uninhabited since the outbreak of war, when the settler-farmer population of a dozen or so had been evacuated. It seems certain that Nerger was well aware that this isolated spot would suit his purpose, no doubt thanks to thorough briefing by German Intelligence. To give his crew their long-awaited shore leave on what was, after all, part of the British Empire would surely make it all the more enjoyable. Nevertheless, even while *Wolf*'s sailors went fishing from her upper deck for big scarlet snappers or yellow and black striped bream, or even sharks, or listened to the ship's band, or rambled around the island, kicking their heels and munching on oranges from the overgrown plantations left by the settlers, and her engineers sweated away to over-haul her boilers, Nerger took no chances. He sent the *Wölfchen* aloft on frequent patrols to check for any Allied warships nosing around the area.

And it was the little seaplane which was to give Nerger his most valuable prize yet. On 2 June, 1917, her pilot spotted a tall-funnelled freighter. She was the *Wairuna*, with a cargo of wool and hides, plus some live sheep and 1,000 tons of coal, a few days out of Auckland and on her way to San Francisco. Knowing that *Wolf*, in the middle of a boiler-clean and with her fires out, could do nothing to capture the Union Steamship Company ship, the aviators swooped low over her masts and dropped a message tied to a sandbag, ordering her to keep wireless silence and put into Sunday Island or be bombed. The plane's observer dangled a pear-shaped object over the side of the cockpit, which he dropped into the sea to explode just ahead of the *Wairuna* to demonstrate his ability to carry out such a threat.

The arrival overhead of a German warplane, here in the South Pacific, must have been one of the things that the *Wairuna*'s master, Captain Harold Crichton Saunders, can have least expected. His course had taken him very close to the island. Indeed he had already spotted the black shape of the *Wolf* at her moorings. His first reaction had been to ignore her. Then, as the seaplane flew off, he took a closer look at her and saw that she had several guns trained on him. Were there other forces lurking in the vicinity? He was not to know that there were not, nor even that the strange ship herself could not put to sea. Could he have escaped? There was a good chance he could have done so. Even if his ship had been damaged by the *Wölfchen*'s bombs in the attempt, it was by no means certain that she would have been seriously disabled. In the event, Saunders took the view that discretion was the better part of valour and concurred with the German's order. He headed towards Sunday Island and capture.

It was an expensive decision. If Saunders had tried to make a run for it, transmitting wireless signals as he fled, surely it would have brought at least one Allied warship on the scene in time to send the trapped and immobile *Wolf* to a watery grave before she could raise steam. In turn, that would have saved many merchant ships from a similar fate.

A German boarding-party approached as the *Wairuna*'s officers hurriedly stuffed the ship's papers and code-books into her furnaces and destroyed the wireless equipment, while the chief steward shared out the store of tobacco among the crew. At least they would not be short of a smoke for a while. "Good afternoon, gentlemen," said a German officer as he came aboard, with drawn revolver, flanked by two blue-jackets, "Your papers, please." It was a very courteous encounter. The Germans took tea with their captive officers in the *Wairuna*'s saloon before politely ordering them over the side into the launch.

The *Wairuna*'s wireless officer was Roy Alexander. Writing years later, he recalled that, as they drew near *Wolf* in the gathering dusk, her silhouette reminded him of the familiar lines of a luxurious P & O steamer, but as they climbed up the ladder and on to her deck this impression changed rapidly. There they saw the torpedo tubes and six-inch guns at close hand, and scores of hard-bitten blue-jackets busy at their tasks. No liner this.

After being thoroughly searched and given a shower, the prisoners were taken aft and ushered down into number four hold, the steel compartment which was to be their home for many months to come. There, amid the dirt, the coal dust and the stink, they discovered their fellow prisoners from the *Turritella*, the *Jumna*, the *Wordsworth* and the *Dee*. There were about a hundred of them, shabby and bedraggled, seamen of a dozen different races, all excitedly clamouring for news of the outside world.

The chatter died down at last and Alexander climbed into his hammock and tried to sleep. This was not easy because, through a rivet hole in a bulkhead, he had seen the mines in the next hold, two hundred of them, sinister, black and round, ready to roll over the stern to await the hull of a passing merchantman. But what if an Allied cruiser landed a shell on them first?

It was Sunday, 22 June, 1917, when they took the red-funnelled *Wairuna* to sea to sink her. Stripped of everything in her cargo which would be of use to Nerger, she refused to submit to the bombs that had been placed in her bilges and it was not until shell after six-inch shell had ripped into the plates along her waterline that she slowly rolled over and disappeared.

The previous day the Germans had spotted the American sailing schooner *Winslow* gracefully passing by with all sails set for Samoa. The US had declared war on the Kaiser on 6 April and therefore she was now fair game. Nerger, having intercepted wireless messages, knew that she carried a valuable cargo of 350 tons of coal, petrol for the *Wölfchen* (which could fly for an hour on only nine gallons) and fire-bricks to repair his own work-worn furnaces. He set off to chase her. It was an easy capture and the schooner was brought back to Sunday Island. Her cargo, her skipper, Captain Trudgett, and his crew were transferred to the raider and she was towed out to be sunk. Again Nerger had a stubborn ship on his hands and it took a whole afternoon of shelling before the *Winslow* disappeared. Even then, burning baulks of her timbers continued to float in the sea long after she had gone to the bottom. That evening at dusk *Wolf* sailed from Sunday Island for the last time. Down below the prisoners had endured hours of deafening noise inside their reverberating metal box as her guns pounded the sailing ship to destruction.

But two of their shipmates were absent. Chief Officer Steers and Second Engineer Clelland, both of the *Turritella*, had decided to escape. The 7,000 acres of overgrown vegetation of Sunday Island would surely provide a good enough hideout. At an opportune moment they climbed down a rope and hung onto the ship's rudder, out of sight under the counter of her stern, waiting for darkness before striking out for the shore. Neither of them were ever seen again. It is not hard to guess what fate befell them. There are many sharks around Sunday Island.

When the absence of Steers and Clelland came to light, the officer on duty at the time was a certain Leutnant Von Oswald who now displayed all the caricatured mannerisms of the Prussian officer, with his beautiful uniforms, haughty speech and over-dignified bearing – and, of course, his ability to rant and rave. Roy Alexander remembered the occasion with relish. Von Oswald's behaviour was "reminiscent of a Port Said hawker who had been robbed of his wares". He roared, raged and cursed in German and scarcely intelligible spluttered English. He ran up on deck and came down below again, still gesticulating, with bulging eyeballs, and with "abuse flowing from him in a shrill stream". The exertions of all this made him sweat profusely, bringing dark damp patches to the once immaculate white and gold uniform. The prisoners, he screamed, were most ungentlemanly for helping two of their number to escape. In fact, they were impolite blighters! Henceforth their status would be reduced from "guests" of the German Admiralty to "prisoners"! And they would be confined to the hold for one month as punishment. He vanished up the ladder with the yells of laughter from the ex-"guests" ringing in his ears. No more was seen of him for quite a while. Nerger, who was in a class of his own when it came to ranting and raving, was furious when he learned of the escape.

Three days out from Sunday Island *Wolf* approached the North Cape, the northernmost tip of New Zealand. All day long the prisoners had heard the crew fixing the mine-laying rails on the deck above them and watched through the bulkhead rivet holes as the mines themselves were prepared for use. Darkness fell. It was a moonless squally night; ideal for the black-painted *Wolf*, with all her lights doused, to go about her business. Nerger took her towards the coast and picked up speed. The prisoners could hear the regular rumbles as clusters of four or five mines at a time slid down the rails and dropped over the stern.

Down below, while most of his fellows swung asleep in their hammocks, one of the prisoners, a Welshman named Rees, was engrossed with a piece of paper and a pencil. He was keeping a careful tally of each mine laid. It was a practice that he was to adopt, meticulously, every time *Wolf* laid mines while he was on board. In time this was to earn him the OBE.

Nerger headed south, staying well out of sight off the western coast of North Island. Two days later the prisoners heard the now familiar sounds of preparation for more mine-laying. That night *Wolf* went to work again. This time they were off Cape Farewell, in the approaches to the Cook Strait which separates the two main islands of New Zealand. It was, and is, a very busy stretch of water, and the strain for both crew and prisoners alike grew in its intensity as *Wolf* laid her mines, of which Rees counted forty-five. A slip in the handling of just one of them, or just one shell from a patrolling cruiser, could have sent every man on board to Kingdom Come in an instant.

By daybreak, the mine-laying stint complete, they found themselves out of sight of land again, heading towards the horizon and leaving a poker-straight wake behind them. It was a simple matter for the experienced mariners among the prisoners to calculate their position and bearing. Many of them were old-time sailing-ship men, well accustomed to scanning the sun and the stars. A snatched look from under the hatch-cover, or a report from the stewards as they returned from the galley with the cans of dreadful coffee and nauseous hunks of sticky black German bread or rice that made up their staple diet, was enough to tell them where they were. On this occasion, however, even the greenest cabin-boy could have provided the answer. With the rising sun showing astern, it was obvious that they were heading west towards Australia across the Tasman Sea.

Nerger made no attempt to avoid the busy Wellington–Sydney and

Melbourne sea-lanes. His ship, with her seaplane dismantled and stowed away and all her elements of disguise employed, appeared just like any other peaceful freighter. All the same, action alarms were frequently called whenever other ships passed uncomfortably close. Her gun and torpedo crews would 'close up' behind their hinged screens, fully ready to fire if necessary. Nerger could have made killings galore in the Tasman Sea, but he was wise enough not to do so. An instant hue and cry would have gone up as soon as the first victim went down, and *Wolf*, now slowed down by her well-worn engines and barnacle-encrusted bottom, and very low on coal, would have had little chance of winning a long sea chase if pursued by a squadron of 20-knot six-inch cruisers. This caution was justified when wireless messages were intercepted which indicated that Allied warships were patrolling the Australian coast. Nerger's immediate plan, to lay mines across the Sydney–Melbourne lane, a six-day steam away, was to need even more impudent courage than usual.

As soon as darkness fell on the evening of 3 July *Wolf* slipped towards Cape Howe and started work. Rees had counted to about twenty-five when an almighty rumpus of thumping feet was heard from the deck above, and loud crashes against the ship's sides as the hinged gun screens clattered down. She heeled over as Nerger changed course violently at full speed. With all those mines still unlaid! What if one of them had rolled over and broken one of its horns! It was obvious that something dramatic had happened to bring the gun crews into action readiness in the middle of the dangerous mine-laying operation.

The minutes ticked by, then an hour, as *Wolf* raced into the safety of the open sea. Then they heard the screen being raised to hide the guns and they breathed more easily. Luckily, Nerger had spotted an Allied warship in the distance and had fled before she had seen him. It was the light cruiser HMAS *Encounter*. He had saved all their lives without much doubt.

What would he do next? His now south-easterly course appeared to be taking him well to the south of New Zealand. Had he decided that the time had come to go into internment in South America? Chile already held many German internees. The prisoners contemplated the prospect of such a voyage with gloom. It was early July, in the middle of winter, which was not an ideal time to linger in the Roaring Forties. The *Turritella*, *Wordsworth* and *Dee* men had already had a generous helping of life in those latitudes three months before. It was freezing cold in that battened down, unheated steel compartment. By now it stank with the accumulated sour sweetness exuded by the mass of seldom-washed bodies in its confined space and, to make matters worse, *Wolf* was rolling her guts out in a fearsome storm.

But Nerger needed coal again and, even if he was lucky enough to capture a collier, it would be impossible to transfer her coal at sea in these parts, with such rough weather blowing up from the South Pole. He had to find it in calmer waters. He turned north, heading back up the middle of the Tasman Sea. Four days' steaming took *Wolf* across the Sydney–Suva lane. Here the sun brought some welcome warmth and the seas were less mountainous. She did not have long to wait before the ancient 500-ton American barque *Beluga* appeared on the skyline with a cargo of benzine from 'Frisco to Sydney.

Nerger had hoisted the German ensign and his boarding party were bringing their boat alongside their latest capture when a dense cloud of smoke was seen on the horizon. Without hesitation, he turned *Wolf* away, leaving his blue-jackets with their prey. But the newcomer was not an Allied cruiser. It was only the *Fiona*, a harmless elderly steamer belonging to the Colonial Sugar Refinery, trudging her way to Australia from the Fiji sugar mills. Assured of safety by the seaplane's report the following morning, Nerger turned back to the *Beluga*. She had no coal, of course, but her cargo provided ample fuel for the *Wölfchen*. Whatever his reasons were for not waylaying the *Fiona*, which could not have been far away, and *did* have the coal to solve his immediate problems, we do not know.

The prisoners were allowed on the upper deck to witness the funeral pyre of the *Beluga*. Roy Alexander said that of all the sights he witnessed roaming the seven seas it was the one that would never leave his memory. Nerger simply had to shell her to ignite the cased benzine he had left in her holds, which ran streaming from her sides into the sea, forming huge burning lakes. In minutes she was alight from stern to bow and right to the tips of her masts. Even hundreds of yards away from her, the sea was on fire where pools of benzine had been flung by the explosions which erupted within her. Night was falling and the glare reached high into the rapidly darkening tropical sky. It must have been visible for many miles. For the bandit twenty-six and a half degrees south and a hundred and sixty-six and three-quarter degrees east was no place to hang around. She fled again. It was 10 July, 1917.

By now the shortage of coal was critical and Nerger was maintaining only a slow speed to conserve supplies. On the bright side, thanks to the *Beluga*'s benzine, he could make full use of the seaplane's reconnoitring flights to keep him away from trouble and hopefully spot a steamer with coal to filch. He sent her up twice a day, morning and evening. She was on her evening flight on 14 July when her engine failed at about 2,500 feet. She crashed awkwardly into the sea about a mile from the ship. The flimsy machine was seriously damaged by the impact and nearly sank before her rescuers could reach her. They found her pilot, Fabecke, who was popular with the prisoners, and his observer, Stein, sitting on the tail quite unhurt, but it was clear that the *Wölfchen* herself would not be taking to the skies for a while.

Not far away over the horizon, enjoying what was, unbeknown to them, their last day of freedom for a long time, were the men of the *Encore*, another American sailing ship, heading for Sydney with a cargo of 900,000 feet of Oregon pine timber stacked high on her decks. She carried little that was of any great use to Nerger, except the excellent stores of food which her owners, the Simpson Lumber Co. of San Francisco, had provided for her crew. She met the same fate as the *Beluga*, shining a massive torch of light into the night sky as the flames consumed her. This time Nerger had really pushed his luck. The inferno could well blaze for days, smack in the middle of a busy sea route. Again he fled, as fast as he dared without wasting too much valuable coal. And again he was lucky to do so, because his wireless officer, trawling the wavelengths to eavesdrop for useful information, had intercepted a message to the effect that there was a Japanese cruiser very close at hand.

But the need for coal remained and he was having no luck in that respect. As they crawled along at no more than a few knots, heading west-north-west, between the New Hebrides and the Solomons, the gossip in the hold was that he would lay his remaining mines off New Guinea, and then go for internment in the Dutch East Indies. But was there enough coal to do even that?

Here, in this tropical paradise, as they sailed among palm-fringed coral islets with brightly coloured birds fluttering above them in the dazzling blue sky, and watching exotic fish darting through the clear water, morale sank. Quarrels became frequent. Everybody was on edge. As they headed for captivity, the prisoners had taken whatever of their possessions they could carry with them. Amazingly, Captain Saunders of the *Wairuna* had even managed to take his armchair! When he returned one day to find it occupied by a cheeky young steward, grinning as he rolled a smoke, the Captain's temper exploded and the youngster found himself dumped on the deck with little ceremony. After that dust-up the hold was divided into three "messes", with empty packing cases forming the walls; one for senior officers, one for junior officers and the other for the lower deck. What with the heat and the tense uncertainty, the hellish voyage was getting them down. Even the Germans seemed irritable with each other.

At last salvation came on 28 July when the wireless office intercepted a message that the regular steamer service had sailed from Sydney for Rabaul in New Guinea. "Burns Philp Rabaul. Donaldson left Sydney on 27th via Newcastle Brisbane. 340 tons general cargo. 500 tons Westport coal Rabaul. 236 tons general cargo Madang. Burns."

The reply came the following day. "7.43 p.m. VHV to VIB. Burns Philp Brisbane. Cape Moreton noon Monday. Donaldson."

Five hundred tons of Westport coal! Another day or so would bring them to the Brisbane–Rabaul track in the middle of the Coral Sea. All Nerger had to do was to loiter there and wait for her to show up, whoever she was. But first he needed to bring the damaged seaplane back into commission so that the steamer could be spotted. Wolf's carpenters and engineers worked round the clock on the Wölfchen. She was winched up from below and assembled ready to be swung over the side and launched on a trial flight. She took off without mishap, soaring into the clear blue sky to the cheers of the watching crew. Even the prisoners cheered. A shell is a shell, whether it is British or German. And with the seaplane keeping watch above, they were less likely to be blown to bits by one of their own.

The single-screw steamer Matunga, 1,618 tons, Captain A. Donaldson, owned by Burns Philp Ltd of Sydney, and indeed carrying 500 tons of Westport coal, general cargo, mails, some passengers, including a platoon of Australian troops, and manned by a crew of forty-five, was the unwitting prey for which Nerger waited. Her capture was a classic piece of Q-ship-ology, a skill Wolf had not needed to practise to any high degree since she had steamed towards the Wordsworth five months and many thousands of miles ago.

The Matunga would be only a day or so away from her destination and would therefore be posted as 'overdue' within a very short time of non-arrival on schedule, thus triggering off an immediate search for her. There was also an abundance of wireless stations within easy earshot. These factors created an overriding need to carry out the kill without allowing any distress calls to be made by the victim. The surest way of achieving that was to put a shell through her wireless office at the earliest opportunity. The first thing was to get as close to her as possible without raising her suspicions.

The presence of the seaplane would be an obvious give-away, and, after she had spotted the *Matunga*, guided *Wolf* on to the correct course to intercept her and returned to the raider for fuel, Fabecke took off again to hide below the horizon whilst Nerger went to work. It was late in the evening of 5 August when the lights of the *Matunga* came into view. *Wolf* spent the rest of the night edging closer to them. By daybreak the two ships were almost within hailing distance. The newcomer did not give Captain Donaldson any cause for alarm. Doubtless, within a few minutes he would be exchanging pleasantries with the other merchant skipper in the time-honoured fashion of ships that pass each other on their peaceful occasion. His passengers were taking early-morning tea on deck at the time, idly observing the big black ship which had joined them. That she could have been a raider was far from their minds. But at 7.00 a.m., when they were only a couple of hundred yards apart, the black and white German ensign flew up, the screens came down on to her steel sides, a single salvo roared out across the water and the seaplane reappeared to circle low around the *Matunga* to discourage Donaldson from breaking wireless silence. The *Matunga* was Nerger's. It was 6 August, 1917, about 250 miles south of Rabaul.

The new arrivals in the hold, smart in their tropical uniforms or well-tailored white suits, were set back on their heels by the pungent stench which hit them. Roy Alexander was surprised to see an old friend among them and went to greet him, but the man stared at him blankly, not recognizing him immediately. Then he exclaimed, "Good God! What in hell have they done to you?" It was then that Alexander realized the sorry picture that he must have made. Sartorial matters had long ago ceased to be of much concern to any of the prisoners. He was clad in nothing but a pair of ragged shorts; he had lost so much weight that his ribs and shoulder-blades protruded and he had chopped his hair short to discourage the lice.

Nerger quickly put a prize crew aboard the *Matunga* under Leutnant Rose, a tall, breezy officer, popular with his men and not at all of the same ranting breed as the martinet Von Oswald. Both ships steamed away north, leaving Rabaul itself on their port side, and then heading westwards, hugging the equator through the Bismarck Archipelago.

This was a clever move. By now the search would be on for the missing ship, and, in steaming directly beyond the point of her destination, Nerger had minimized his chances of being caught, even if it had occurred to any of the searchers that they should be looking for a raider at all. The two ships sailed onwards for several days, showing no lights at night and keeping wireless silence as the *Wolf* searched for a suitable lair where she could strip her kill in safety.

Conditions in the hold worsened as the bandit nosed her way along the equator. There were now two hundred bodies crammed into a space which only gave them the equivalent of half-a-dozen kitchen fridgefuls of air each, and the prisoners were forced to sling their hammocks in two tiers. The heat and the stink were unbearable.

Then, exactly a week after the capture of the *Matunga*, the throb of the engines stopped. They were off the island of Waigeo on the northwest tip of New Guinea. The *Wölfchen* was sent up to scout the surrounding area, and when she returned the two ships headed towards an almost invisible cleft in the lush green jungle which hung like a pelmet between the higher ground inland and the beach. It was almost as if Nerger was as 'at home' in these parts as he was in the Kattegat, and that he had known exactly where he was going all along. Maybe he did. Germany had possessed several colonies in the Pacific before the war, including part of the island of New Guinea. The coastlines thereabouts would have been well charted by the Germans and Nerger probably left Kiel well equipped with cartographical information.

The narrow channel opened out into a beautiful landlocked bay. It presented some of the most breathtaking scenery that one could find anywhere in the world. Parrots squawked and flew about in vivid splashes of colour. Luxuriant vegetation reached almost to the water's edge. Some fuzzy-haired brown men were fishing from a canoe. It was a perfect hide-out for a pirate. Captain Kidd could not have wished for a better one. But it was an evil beauty. The high hills all around and the narrow sea-entrance meant that the place was airless and dank. The stink of rotting vegetation was little better than the ripeness of the hold. Crocodiles glided through the green water. Many more sunned themselves among the mangrove roots on the shore. Mosquitoes buzzed in swarms. It was a spot God made for malaria. It was called Offak Bay.

If he had been caught here, of course, Nerger would have been a sitting duck. He sent an armed party ashore to set up an early-warning observation post on some high ground.

As for the prisoners, any thoughts of escaping were instantly put out of mind by the presence of crocodiles. But again Nerger took no chances. He ordered them below and battened down the hatches. The hold was now a hellish jail. Warm moisture dripped from the deckheads onto the suffering men. The steel sides of the ship were so hot that they were untouchable, even hours after sunset. Men were on the point of suffocation. And still there was the over-powering sickly stink.

Eventually the giant Captain Meadows of the *Turritella* had had enough. Paying little heed to caution (his actions could have earned him a bullet), he shoved his way towards the guard, who was almost fainting himself, and bullied the man into taking a message to the officer on duty. Von Oswald appeared, with the ship's doctor, and in fairness it must be said that he showed sympathy for their plight. All Nerger would agree to, however, was to open the hatch cover a few inches. He was not being cruel, but thoughtful. Some of his own men had got into the *Matunga*'s liquor. They were roaring drunk, and the last thing Nerger wanted was a mutiny or a murder on his hands, which could well have resulted if the prisoners had confronted them. In any case, they would be sober in the morning, and it would be time to go to work.

Crate after crate of canned food, tons of frozen meat, cases of whisky, all swung their way over on the derricks from hold to hold. And then there was the coal. Five hundred beautiful tons of cargo coal, plus all that in the bunkers of the *Matunga* which she would not now be needing. *Wolf* had struck it rich, but there was still much to do before she was ready to sail. Her boilers needed another clean, her engines required an overhaul and her hull was festooned with weeds and barnacles. Her crew swarmed like ants, lifting, hauling, painting, scraping and shovelling.

Captain Trudgett, of the *Winslow*, made no attempt to hide a smile as he watched all this activity. His ship, as with many American vessels, had carried some Scandinavian sailors in its crew. On capture, these men had claimed neutrality, as had those from the *Beluga* and the *Encore*. The USA had huge administration problems with the masses of immigrants arriving from Europe. These men were still waiting for their naturalization papers to come through, and all claimed to be still Swedish or Danish, and not to be treated as prisoners. Nerger, as ever the diplomat, had sent them forward to mess with his own crew, but now he demanded that they worked. And Trudgett, leaning on the rail, chuckled as they heaved coal in the insufferable heat.

Wolf sailed from the steamy hell of Offak Bay, followed by the empty *Matunga*. Ten miles off the coast the skeleton crew left the doomed ship and two explosions blew the bottom out of her stern. She sank in minutes. *Wolf* turned away and steamed to the south-west. It was the morning of 26 August, 1917. She was nearly nine months out of Kiel.

To wander at leisure through the beautiful Spice Islands of the East Indies, with your nostrils savouring the scented breeze, is a privilege that can only be enjoyed by a fortunate few. It must have been comparatively enjoyable for all on board *Wolf* too, after the excruciating conditions in Offak Bay. They meandered through the Moluccas and past Banda Island. Then westward through the Flores Sea, clearing the big island of Celebes on their starboard side. When they entered the Java Sea, among the big oil-tankers in and out of Batavia and Macassar, crowded inter-island ferry-boats, plodding freighters and tramps flying any one of a dozen flags, it was easier, and far less conspicuous, simply to join the flow of traffic. Nerger made no attempt to avoid them and dipped whatever flag he was showing as he passed each one.

By now the "internment in Batavia" theory had gone out of fashion. Information seems to have leaked out, somehow, that the plan was to lay the remaining mines off Singapore. It was common knowledge. Singapore? Surely, even the bold Nerger would never risk sailing that close to disaster. Nearly every trade route to and from the Far East converged on Singapore, besides which it was a main base for the Royal Navy. Maybe it was the sheer impudence of such an escapade that made it so irresistible. What a final flourish it would be!

Wolf had made the busy, and heavily patrolled, Karimata Strait which separates the islands of Borneo and Sumatra by the night of 2 September. The moon glared on the flat sea, making it glint like burnished pewter. It was not a comfortable setting. Just after midnight the alarm buzzer sounded. Action stations! the lookouts had reported a ship ahead. It was approaching them on their port side, on the opposite course. It was a cruiser! Feet thumped urgently along the decks above the prisoners' hold as the raider's gun and torpedo crews took up their positions behind their screens. And then all was silent except for the rhythmic throb of the engines and the quiet hiss of compressed air from the waiting torpedo tubes.

The unlit warship drew nearer. She could not have failed to have seen the 6,000-ton black bulk sitting on the water, even though it too was without lights. The German sailors were tense. Any minute now, for sure, they would be caught in the glare of the cruiser's searchlights and a loud-hailer would order Nerger to stop. But no, whoever she was, she gave no indication that she had ever seen them. She held her course and her grey shape was eventually swallowed astern into the night. Nerger's amazing influence on Lady Luck had stood him in good stead yet again.

He must have been sorely tempted to give the unalert cruiser a couple of torpedoes. The range was point-blank, broadside on. But that would have sealed his own doom in these enclosed and busy waters. The whole of the Royal Navy's East Indies station would have been on his tail and he would never have got to plant his mines off Singapore.

In the morning, although *Wolf* was through the strait and among the Dutch islands to the east of Singapore, the strain of the previous evening's encounter still showed on the faces of her crew. They could not believe their luck as they spent the day preparing the mines for the coming night's operations, watched as ever through the bulkhead rivet holes by the prisoners in the hold. It was a full two months since Rees, now much thinner, had kept his tally of mines as they tumbled over the stern off the coast of New South Wales. They started at midnight and it was not until nearly dawn that the Welshman folded his dog-eared piece of paper and put it away. A quiet cheer went up from the crew. The mine racks were all empty. The eggs had all been laid, a hundred and ten of them, between the Anamba Islands and the eastern approaches to Singapore itself. It was the morning of 4 September, 1917.

As ever, Nerger's tactics immediately following a raid were straight out of the text-book. He had laid his mines to the north of Singapore, plumb on the track to Hong Kong and Japan, and now he steamed in exactly the opposite direction to where any search for him would probably be concentrated, making no attempt to avoid the traffic in the busy seaway. But what would he do next? Were they heading for internment in Batavia after all?

For five days *Wolf* retraced her course, sailing back through the Java Sea. Then, on the fifth night, every light was extinguished, even the dim blue ones which were always kept on for reasons of security, leaving the hold with its two hundred occupants in absolute darkness. It was impossible to see from one hammock to the next. The total blackness seemed to emphasize the heat and the stench.

Came the dawn and the ship had taken on a different motion. The rhythm of the waves told them that they were in another sea. Sailors know these things. It was an ocean, in fact – the Indian Ocean. Nerger had performed another amazing feat of seamanship. He had taken his blacked-out ship through one of the narrow passages in the chain of islands which separates the Java and Flores Seas from the Indian Ocean. The navigators among the prisoners said they had probably passed through the Lombok Strait, between the islands of Bali and Lombok. *Wolf* had broken free and now had thousands of miles of open water in front of her.

So that was to be the plan! Get lost in the wide blue expanses of a little-used part of the Indian Ocean; relax after all the stresses and strains of raiding; cruise around for a while until the mines achieved some results and then go for internment in one of the Dutch Javanese ports. There was little likelihood of meeting any shipping in this quiet corner of the ocean. The prisoners were allowed on deck to lounge around and enjoy the fresh air and sunshine, sometimes even all day, and they all felt much better thanks to the good food pilfered from the *Matunga*. The ship's band would play bouncy German oompah tunes to the robust accompaniment of the crew, and whenever Nerger appeared on the wing of the bridge they would burst into wild cheers whilst he basked in the adulation.

But internment was the last thing on Nerger's mind. As *Wolf* maintained a westward course, the cheeriness faded as the pirate nudged her way towards the busy Australia–Colombo track. The pleasure cruise was at an end and, what was more, the old problems had recurred – shortage of both coal and fresh food. With six hundred people to feed, the *Matunga*'s fresh food stores had not gone far when divided among such a number, although there were plenty of tinned provisions. And *Wolf* needed over thirty tons of coal per day at seven knots, which meant that most of the *Matunga*'s paltry five hundred tons had already been turned into ash. Nerger had no alternative but to go hunting again. On 25 September they were south of Ceylon. Nearly ten months out of Kiel.

The *Wölfchen* was hoisted up and re-assembled. Now a veteran of dozens of sorties and a disastrous crash, she was work-worn and shabby. Her fabric had been patched and mended as well as possible, but a complete recovery was what she really needed if she was to continue her services, and there was no new material for such a job. Nevertheless, Fabecke nursed her into the air and they disappeared from view. The spluttery roar of her engine had scarcely gone out of earshot when she came back. Fresh prey had been spotted.

Nerger used the same tactics as when he had captured the *Matunga*. The seaplane was swung in-board while the bandit steamed towards her quarry, and then took off again to disappear from view before they came into sight of their victim. Again the silent gun and torpedo crews crouched silently behind their screens. But this time, for some reason, the prisoners' hatch cover was left open and they were able to see along part of the deck.

It was mid-afternoon when they saw the *kriegsflagge*, with its black eagle, running up the mainmast and a single gunshot was heard. Then all was quiet for a minute or so. "She's surrendered," the watching prisoners whispered to each other. But then they heard the screens crashing down with a resounding clatter and instantly *Wolf* let fly a four-gun broadside, deafening their ears. She was not a purpose-built warship, of course, and her flimsy frame was not designed for such work. She heeled back with the recoil and great clouds of dust, slats of wood and flying rivets filled the hold. Another broadside boomed out and she shuddered again. The prisoners were all on their feet now, anxious and afraid. It is not a comfortable experience to be herded into the hold of a ship engaged in a fight. This time the victim was not going to go quietly. For the first time Nerger had found a really stubborn one.

Roy Alexander managed to sneak a look over the starboard beam. There, less than a mile off, was a grey passenger steamer. Already, some of her lifeboats were in the water and pulling away. She had several holes in her side and her black funnel was tipsy and half shot away. Like many steamers, she had been fitted with a stern gun and the crew were racing towards it, crouching as they ran. But another salvo of four shells smashed through the upper-works of the steamer and wiped them out before they reached the gun.

Wolf's gunners kept up their fire as Alexander watched with horror. The steamer's boat-deck was hit, killing and maiming people who were clustering round a lifeboat. Another boat was hit as it was being lowered. It capsized, tipping all its occupants into the sea to the mercy of the sharks. At last the passenger boat stopped, with dead and injured people slumped all over her decks. Other passengers were in the water and some in her lifeboats, one of which was sinking, full of terrified people frenziedly bailing her out as best they could.

She was the *Hitachi Maru*, 6,700 tons, from Yokohama to London via Cape Town; Captain Tominaga, with mails, passengers and general cargo, call sign LCBS, owned by Nippon Yusen Kaisha of Tokyo. It was 26 September, 1917, 400 miles south-west of Colombo.

Carnage of this degree was not Nerger's usual style. But Tominaga had made a dreadful mistake. He had persisted in transmitting distress signals by wireless for far too long. This led to the deaths of many people who were in his care on an ocean voyage. Later, as we will see, he was to pay for this in the traditional Japanese way of one who has brought dishonour upon himself. Nerger, once committed, had had no choice but to keep shelling the helpless ship until he managed to silence her wireless transmissions, which was not until a shell had passed through the *Hitachi*'s wireless room, just missing the head of the Japanese operator.

He sent a boarding-party over and lowered his own boats to help with the rescue work. The mine compartment, now empty, was used to house the bewildered new arrivals. Only an hour or so ago they had been relaxing on a liner in mid-ocean, thousands of miles from any war zone, and now they were being herded like cattle into the grim hold of an enemy raider. There were English civil servants, Japanese business-men, Anglo-Indian officials, Portuguese soldiers from Macao, Chinese, Indians, Americans, women and children.

The two ships were sitting right on a very busy sea-lane. Here was no place to strip his latest conquest of her wealth. Nerger had to take her 6,500 tons somewhere quiet, out of sight of the prying eyes of passing ships. But first he had two immediate problems to face. His guns had damaged the *Hitachi*'s rudder, making it impossible for her to steer. Urging them to work with utmost speed, he dispatched his own ship-wrights to set about some emergency repairs. And about thirty people had been killed by the shelling. These had to be decently buried. The bodies were sewn into hammocks, or, as Roy Alexander put it, "a certain amount of body was placed in each hammock – some were unrecognizable dollops of flesh". Against the background of a beautiful sunset which turned the sea into a treacly lake of glowing pinks and orange-yellows, a mass burial service was held, with Nerger and his men formed up in respectful lines on deck as the prayers were said and the line of bodies slid over the side. With no time to waste, the two ships turned away.

Many thousands of miles away, off the coast of Ireland, willing hands were reaching down to rescue Lieutenant Smiles and the other survivors from Blackwood's *Stonecrop* after their six-day ordeal on a raft of planks in the Atlantic.

The Suvadiva atoll is just below the equator at the southernmost tip of the long trickle of specks which form the Maldive Islands, dangling like a necklace of green beads from the throat of India. It was towards Suvadiva that Nerger set course, arriving offshore the following morning. He sent the seaplane ahead to scout for any unwelcome visitors, and, given the 'all-clear' on Fabecke's return, he took his ship, followed by the *Hitachi*, through a gap in the coral reef which surrounded the atoll and they anchored in the peaceful lagoon. This was another piece of superb seamanship on the part of the German captain. To take two big ships through a passage that would normally require the services of a local pilot was a show of skill which earned the genuine admiration of his fellow professionals locked in the hold.

The *Hitachi*'s cargo was extremely valuable. She carried a huge amount of undyed raw silk, tea, rubber and copper, plus thousands of crates of the tinned crab which would eventually form the staple diet of both crew and prisoners alike for months on end, rendering some of them unable to face such fare for the rest of their lives. But she carried no coal, except that in her own bunkers, and that was the sticking-point in a spectacular plan that was forming in Nerger's brain. This cargo would be of inestimable value if only he could get it home to Germany. What a glorious sight they would make, the two of them steaming into Kiel, captor and captive. But Kiel was at least 15,000 miles away. He needed coal. Enough to take the two ships more than halfway round the world. That was the key.

Coal may have been the key, but the door to Germany would still remain bolted by the firm hand of the Royal Navy. To smuggle one ship through the blockade called for a good slice of luck. But to try it with two, was that not pushing one's fortunes a little too optimistically? Not at all. Nerger was a positive thinker. With two ships, the chances of one of them getting home were doubled. The risk was halved.

He put his shipwrights and engineers to work again on the *Hitachi*, making her seaworthy for the long trip ahead, while good supplies of stores and some of her bunker coal were transferred to the waiting *Wolf*. There were nineteen women on board the raider, including the wife and small daughter of Captain Cameron of the *Beluga*. These were all put on board the Japanese ship, accompanied by the delighted Cameron, a medical officer, one Major Flood, and half a dozen old men and boys, mainly from the crew of the *Dee*. There was never any suggestion that the German crew had ever treated the women with anything other than proper respect, but all the same Nerger was pleased to see them go. He had made no secret of his opinion that to have women on board a ship full of sex-starved men was to court trouble.

For three days the work went on. It was an idyllic spot; a paradise of coconut palms, white sand and turquoise sea, but just as at Offak Bay, its beauty concealed an unpleasant side. The inhabitants were hordes of land-crabs and scurrying teams of rats, probably the descendants of escapees from the pirate ships who had frequented these secluded atolls two centuries before. As for the emerald green waters of the lagoon, they were full of sharks. But the crew were happy. They went about their work with gusto, singing lustily as the ship's band played their favourite tune, the *Nach der Heimat* (Homeward Bound) song. A cynic may have mused that they had last sung it when they thought they were going to intern in Batavia nearly a month ago.

Leaving a heavily armed party on the *Hitachi* in the lagoon, *Wolf* went hunting for coal. It was an urgent mission, because soon the Japanese ship would be reported overdue at Lourenço Marques and Nerger wanted to be clear of the area before a posse of warships came looking for her. He headed straight on to the Colombo–South Africa track, which was the most likely place to find a collier. It was risky, but it was a risk that had to be run. At any time he may have met a patrolling cruiser. Indeed, he was overtaken by a large fast ship on the second night. He called his men to action stations, but the unlit stranger passed by without pausing.

The *Wolf* prowled the area for a week. Several times a likely victim was spotted in the distance, but as the pirate tried to sidle closer the other captain would turn away and put on speed to lose him. Merchant captains had become more cautious. It was a lesson which had been learned the hard way. Coalless, Nerger headed back towards Suvadiva.

Rather than break wireless silence, he sent *Wölfchen* ahead with orders for the *Hitachi* to put to sea and join him. Together, they steamed south-west towards Madagascar, skipping on and off the main track to lessen the chances of meeting a patrol. He was not to know it, but again he had enjoyed astonishing luck, because only a few days later an inquisitive French cruiser decided to pay Suvadiva a visit. The hunt for coal continued, but every time a ship was seen her wary captain gave *Wolf* a wide berth. The situation was becoming critical.

106. Sehnsucht nach der Heimat.

Nach der Hei-mat möcht' ich wie-der, nach dem
teu-ren Va-ter-haus, wo man singt die fro-hen
Lie-der, wo man spricht ein trau-tes Wort. Teu-re
Hei-mat, sei ge-grüßt! In der Fer-ne — sei ge-
grüßt! Sei ge-grüßt in wei-ter Fer-ne, teu-re
Hei-mat sei ge-grüßt!

Deine Täler, deine Höhen,
Deiner heil'gen Wälder Grün,
O, die möcht ich wieder sehen,
Dorthin, dorthin möcht ich ziehn!
Teure Heimat usw.

Doch mein Schicksal will es nimmer,
Durch die Welt ich wandern muß.
Trautes Heim, dein denk' ich immer,
Trautes Heim, dir gilt mein Gruß.
Teure Heimat usw.

Another crisis had arisen following the capture of the *Hitachi Maru*. Beriberi, dhobie rash and syphilis all arrived on board with the people from the Japanese steamer. And there were two cases of dreaded typhus. For the moment the danger of meeting an enemy warship was put to the back of Nerger's mind. Typhus is spread by lice and fleas. Unlike typhoid, typhus is not controllable by inoculation. Typhus could run like wild-fire through the ship's company. With typhus, you can wake one morning feeling quite fit, and by the next week your insides can have turned to water and you are nothing but a corpse. There was no point in allowing *Wolf* to be found as a floating derelict, full of dead bodies. Nerger ordered everybody on board to be inoculated against typhoid and all hands set to on a vicious anti-flea cleaning-up exercise, scrubbing and washing every suspicious article, even the decks and bulkheads of the hold itself. As for the two Japanese typhus cases, they disappeared and were never seen again. We can only guess what Nerger did with them.

The hunt for coal continued to be fruitless and by now *Wolf's* bunkers were almost empty. Without fuel, Nerger's dream of taking the *Hitachi* home to Kiel would never materialize. He would not even make it into the Atlantic himself. There was no alternative. He would have to sink his captive. He took her to a group of small islands, bounded by huge coral reefs, about three hundred miles north of Mauritius, called the Cargados Carajos, or, as they were known to English seafarers, St Brandon's Rocks. It was a poorly sheltered anchorage, exposed to heavy seas, but it was well away from any well-used sea-lane. The *Hitatchi* was stripped of the most valuable parts of her cargo, which were then stuffed into the lower holds, and the women and other prisoners taken back on board the raider. Four hundred people were now cramped together in the two holds. It was not going to be a comfortable trip.

The two ships put to sea and a few miles out the prize crew left the doomed *Hitachi Maru* and the time bombs in her forward compartments exploded. It was nearly half an hour before she put her bows down, showed her propellers to the sky and vanished. Nerger turned away to the south-west. It was Wednesday, 7 November, 1917, eleven months and one week out of Kiel.

The problems with disease had not been completely resolved and *Wolf* herself had been the cause of the difficulty. The onslaught of shell-fire with which she had greeted the *Hitachi* had damaged the refrigeration plant of the steamer. This meant that her stores of fresh provisions, including fruit and vegetables, had been spoilt. But for this, much of the sickness on board may never have arisen. Beriberi, for one thing, whilst a gruesome and, if unchecked, a fatal condition, is merely caused by dietary deficiencies. And now, another dietary disease appeared, one that had been feared by ocean-going sailors throughout the ages, scurvy.

But for the moment even the scurvy was forgotten, because on the second night out from St Brandon's Rocks another traditional dread appeared – fire at sea. It had erupted among the few tons of coal in the bunkers, and bunker fires are notoriously difficult to put out. This one did not pose any real danger, but it was consuming a precious commodity. That night the prisoners swung into their hammocks happily. Nerger's stupendous good luck had surely run out. It looked as if he would have to run for Madagascar and the hell-cruise would be over.

In the morning their hearts sank. They awoke to see a grey ship with a yellow funnel bearing the monogram SA in red lying a short distance abeam of the *Wolf*, whose guns were trained on her. The stranger wore a Spanish flag and was therefore strictly neutral. But she was carrying cargo to a British port and therefore Nerger was legally entitled to seize it as contraband. She was the *Igotz Mendi*, built in Bilbao only a year ago, 4,650 tons, bound from Lourenço Marques to Colombo. And in her holds she carried over 6,500 tons of coal! It was 10 November, 1917, latitude 21 south, longitude 53.3 east.

Nerger put the affable Leutnant Rose on board the Spaniard with his well-practised prize crew and the ships headed back to St Brandon's Rocks. It is not difficult to imagine the grim smile that must have played on the German captain's face as they set off. Lady Luck had been teasing him yesterday with the fire in the bunkers. Now she had bestowed on him what was probably her most generous gift so far – six and a half thousand tons of black diamonds.

Chapter 17

Back to the Lair

Now in possession of plentiful coal, Nerger took the opportunity to deal with other important matters while his crew were loading it into the bunkers. The Spaniard was conspicuous in her garish colours and she was given a hasty coat of warship grey, ready for the voyage up through the Atlantic which she would make in place of the *Hitachi Maru*. There was capacity for only a limited amount of coal because so much space was taken up in *Wolf*'s lower holds by the loot taken from the Japanese. She would need to re-coal again from the Spaniard long before reaching the North Atlantic. In further preparation of such a trip, and here is more evidence of Nerger's inherent decency, he sent teams of engineers down into the prisoners' holds to fit steam pipes. Without these they would have surely frozen to death.

Fabecke's sixty-odd operational flights in the *Wölfchen* had made aviation history, but they had left her fabric in dire need of repair. She had been patched and mended as best they could, but it was far from satisfactory, not to mention unsafe. For weeks, ever since the capture of the *Hitachi*'s silk, Fabecke had been imploring Nerger to allow some of this to be used in giving the little seaplane a complete recovering, but the captain had refused, saying that it was an experiment which could fail, and without her eyes in the sky the search for a collier would be severely restricted. Now that the coal problem had been solved, he gave his permission for the silk to be used, but on the first scouting flight in her new coat the *Wölfchen* ran into a storm and returned in tatters. She was dismantled and stored below, never to fly again on the voyage.

Time and again the Allies had had *Wolf* within their grasp and time and again she had either escaped unnoticed or they had missed her by a whisker. The list is astonishing. The unwitting *Cornwall* (some accounts say it was HMS *Berwick*) had passed her off the Cape of Good Hope; Captain Meadows of the *Turritella* had been hailed by the 25-knot six-inch cruiser *Newcastle* only a few hours before his ship was captured north of the Maldives; laying mines off the coast of New South Wales, *Wolf* had run away from HMS *Encounter* without being seen; an unidentified cruiser, her lookouts surely asleep in the white moonlight, had ignored her in the Karimata Strait (probably it was HMS *Psyche*, the same ship from which Hallwright, the late captain of *Heather*, Q-16, had been dismissed four years before); a French cruiser had been only days too late to catch her red-handed with the captured *Hitachi* at Suvadiva, and a large darkened ship, almost certainly a patrolling cruiser, had passed close by at speed when she was hunting for coal on the Colombo–South Africa track.

And now, here at the lonely St Brandon's Rocks, she was to have another close shave. Coaling from the *Igotz Mendi* was still going on when the raider's wireless crackled. From the volume and clearness of the intercepted signal, the operator could tell that it came from a ship very close by. Not only that, but it was from a cruiser. And she was looking for the *Hitachi Maru*!

Nerger called his crew to action stations as darkness was falling. Only partly coaled, should he leave the *Igotz Mendi*, run for the open sea and take his chances? Or should he lie doggo and pray that the dawn would not find him facing the muzzles of a broadside of six-inch guns? He gambled on the latter. All night long the German gunners waited at their stations, but when morning came they saw that their captain had backed another correct hunch. The horizon was clear. There was no cruiser. She had passed on her way in the night.

By the end of the next day the coaling was done, the women transferred to the *Igotz Mendi* and they steamed off together to the south-west. It was not sensible for the two ships to be seen in close company and Nerger ordered Leutnant Rose to take the Spanish steamer on ahead and rendezvous in the Atlantic. *Wolf* gave the Cape of Good Hope a wide berth before turning northwards. And as she did so, another innocent victim sailed right into her path. She was the 1,200-ton American barque *John H. Kirby*, rolling down to South Africa from the USA with 270 of Henry Ford's motor cars. The sailing ship was in no position to offer resistance and she hove-to when ordered. She carried little that was any use to Nerger, except a supply of soap. He showed a wry sense of humour when he announced to his crew that they could each take one of the £400 cars as a prize, but they could not use the ship's boats to get them! No wonder he was in such a light-hearted mood. It was 30 November, 1917. One year since they had sailed from Kiel!

With her master, Captain Blom, and her crew of nineteen crammed into the already packed holds of the raider, the beautiful *John H. Kirby* went to the bottom with her sails still set. As far as is known, she still has 270 brand-new 1917 Fords with her on the floor of the ocean.

Wolf was going home. She had access to plenty of coal. Discipline was relaxed and the prisoners were allowed to spend much time lounging on the upper deck, watching the big South Atlantic rollers swing along her sides as she buffeted her way north. But there was one vital thing that the prisoners lacked – fresh food. Scurvy broke out in a big way and dozens went down with it. The little sick-bay was not big enough to take them and a makeshift 'hospital' had to be rigged up in the hold. Roy Alexander paid special tribute to Staff-Sergeant Alcon Webb of the Australian Medical Corps, who, racked with malaria himself, devoted himself to the care of the scurvy sufferers with very little medication to help him.

Scurvy is a horrible disease and its presence did not improve conditions in the hell-hold. It starts with a listless nausea. Then teeth begin to fall out. The skin erupts with multi-coloured spots, some green, which itch maddeningly, but if touched turn into great ulcers. Some patients go blind, with eyes turned to fungus. Everything about them stinks, because, quite simply, they are rotting alive. Even the brain rots, sending them mad. In the end the lungs rot and death brings a merciful end. All for the lack of a bit of fresh fruit or a few vegetables.

The determined Nerger was well up into the Atlantic when he caught the large French barque *Maréchal Davout*, 2,000 tons, on 14 December. She was bound from Australia to Dakar with a cargo of wheat. The German spotted her cloud of white canvas at dusk and tagged along behind her all night, signalling her to heave-to at dawn. Seeing that she was well armed with two 12-pounders and equipped with wireless, Nerger took no chances with her, wisely keeping his guns trained on her until his prize crew had taken control. She carried nothing of any use to him, except what had been intended as Christmas fare for her crew, including a pig, poultry and several casks of French wine. Captain Louis Bret and his men were squeezed into the hold of the raider and his barque was dispatched in the same way as the *John H. Kirby*.

Nerger needed coal again and steamed towards his rendezvous with the *Igotz Mendi* at a point half a day's steam south of the remote Trinidade Island, some 500 miles off the Brazilian coast about 1,200 miles south of the equator. Trinidade has very few attractive features, being composed of little else but three miles of putty-coloured rocks and some spindly shrubs. But its sheltered anchorage had made it a favourite hideaway for pirates for centuries. In the early stages of the war, in keeping with this tradition, German raiders such as *Möwe*, *Kronprinz Wilhelm* and *Dresden* had all visited; the latter to lick its wounds and take on coal from a waiting collier after the Battle of the Falklands, in the lee of Trinidade's Nine Pin Peak. And the 18,000-ton ex-Hamburg – South American Line armed liner *Cap Trafalgar* had actually been surprised while coaling at the same spot by her Cunard equivalent, now HMS *Carmania*, which had sent her to the bottom in the ensuing battle; the longest single-ship fight of the war. But that was all in 1914, when Brazil was neutral and Trinidade was uninhabited.

Now it was December, 1917, and Brazil had declared war on Germany on 26 October. German fondness for Trinidade was well-known to the Brazilians, and it was no longer uninhabited. Now there was a wireless station and a company of troops there. Nerger knew none of these things until *Wolf* and *Igotz Mendi* were only a few miles from the island.

At that moment Admiral Adelino Martins, the Brazilian Navy's Chief of Staff, chose to send a wireless signal to the island, *en clair*, which was intercepted by *Wolf*'s ever-alert operator. The Nerger luck was stranger than fiction! If that message had not been sent he would have sailed on innocently through the night, only to find himself anchored in full view of the Brazilians at dawn. Re-coaling at Trinidade Island was not an option. He turned his ships around. It was the night of 20–21 December, 1917, nearly thirteen months out of Kiel.

There was no other safe haven for thousands of miles, and there was nothing for it but to heave-to away from the shipping lanes and coal from the Spaniard in the open sea. But the weather was boisterous and the seas were heavy. The two ships steamed around aimlessly, waiting for calmer conditions. They waited in vain. Then it was Christmas. The crew celebrated the occasion noisily, and the prisoners enjoyed, if that is the right word, an extra issue of the dreary tinned crab and a cup of the *Maréchal Davout*'s wine. On Christmas afternoon Nerger decided that, swell or no swell, he must have coal, and Leutnant Rose brought the *Igotz Mendi* alongside.

In any other circumstances such a manoeuvre could have only been described as suicidal. The sides of the two ships met with such tremendous impact that Roy Alexander, in the sick-bay again, was thrown from his cot, landing in a heap on the deck. The coalless *Wolf* was much larger than her heavily laden companion and therefore sat much higher in the water. Each time they crashed together it was the Spaniard who came off worst. Her boats were damaged, her davits and upper-works were twisted and one enormous crash stove in the wing of her bridge. In the holds of the collier the heavers struggled to keep their feet as they flung the coal into the baskets and it was hoisted up through the hatches to be swung over and dumped in untidy heaps all along *Wolf*'s deck. To get it aboard, anyhow, was all that mattered. The crews of each ship watched and prayed as the thousands of tons of steel and coal swung away from each other and then hurtled together again with mighty crashes. Every available fender hung over their sides, but they provided no protection at all. Plates buckled. Rivets popped. It went on all night. By morning they had managed to transfer five hundred tons.

In itself, this was a miracle, but *Wolf*, now caked with wet coal-dust and with great dents in her sides, as if she had been kicked by a giant's boots, was leaking badly. Twenty tons of seawater were entering the parted seams in her hull every hour. The pumps could cope with this, but she would still need to coal again long before she reached the Kattegat. Nerger pointed her bows homeward. Perhaps the weather would be kinder nearer the equator.

New Year's Day, 1918, came and went as the ships laboured northwards. *Wolf* was hampered severely by her condition, making barely seven knots. Scurvy was now rampant in the prisoners' hold, mainly affecting the men from the *Turritella, Jumna, Wordsworth* and *Dee,* who had suffered there the longest. The weather was warmer, but still the sea ran high.

On 4 January the tops of some sails were spotted, alternately appearing and disappearing from view as the grey horizon fell and rose. Nerger was preoccupied with getting his ship home. He had chalked up enough conquests to please the Kaiser. Flying the British Red Ensign, he exchanged the usual compliments by signal with the big four-masted stranger as she drew near, wearing a large Norwegian flag painted on her sides. Each passed on their way.

But Nerger felt uneasy. In her damaged condition, *Wolf*'s disguise as a British merchantman was not as convincing as it should have been. If the Norwegian was suspicious, and reported having seen him when she arrived in port, then his already slim chances of reaching Germany would surely disappear. By now she would be only an hour or so astern. He hoisted German colours, turned round and caught her up. She was the *Storo Brore*, 2,000 tons, bound from Martinique to Montevideo in ballast. Her surprised and bewildered captain and crew were somehow squeezed into the hold of the raider and, without more ado, she was sunk by time bombs in her bottom. As a neutral ship, her sinking was illegal, but Nerger excused himself on the absurd basis that she had once long ago been the British *Afon Alaw*.

They lumbered on for another week and were now well north of the equator. In another few days they would be crossing the busy east-west North Atlantic sea-lanes. To stop anywhere in those latitudes to take on the coal she needed would be suicidally dangerous. She would have to do it here and now. But *still* the calm seas that Nerger prayed for had not materialized.

Again Rose brought the battered *Igotz Mendi* alongside. Again the ships hurled themselves against each other with frame-shuddering crashes as basket after basket of coal swayed its way over on to the pitching deck. Again plates buckled and rivets popped. Round the clock this terrifying mutual mutilation went on until another five hundred tons had been taken. At long last they swung apart. The *Igotz*'s side had been scraped bare of paint for her full length and the starboard wing of her tipsy bridge seemed as if it was about to fall in the sea. As for the *Wolf*, she now had enough coal to make it home. Great heaps were burying her guns and deck machinery. But she was in a sorry state, leaking forty tons of water every hour.

The ships parted company, each to take its own chance of a successful run through the blockade. The women on board the Spaniard waved goodbye tearfully, convinced that their friends on board the prison ship were destined to drown even before they ran the gauntlet.

Wolf was labouring now, steaming at no more than seven knots as she wallowed through the rollers. The weather had not relented for weeks. On the contrary, it had worsened, and soon the howling wind had whipped the sea up into a never-ending range of tumbling piles over

238

which she slid and shuddered from one to the next. And the farther north she clawed her way, so the gales intensified into storm and hurricane forces. In fact, the atrocious conditions in the North Atlantic in January, 1918, were to be remembered by seamen as the most awful in living memory.

For all its discomfort, for Nerger the ugly weather was a blessing in disguise. In such mountainous seas, in the middle of an ocean, a ship is but a very small thing. The chances of *Wolf* being seen by a Royal Navy cruiser were greatly lessened in these conditions. She would be even less likely to be spotted and torpedoed by one of her own U-boats too, which would have been an ironic end. These would not be hunting in mid-ocean in this weather. In fact, he knew that they were scavenging in packs around the western entrance to the English Channel and off the Irish coast, because *Wolf*'s wireless operator, eavesdropping anxiously, had picked up several distress calls from their victims. Nerger kept well to the west, out of the way of all this drama, retracing the steps he had made on his outward journey.

But if not a cruiser or a U-boat, would it be the Atlantic itself that sealed the pirate's fate? Her plates had parted further and the pumps had become clogged with ashes and coal-dust. They were barely working at all. In her stokeholds the stokers struggled to keep their feet as they fed the furnaces with a flood of water slapping round their shins. And it was rising. She was rolling to a terrifying angle, scuppers awash, made worse by the water within her hull as it rushed from side to side. Her nose buried itself deep into each charging wall of black water, sending torrents of boiling foam racing along her deck. And she was listing. She could not stay afloat once the water got into her furnaces. The only chance of survival was to clear the pumps. They tried to dam the worst of the leaks with sacks, hammocks and bedding. Teams of men went down to try to clear the bilge pumps, working up to their waists in the freezing water. Outside, the hurricane had risen to a scream, shedding great licks of scud from the top of each surging hill of water. It was 27 January, 1918, the Kaiser's birthday.

The black *Wolf* celebrated the occasion by surviving. Her crew worked all night in the bilges, each team spending as long as it could in the icy water, deep in the guts of the lurching ship. By morning they had cleared the pumps and the worst of the weather seemed to have blown itself out. She rode more easily now, even increasing her speed by a knot or so.

She was now well north of the latitude of Scotland and snow was falling, bringing visibility down to no more than a few paces and burying her decks and upperworks in a thick blanket. Then the snow turned to freezing sleet and the ship's snowy duvet became a sheath of glistening ice. Huge icicles hung from her upper-works and all along her rails. And they caught their last glimpse of the *Igotz Mendi*. She too was in a bad way and Nerger sent across some extra clothing in a boat, but to loiter here was dangerous. He left her and hurried on into the Denmark Strait, to go north of Iceland and butt his way through the ice-packs.

The prisoners, now all battened down in their hold, listened anxiously as the floes bumped and jolted along the sides of the ship with increasing frequency. Would one of them turn out to be not ice, but a mine? Had they come all this way to be blown to smithereens? They tried to keep cheerful. Somehow or other, a decrepit piano had been saved from the *Matunga* and somebody had a concertina. There were singsongs with all the old sailors' ditties and even a comic act or two. But one of their company had been in torment ever since his ship had been taken. The Japanese Captain Tominaga, overcome with remorse for the clumsy way in which he had handled the *Hitachi Maru*, causing so many innocent deaths, could no longer cope with his mental anguish. He jumped overboard into the freezing sea, to an almost instant end.

The scurvy cases lay in their dozens on the mattresses on the deck in the 'hospital' section, still attended by the intrepid Staff Sergeant Webb. Webb was a shining example of devotion to duty. Clad in a ragged dressing-gown, and quivering with malaria himself, he seemed never to sleep, patiently plodding from patient to patient. The stench, intensified by the putrescence of the scurvy, was unspeakable. But thanks to Nerger's steam-pipes, at least it was warm.

Nerger knew of the problems of the winter ice-pack north of Iceland, but it was by far the safer route to take. If only he could find a way through. He bludgeoned his way through endless black openings in the white moonscape, only to find that every one was a dead end. It was no use. He turned back, forced to take the southern, and far more perilous, track.

A week's nail-biting journey lay ahead. At little more than walking pace *Wolf* crawled due east. She carried no identification marks and was a sitting target for a submarine of either side. Nerger had no recent charts of minefields and, for all he knew, he could have been sailing straight through one of them. How he avoided being challenged by a Royal Naval patrol was yet another miracle. But a miracle it was, because the welcoming coast of Norway came into sight. It was 14 February, 1918, fourteen and a half months out of Kiel.

Excitement grew as they slipped down the coast of Norway, safely in neutral waters, and into the Skaggerak the following day. Hardly any man on board, crew or prisoner, could sleep through such a time of tension. This stretch of water was the bottleneck through which ships had to pass to reach any of the Baltic ports. The Allies had effectively shut it up securely with heavy patrols and dense minefields, but there was clearly a flaw somewhere in their operation because *Wolf* proceeded unchallenged – straight through. It was truly another miracle.

Into the Kattegat, between Sweden and Denmark. This was the Baltic! Or as good as. They were going to live and a German prison camp was infinitely preferable to an icy grave in the North Atlantic or being blown sky-high by a mine in the Skaggerak. A German cruiser, low and grey, slid towards the black stranger, demanding identification. SMS *Wolf?* It was impossible. This could not be *Wolf*. She had not been heard of for over a year. They had given her up for lost many months ago. But it was. It was SMS *Wolf!*

Other ships arrived to escort her into German waters. Nearly four hundred prisoners, all those who were fit enough, spent a very pleasant Sunday morning on deck enjoying the cool fresh air as they watched Denmark slide past. It was the first time that many of them had seen any land outside the tropics. It was 17 February, 1918.

The surprised Kaiser was beside himself with joy. Every member of the raider's crew was to be presented with the Iron Cross, but, ever one for theatricals, he issued orders that Nerger was to wait until a suitably festive greeting was arranged for his ship before bringing her into Kiel. She anchored in Flensburg Fjord, spending a whole week there while men swarmed all over her travel-stained and battered body, scraping away the rust and giving her a gleaming new coat of black paint. The little *Wölfchen* was not to be forgotten. She was hoisted up, re-assembled, renovated and installed in her old position on top of Number Three Hatch cover. The ship's doctor, who had guided Staff Sergeant Webb in his care of the scurvy cases, ordered an immediate supply of fresh food for them. This arrived in the form of a load of rhubarb, which was the best that a half-starved Germany could do. In exchange, the prisoners were delighted to offer generous donations of the despised tinned crab.

At last came the day for the grand entrance. Nerger weighed anchor for the last time and *Wolf*, wearing a large Ensign and a long paying-off pennant, set off through the winter mist on the short final leg of her epic voyage. Nearer Kiel, she steamed through a double line of warships, some of them veterans of Jutland which had been brought through the canal from Wilhelmshaven to greet her. Battle-cruisers, light cruisers and a host of smaller ships and U-boats, all were there. Bands blared out triumphant music from the decks of the larger ships and hundreds of sailors lined the decks to cheer wildly, forgetting for the moment the festering grievances that would soon lead them to mutiny at this very port. And Nerger's crew, now in new uniforms and wearing *Wolf* cap tallies for the first time in admission of their true identity, waved and cheered back. Fire boats in the harbour sent jets of water arching into the sky and blew their hooters. Small boats crammed with sightseers came out in their dozens, causing fears of collision. Still more crowds flocked to the Kiel shoreline. And, to add a final touch to the scene, the *Wölfchen* took to the sky once more, to perform a lap of honour around the mastheads of her proud parent.

Nerger brought *Wolf* to anchor alongside some distinguished company. There was the Kaiser's yacht, *Hohenzollern*, waiting for her, with the flagship *Bayern* and none other than her fellow raider, the famous *Möwe*. It was 24 February, 1918, a week short of fifteen months after she had quietly slipped away from this place to steam 64,000 miles.

The *Igotz Mendi*? She came to the end of her voyage on the same day as *Wolf*. But it was not in Kiel. In dense fog, the same soggy curtain that had screened *Wolf* on her way through the Skaggerak, she went aground at the very northernmost tip of Denmark, at the Skaw. Leutnant Rose, dressed in civilian clothes, tried to hoodwink the Danes into believing that he was a merchant captain, bound from Bergen to Kiel, and asked for a tug to pull him off. It was a noble effort, but it failed to convince the Danes, and when their boarding party heard the prisoners shouting for help and making as much noise as possible the game was up. The Spanish crew and the prisoners were placed in the care of their various consuls and the German naval prize crew were taken into internment.

For the prisoners it was an uncertain time. Their feelings were understandably mixed. They had been paraded on the deck of the raider as she had come to anchor, like trophies won in the hunt, which indeed they were. On the other hand, they were glad to be alive. They were sent to various camps and hospitals, each with their individual memories of their cruise through hell. Roy Alexander said that, strangely, he had almost ceased to think of the *Wolf* as an enemy ship. She had brought him safely through hell, and he always remembered her, sitting quietly at last in her berth in Kiel, dignified and famous.

As for Karl Augustus Nerger, this heroic leader of men, often fiery, but never losing his sense of purpose, never shrinking from the need to make hard decisions, but always tempered with humanity, and surely one of the greatest seamen ever to set sail, was given Germany's highest accolade, the blue enamel cross of the Pour le Mérite; an extra 800 marks a month (soon to be almost worthless) and appointed to the command of the North Sea division of Armed Trawlers. According to many, this was regarded as the worst job in the German Navy.

POSTSCRIPT. As was the case with all the "Q-ships" of both sides, the exact amount of tonnage destroyed or damaged by *Wolf*'s exploits can never be known for sure. The minefields she laid were still doing their work long after she had left each region. One victim, the Huddart Parker passenger liner *Wimmera*, did not meet her fate until long after the raider was back in Kiel. She was commanded by the criminally obstinate Captain Kell, who insisted on sailing through a known minefield. Bound for Sydney, she went down off Auckland on 16 June, 1918, with the loss of twenty-seven lives, including that of her mulish captain.

Many of *Wolf*'s victims have already been mentioned in the story, but the minefields also claimed those in the following list. Almost certainly there were still more, although strangely there seems to be no record of any damage being caused by Nerger's mines laid off Singapore.

Off South Africa:
City of Athens. 5,600 tons. Sunk August 1917.
Bhamo. 3,250 tons. Damaged August 1917.
Ciudad de Fizaguirre. Spanish vessel. Sunk.

Off Bombay:
Croxteth Hall. 3,900 tons. Sunk June 1917.
City of Exeter. 9,400 tons. Damaged June 1917.
Mongolia. 9,300 tons. Sunk June 1917.
Unkai Maru. Japanese vessel. Sunk.

Off Australia and New Zealand:
Cumberland. 9,600 tons. Sunk July 1917.
Port Kembla. 5,000 tons. Sunk September 1917
Wimmera. 3,500 tons. Sunk July 1918.

Chapter 18

The Eagle of the Sea

The *Pass of Balmaha* was a beautiful clipper ship, 1,600 tons, 275 feet long and with room on her lofty masts for a huge cloud of canvas to push her along at a brisk rate of knots. She had been built in Scotland by Duncan & Co in 1888 for the River Plate Shipping Company. Sometime in 1915, then American-owned, she was on a run from New York to Archangel with a cargo of cotton when, approaching European waters, she was stopped by a British patrol vessel. Before allowing her through the blockade, the Royal Navy decided to escort her into Scapa Flow for inspection. On the way they were ambushed by a U-boat. The cotton being too valuable a commodity to send to the bottom of the sea, especially in wartime Germany, the submarine captain put a prize crew on board with orders to sail her to Cuxhaven.

A sailing ship needs no coal. Its only requirement is a breath of wind, which comes in ample if unreliable supply on the oceans of the world. Therefore, its range is limited only by the amount of food and water which it can carry to sustain the crew. It followed that, suitably disguised, a sailing ship would make an ideal commerce raider for Germany, free of the constant worries about fuel that the coal-burners carried with them, and able to operate for long periods many thousands of miles from any friendly port. It is surprising that nobody within the Imperial German Navy appears to have thought of this before 1916.

When at last the suggestion was made, the idea was taken up with enthusiasm. They would create a classic example of a decoy raider. Her disguise would be superb. She would be manned by crack, selected personnel. She would be comfortable as far as possible, in view of the huge distances she would be required to travel. She would be crammed to the gunwales with ingenious gadgetry. Orders were issued to select a suitable candidate for conversion and put the job in hand. They chose the *Pass of Balmaha*.

They took her round to Bremerhaven, put her in dry-dock with a guard of armed blue-jackets around her and went to work. Her after-hold became an engine-room. A 1,000 horse-power diesel engine was lowered through the hatch to drive the single propeller which now hung under her stern. Now she would not always be solely dependent on the wind, but with her auxiliary engine thrusting her along at nine knots when need be, she would be able to approach her victims from several miles off, in even a calm sea. Skilled carpenters and metalworkers installed a baffling array of false bulkheads and doors. It was only through one of these that access to the secret engine-room could be gained. More panelling hid her diesel and fresh water tanks. Accommodation for her crew and their prisoners was to be roomy and spacious enough for her to carry 400 of the latter. The space forward of the engine-room in the after-hold was converted into cabins for the officers and hung with hammocks for the men. It was also to serve as a hiding place for the extra crew if she were to be stopped for inspection by the British. And nestling amidships, under tarpaulin covers, were two 4.2 inch guns.

The main architect of all this inventiveness was the man who was to be her captain. His name was Count Felix Von Luckner, a thirty-four year-old aristocrat from Halle, whose family had a long military tradition. At the age of thirteen he had run away to sea after quarrelling with his father, a straight-backed Prussian cavalryman, over his ambition to follow a naval career. The cavalry was not for Felix. He vowed never to return until he became a naval officer.

Calling himself Phelax Luedige (his mother's maiden name) he sailed the seven seas for seven years in all manner of merchant ships from giant windjammers downwards. The tales of his adventures, which he would relate with relish, were doubtless embroidered with the imagination that all sailors possess when spinning a yarn under a swinging lamp in mid-ocean. If they were only half-true they would still be astounding. He had fallen into the sea from the top-mast of a Russian square-rigger and would have drowned, but managed to hold on to the foot of a passing albatross until help arrived. He had jumped ship in Australia and worked as an assistant lighthouse-keeper, had been a boxer and a kangaroo hunter and had worked in a troupe of Hindu fakirs. He had even sold religious pamphlets for the Salvation Army. He had gone back to sea, been shipwrecked, been in jail in Vancouver, nearly been murdered in Hawaii, had missed his ship in Tampico, had served as a Presidential guard in Mexico City and had been jailed again in Chile for stealing a pig.

On one voyage, it was true, he had nearly died of scurvy when the four-masted British windjammer *Pinmore*, bound from Vancouver to Liverpool, ran out of food and water while trying to battle her way round the Horn. Another trip, from Havana to Australia and back to Liverpool in a Norwegian ship, was to have a lasting influence on his later life, as will be seen, because in the course of the long voyage he became fluent in the language of his shipmates.

In 1901 he returned to Germany, took a course in navigation, joined the Navy and obtained his commission. Phelax Luedige ceased to exist. He could be Felix Von Luckner again and return home. His family had long ago posted him as a missing person and were amazed when the maid announced a visitor and a Naval Lieutenant, in full dress uniform, entered the room.

Luckner worked and studied hard to advance his career, eventually becoming a favourite of the Kaiser by way of a strange piece of opportunism. He had learned various conjuring tricks when travelling around Australia with the band of fakirs, and once, at a party in honour of various dignitaries, he calmly produced an egg from the inside coat pocket of the King of Italy! From then on Luckner could do no wrong in the eyes of the Emperor.

Having been awarded his captain's certificate, he fought in the Battle of Heligoland, and at Jutland, where he was wounded, he was Gunnery Officer in the battleship *Kronprinz*. Once recovered, and no doubt due to influence from the Kaiser, the German Admiralty decided that they had no officer better suited to take charge of a sailing ship about to embark on a hazardous mission. He was appointed to take charge of the *Pass of Balmaha*, which, for the time being, for the sake of prying eyes in the dockyard, had been called the *Walter*.

Soon she was to be famous under another name, SMS *Seeadler* – the Sea Eagle. Luckner set about completing her disguise. *Seeadler* was to pose as a Norwegian. Luckner spoke the language perfectly and selected a couple of dozen officers and ratings who could also speak it. One of them, a seaman named Heinrich Hinz, recalled, "The crew dressed like Norwegian seamen with Trasko wooden shoes, thick woollen Icelander sweaters and blue shipmen's caps, and carried Norwegian tobacco, Skraa chewing tobacco and above all Norwegian identity papers. Many suddenly got 'fiancées' in Norway who wrote letters full of longing. We grew beards and took Norwegian names."

Luckner, a pipe smoker, gave up his pipe to practise the 'art' of chewing tobacco, a well-known habit among Norwegian sailors. He said, "A chew of tobacco gives you time to think. If somebody asks you an embarrassing question, you can roll the quid around in your mouth, pucker up your lips slowly, and spit deliberately and elegantly."

It being a common custom for the wives of the masters of merchant ships to accompany their husbands to sea, a youthful Norwegian-speaking German sailor, "that rascal Schmidt," was fitted out with a blonde wig and a dress to act Luckner's spouse "Josephine".

At last, with all her machinery, barometers and compasses stamped with the names of Norwegian or Danish manufacturers, pictures of the Queen of Norway and King Edward VII gazing from the panelled bulkheads in the captain's cabin and her galley well stocked with Scandinavian food, *Seeadler* slipped away from Bremerhaven. Only a few miles offshore, she rendezvoused with a tug pulling a couple of lighters laden with timber. The final touch was to be added to her disguise – her "cargo". Great piles of sawn planks, each stamped with the name of a Norwegian timbermill, were swung over by boom-hoist, to be stacked along her deck and on top of the hatches in the usual fashion of timber cargoes, and carefully arranged so as to hide her motor-boats and guns. She was ready.

At last, under her tobacco-chewing, hard-swearing "Captain Knudson", she made for the open sea, allegedly bound from Norway to Melbourne with her cargo of timber. About 180 miles south-east of Iceland she ran into a British patrol in the shape of the auxiliary cruiser HMS *Avenger*, which ordered her to stop. "Knudson" invited the boarding officers to his cabin to inspect his papers, adding a suitable string of sailorly Norwegian oaths. They found it full of acrid kerosene smoke and "Josephine" prostrate on a bunk with a large scarf tied over her blonde head, moaning pitiably. "Knudson" apologized to the British officer for the smoke. He was having problems with his stove and, on top of this, his wife had toothache. In response to the officer's apologies for disturbing her, "Josephine" played her part with brilliance and came in on cue with a shrill "Aargh!" "Have a drink, Mister Officer," invited "Knudson", "Always give a British sailor a drink, or

1.	*Gladys Royale*, 9 January, 1917	8.	*British Yeoman*, 26 February, 1917
2.	*Lundy Island*, 10 January, 1917	9.	*Rochefoucauld*, 27 February, 1917
3.	*Charles Gounod*, 21 January, 1917	10.	*Dupleix*, 5 March, 1917
4.	*Perce*, 24 January, 1917	11.	*Horngarth*, 11 March, 1917
5.	*Antonin*, 3 January, 1917	12.	*A.B. Johnson*, 8 June, 1917
6.	*Buenos Aires*, 9 February, 1917	13.	*R.C. Slade*, 18 June, 1917
7.	*Pinmore*, captured 19 February,	14.	*Manila*, 8 July, 1917
	sunk early March, 1917	15.	*Seeadler*, wrecked 2 August, 1917

a German sailor, or an American sailor, or any kind of sailor . . .". The drinks were poured and the papers examined. All was in order and the British officer bade "Knudson" farewell. HMS *Avenger* steamed off, leaving a boiling wake and signalling an innocent "bon voyage" as she went. It was Christmas Day, 1916.

Once in the wide expanse of the North Atlantic, *Seeadler* did not have to wait long before she met her first victim. The 3,300-ton collier *Gladys Royale* was ploughing down to Argentina from Cardiff, full of good Welsh coal. It was ironic that *Seeadler* should have no use for such a cargo and that she should find such a mountain of it on her first "kill". The *Gladys*'s captain, W.S. Shewan, had no reason to be alarmed as the harmless-looking "Norwegian" sailing ship approached on her starboard bow, with signals fluttering which asked for chronometer time. This was not at all unusual. Elderly sailing ships often did not have a decent chronometer, or wireless, and would check with passing steamers. The British captain slowed, in order to grant the requested favour. It was then that he received the surprise order to stop and saw that the German ensign had replaced the Norwegian flag at the stranger's masthead. When a shot exploded across his bows, he decided to make a run for it. He turned up-wind to escape from the raider, assuming that she had only her sails to drive her, and rang down the order "Full ahead". But he was well within range of Luckner's guns, and the German had taken in his sails and started his diesel engine. Shots from *Seeadler*'s 4.2s straddled the merchant ship. Three shells hit her, aft, one of which set Shewan's cabin on fire. Wisely, he decided that the *Gladys* had insufficient speed to escape and hove-to. As his crew were shown below to the hold which was to become their quarters he told Luckner, "You fooled me bloody well". That night explosive charges ripped out the collier's bottom and, amid clouds of steam and smoke, she went down to settle on the seabed 100 miles east of the Azores. It was 9 January, 1917.

The next day more smoke was seen on the horizon. It was another British freighter, the 3,000-ton *Lundy Island*, with sugar from Martinique to Nantes. Again, Luckner signalled asking for chronometer time, but this time the steamer ignored the request and kept on course. In fact, she was heading straight for the bandit, in blatant contravention of the "rules of the road" which gave "sail" the right of way. Luckner managed to avoid the collision by veering away at the last minute, and at the same time hoisted his German colours and fired warning shots. The British ship turned to run, but received shells at point-blank range, holing her side and funnel. That was enough for her captain, David Barton, and he decided to surrender. He stopped his engines and ran to the galley with his confidential ship's papers to stuff them on the fire.

There was a strange coincidence in connection with the capture and sinking of the *Lundy Island*. It turned out that Barton had been suspicious of *Seeadler* as she approached and had good reason to be more worried than most. He had already lost one ship, the *Corbridge*, to the raider *Möwe*, as we have seen, and had given his parole that he would not engage in further wartime activity at sea. Understandably, he was apprehensive about being caught again and could picture himself being strung up from a yardarm for breaking his word. His horror can be imagined when he came face to face with *Seeadler*'s medical officer, who had been serving aboard *Möwe* and who knew him well. But Luckner, always chivalrous and respectful of human life, did not hang Barton. Instead, he sent him below to join the other prisoners, where he was to spend many hours playing chess with the captain of the *Gladys Royale*.

And while Luckner was making his first two "kills" in the sunshine, the helpless Q-ship *Mary Mitchell* was being battered by the elements 1,000 miles away to the north-east, as she awaited rescue and a tow into the safety of Brest.

For some days, Luckner sailed steadily south, but no traffic was seen. The ocean appeared to be deserted. Eager to add to his score, he offered a £25 reward and a bottle of champagne to the first man to sight a ship. His crew, joined by the British prisoners, even the captains, all clung to the raider's rigging, scouring the horizon with binoculars and telescopes. "Never," he laughed, "has a ship had such a good lookout!" It was not until 21 January, in the narrowest part of the Atlantic, where the westward bulge of Africa reaches out towards the eastward point of Brazil, and only a couple of days before *Wolf's* first victims were to meet their fate in Nerger's minefields off Cape Town, 3,000 miles away, that a sail was spotted. *Seeadler* was about to embark on an orgy of destruction.

In the space of the next forty-eight days, and all in an area of the Atlantic no bigger than the British Isles, the German was to sink no fewer than nine Allied merchant ships. The first was the 2,250-ton French barque *Charles Gounod*, with grain for Bordeaux, sunk on 21 January. Then, three days later, came a little Canadian schooner, the 370-ton *Perce*, which was rolling down to Brazil from Halifax with a cargo of dried fish and timber.The *Perce's* captain, Carl Kohler, had married shortly before sailing and was accompanied by his wife. Luckner, chivalrous as ever, sent his motor launch over to collect the happy couple and installed them in a special state room for the continuance of their honeymoon!

On 3 February *Seeadler* met the big French windjammer *Antonin*, 3,100 tons, with saltpetre for Brest. The Frenchman decided to try to outsail her, but by crowding on all sail the bandit overhauled him and a burst of machine-gun fire was enough to secure another capture. The following week, on 9 February, the 1,000-ton Italian sailing vessel *Buenos Aires*, bound for Gibraltar with a cargo of saltpetre, went to the bottom.

And on 19 February, at the same time as Lieutenant Frank and his *Lady Olive* crew were rowing their open boat wearily through the grey Channel drizzle, a situation arose in the South Atlantic which was to affect Luckner greatly, tearing him between his natural emotions as a

251

seaman and his duty as a patriot. *Seeadler* met the *Pinmore*, the same *Pinmore* in which he had sailed as a youth named Phelax Luedige. He had rounded Cape Horn in her, suffered from scurvy in her, learned much of his seamanship, and gained much respect for British sailors in her. And now she was his captive, a stately old lady, gently riding the mid-Atlantic swell as she sat awaiting her fate. After transferring her officers and crew to their quarters on board the raider, Luckner rowed over to the *Pinmore*, alone. With no one on board, the big ship was quiet. He walked around her decks, full of nostalgic thoughts. In the fo'c'lse, he found his old bunk. There was still a hook on the deck-head above it, on which he had hung a tin can to catch leaking drips. And on the stern rail he could just make out the carved words – Phelax Luedige. Sink her? No, a better plan occurred to him. He would sail in her again. He would take her to Rio!

He had learned from the *Pinmore*'s captain that her owners had no agents in Rio, and now that *Seeadler* had been at sea for some months she was low on certain items of stores, including fruit and vegetables. It was a bold plan, maybe forged through his own memories of the scurvy. And so, leaving his own ship to meander around the equator with a heavily armed guard over the prisoners, he sailed the old *Pinmore* into Rio. With his arm in a sling to excuse the clumsy copying of the signature of the real captain, Mullen, he hoodwinked the Brazilian customs officers and was allowed ashore to order his supplies. Whilst there, he struck up a conversation with a British officer from the cruiser *Glasgow*, which was in port taking on coal, who warned him about a raider which had been operating in the Atlantic and told him that the cruiser was about to sail, in company with her sister HMS *Amethyst*, to try to track the pirate down. Thus warned, and with plenty of fruit and vegetables, 350 lbs of tobacco, 20,000 cigarettes and 50 boxes of cigars on board, he hurried back to rendezvous with *Seeadler*. He stripped the *Pinmore* of everything of value and, with a heavy heart, sent his demolition crew over to her. Two dull explosions told him that they had done their job. He had locked himself alone in his cabin, unable to watch as she went down.

It is recorded that *Seeadler* sank two more windjammers on 26 and 27 February, the 2,000-ton Canadian *British Yeoman* (whose captain's wife, Mrs Neilson, was on board and thus became the second woman among the prisoners) and the 2,200-ton French barque *La Rochefoucauld*. As the *Pinmore* had only been captured five days beforehand, then went to Rio, and was not sunk until the early days of March, if these date are accurate, we can only assume that both these ships were destroyed in Luckner's absence. This may also have been the case with another French square-rigger, the 2,250-ton *Dupleix*, sunk on 5 March. She too had been carrying saltpetre for the French munitions industry.

The balance of probability is that Luckner returned to *Seeadler*, learned of the further 'kills' she had made, disposed of the *Pinmore* and was in the process of running away to find new and safer pastures when he ran across the 3,650-ton British Admiralty chartered steamer *Horngarth*, laden with Argentinian corn for Plymouth. This was too valuable a target to pass by, but the *Horngarth* boasted a 5-inch gun and a glance at her masts told him that she was fitted with wireless. He adopted his standard approach, asking for a chronometer check. When there was no answer, he placed pans full of burning kerosene on top of his deckhouses and hoisted a distress signal amid the clouds of smoke and leaping flames. No ship's captain can ignore another vessel on fire at sea. The steamer came alongside and hove-to. It was of vital importance to put her wireless out of action quickly. A distraction was required while the German gunners brought their 4.2s to bear on the *Horngarth*'s wireless office. And so the lovely "Josephine", her seaboots hidden by a long elegant gown, minced along the raider's deck, waving at the steamer's crew as they lined the rails to ogle her. At that Luckner ran up the German ensign and opened fire. It was at point-blank rage and the wireless office was demolished by a direct hit. The British sailors ran to man their own gun, but Luckner pulled another clever bluff. He had ordered three men aloft, armed with megaphones. At a sign from him, they all shouted, "Torpedoes clear!" He had no such weapon, but the trick worked. The *Horngarth*'s captain, I.N. Stainthorp, surrendered and his ship was consigned to the deep.

On the same day, far to the north, *Möwe* was licking her wounds and burying her dead after the fight with the *Otaki*, and in another ocean *Wolf* was watching the *Wordsworth*'s plain black funnel disappearing towards the sea bed with her cargo of rice. It was 11 March, 1917.

There was a sad element for Luckner in the taking of the *Horngarth*. One of her officers was badly wounded by a flying shell splinter and later died on board the raider. The Germans buried him with full honours, wrapped in a Union Jack. For the rest of his life, until he died in 1966 at the age of eighty-five, it would be Luckner's proud boast that he and his men had destroyed millions of pounds worth of Allied shipping and materials, but they had only caused this one death, and that was by accident.

Nearly a fortnight had slipped by since Luckner had spoken to the helpful officer from the *Glasgow* in Rio. Clearly it was pushing his luck to tarry in these parts any longer. He headed for Cape Horn and the Pacific. By now he had nearly three hundred prisoners to feed and a lengthy voyage ahead. This was going to cause a problem. But on 21 March he found a solution to it in the form of yet another saltpetre-laden French barque, the 1,900-ton *Cambronne*. Her captain was astonished to learn that his ship was not to be sunk. Instead, Luckner sawed off the tops of her masts to slow her down, dumped most of her cargo into the sea and transferred his prisoners to her. Then he placed Captain Mullen of the *Pinmore* in command, with instructions to sail her to Rio. As a parting gesture, he assembled the captured officers for a glass of wine before wishing them good luck, giving Mullen a Red Ensign to fly and returning to him a photograph of his family which the prize crew had taken from the *Pinmore* master's cabin. He thanked the men for the work they had done on board the raider, repairing sails and so on, and was pleased to pay a total of £800 sterling for their labours.

Thousands of miles away, in an ice-bound Baltic, Prince Henry of Prussia was boarding SMS *Möwe* to accompany Dohna-Schlodien on his second triumphant return to Kiel.

Mullen was unable to believe his luck as the handicapped square-rigger laboured her way towards Rio with 300 free and happy souls on board. Once there, he handed command back to her real captain and hurried to inform the British naval authorities that Luckner was headed for the Pacific. Immediately the cruisers *Lancaster*, *Otranto* and *Orbita* were ordered to leave the Peruvian and Chilean ports where they were berthed and to sail south to intercept him.

If Luckner, ever decent and respectful, had not interrupted his flight to pause near the Falkland Islands to hold a memorial service for Von Spee's East Asiatic Squadron, which, bar a couple of ships, had been wiped out there by the British in 1914, *Seeadler* may well have been caught by HMS *Orbita*. As it was, the cruiser did not patrol off Cape Horn as ordered, but carried on eastwards, well past the Islas de los Estados, and Luckner, now with storm-force winds astern which pushed his ship along at breakneck speed, had already been blown well over a hundred miles to the south of the Cape. He was unable to turn the corner to proceed northwards into the Pacific until the weather eased and could do nothing more than continue beating to the westward and wait. By the time the wind dropped at last, he had made a giant stride to the west. If it had abated a few days earlier his course may have brought him smack into contact with *Otranto* or *Lancaster*, which were belching smoke and sparks as they charged southwards down the west coast of South America. When at last Luckner was able to turn north, on 21 April, 1917, he was well to the west of the coast of Chile. Neither German captain was to know it, but on this day *Wolf* and *Seeadler* had been actually facing each other across the thousands of miles of the bleak wastes of the Southern Ocean. The British cruisers racing to catch Luckner were still far away, somewhere off Valdivia, hundreds of miles up the Chilean coast. And the *Seeadler* was at large in the Pacific.

It was a pleasant time for the raider's crew. For several weeks they roamed among the islands of Melanesia and Polynesia in mid-Pacific. These islands are numbered in their thousands and, although many were uninhabited, each island group was under the control of one of the enemies of Germany, and vigilance was ever-important. Nevertheless, it was good to meander through this tropical paradise after the harsh conditions they had endured.

Their Pacific 'catch' was unimpressive compared to their massive haul of ships in the Atlantic. The net bag was just three small American schooners, all bound for Australia. These were the *A.B. Johnson*, 550 tons, sunk on 8 June, the *R.C. Slade*, 690 tons, sunk on 18 June, and the 750-ton *Manila*, which was sent to the bottom on 8 July. It had been four months since they had sunk the *Horngarth*. It was a paltry score, and *Seeadler*'s men were no different from any other sailors; they needed some shore leave.

Luckner's second problem was that he was low on supplies again, especially of fruit and vegetables. And to complicate the situation, beriberi and the dreaded scurvy had broken out on board. He had no alternative but to find a lonely atoll and take a chance by anchoring to allow his men to go ashore and obtain food. Indeed, except for those who had accompanied him to Rio in the *Pinmore*, they had not set foot on dry land for over seven months. He pored over his charts and finally decided to make for Mopelia in the Society Islands, part of French Polynesia, straddling the 150 degrees west of Greenwich meridian about 1,000 miles south of the equator. About six miles long, with lush vegetation, Mopelia was not exactly uninhabited; there were a few native copra gatherers there, but it was visited only every three months or so by a ship which called to collect the harvest. It was worth the chance.

The passage into the lagoon was too small to allow *Seeadler* to enter, so Luckner dropped anchor outside the reef and his men went ashore by boat. They found that Mopelia was indeed a bower of plenty, and that night they dined on turtle soup, gulls' eggs, lobster and coconuts. Off another Pacific Island, 2,500 miles to the west in the Coral Sea, *Wolf* was waiting to ambush the *Matunga*. On the other side of the globe, in the hell of Flanders, the Third Battle of Ypres (Passchendaele) was taking place. It was 31 July, 1917.

For two days Luckner's men and their prisoners basked in the sun on Mopelia and feasted on tropical fare. Then, on 2 August, disaster struck *Seeadler*. There are two versions of what happened. According to the Germans, they were picknicking ashore while she lay at anchor, riding the ocean swell outside the reef, when they noticed what was described as a "bulge" on the horizon. In a matter of minutes the "bulge" had grown into a huge tidal wave which was racing towards them, accompanied by a howling wind. These phenomena are awesome in their power. They are quite capable of picking up even a railway truck and dumping it half a mile away. The few men on board tried to save their ship by starting the auxiliary diesel engine and running into the open sea, away from the coral reef. But they were too late. *Seeadler* was lifted high into the air and dashed down with such force on the hard coral that it broke her keel in five places, stove in her hull and brought down her masts and rigging in a hopeless tangle. However, the American prisoners did not agree with this story. They said that there was no storm, that there was no such tidal wave, and that it was quite simple. The sea was calm, but a strong tide was running, and the German captain, in a rare lapse of skill, had anchored his ship far too near to the treacherous reef to be safe. She had dragged her anchor and simply smashed onto the coral.

The only independent evidence to support either story is from the French weather records for Tahiti, a couple of hundred miles away to the south-east of Mopelia. These make no mention of any tidal waves in the area for the month of August, 1917, although that is by no means conclusive proof that Luckner was lying. But why should he lie, a man known for his integrity? As a master mariner, and veteran of so many tight situations, maybe he was simply embarrassed to have committed such an elementary *faux pas*. On the other hand, photographs of the damaged ship suggest that much more violence was involved than is likely to have been incurred under the force of any normal current. Whatever the truth, the fact was that *Seeadler*, super-bandit of the high seas, would pillage no more. And her German crew and their fifty prisoners, all Americans, were now marooned on a lonely atoll in the Pacific.

As Robinson Crusoe had done before them, they salvaged what they could from the wreck. Timbers, sails, tools, tobacco, provisions and what was left of the *Charles Gounod*'s wine, all were humped ashore in one of *Seeadler*'s boats, together with the wireless equipment and instruments. Soon a village of makeshift tents and hovels sprouted up, made of spars covered with sails and palm leaves. Wondering when, and if, they would ever see their homes again, the Americans dubbed their creations with names such as The Bowery and Broadway, while the Germans countered with a thoroughfare which they called Potsdammerplatz.

But the war was not over for Luckner. He was far from finished. On examining the ship's motor boats, he found that one of them was still seaworthy and decided to take her to sea with a small selected crew, capture the first ship that came along, bring her back to Mopelia to collect the others and resume raiding. He fitted her with a mast and set the sailmakers to work making sails from canvas salvaged from the wreck. Then he loaded her with provisions and weapons, and, with Leutnant Kircheiss as navigator, plus four sailors, set sail into the Pacific haze. They called her *Kronprinzessin Cecilie*. It was 22 August, 1917.

In the thirty-year-old Carl Kircheiss, Luckner had chosen well. One of a family of six children from Harburg, just south of Hamburg, Kircheiss had first gone to sea as a cabin boy in a windjammer at the age of fourteen, rising to be one of Germany's youngest sea captains by the time he was twenty-five. The assistance of such a man, a senior professional sailor in his own right, would be invaluable on the dangerous expedition on which they had embarked.

A little motor boat with six men and a machine gun would have had difficulty in capturing a large freighter, even if it were totally unarmed. The answer was to seek one of the small schooners which wandered around the South Sea Islands collecting copra and coconuts. One wonders why Luckner did not simply wait for the next one to visit

Mopelia itself and waylay it there. Maybe he was driven by impatience, or boredom, or both. Be that as it may, the little *Kronprinzessin Cecilie* sailed westward, for days without sighting another vessel. They had been confident of an early 'kill' and had not planned to be at sea this long. Indeed, provisions were running low when they sighted land. It was Atiu, in the Cook group, administered by New Zealand. Bold as brass, Luckner stepped ashore and asked the Resident Official to let him have some provisions, claiming that they were Dutch-American sailors who were crossing the Pacific in their small boat as part of a bet! He was given enough stores to sustain them for a few days, but, still having seen no ships, he put into Aitutaki, another of the Cook group, this time posing as Norwegians. Here, the Residential Official was suspicious, having spotted the weapons in the visitors' boat. Several local inhabitants urged him to arrest the Germans, but it could not be done. Astonishingly, the fact was that the local police possessed no guns themselves, such was the peaceable nature of the community. All the perplexed civil servant could do, therefore, was to give Luckner some stores, hold his tongue and hope that his 'guests' would soon leave. Eventually *Kronprinzessin Cecilie* did indeed sail away, well-stocked with food, but still seeking a ship to steal. It was not the last time, as will be seen, that Luckner would benefit from the lackadaisical attitude of New Zealand officialdom.

The Germans headed their tiny boat westward, on to the Fiji–Tahiti track. Surely this stretch of water would be busy enough to produce some results. But no. Still they met no schooners. And it was hot. On and on the *Cecilie* glided, between Tonga and Samoa. To be in a luxurious liner in these surroundings would be the fulfilment of the dreams of millions of ordinary people, but for Luckner and his men, in their open boat under the blazing tropical sun, it was sheer torture. Exhausted, scorched and blistered by sun and wind, and showing signs of scurvy, they eventually anchored at Wakaya, in the Fiji Islands. They had sailed 2,250 miles in *Seeadler*'s motor boat. It was 21 September, 1917.

Ashore, their story was that they were shipwrecked Norwegians, which was accepted as genuine by most of the locals. But one of them was not convinced. Sufficiently so, in fact, for him to hurry off to the police station at Levuka to inform the authorities of his fears. A party of policemen, with a Sub-Inspector Hills in charge, set out for Wakaya in a cutter to question the strangers, who had returned to their boat.

But before the police boat had gone far, bad weather blew up and she turned back. Now was the point at which the Germans' luck deserted them, because at that moment the little island steamer *Amra* was chugging into Levuka. Hills requisitioned her, and the following day he and his policemen set out, again for Wakaya. As they drew near, they saw the suspicious craft leaving harbour. The *Amra* lowered a boat and Hills and his men clambered in, all unarmed except for his own revolver. He cut across Luckner's bows and demanded that he identify himself. The German remained cool. "Who are you?" he replied in perfect English. But the policeman was not to be put off so easily. "I call on you to surrender," he shouted across the water, "I do not wish to parley."

Luckner hesitated, and that was enough for Hills. He told the German that if he did not surrender immediately the *Amra*'s gun would sink his boat. Luckner, with his wits no doubt blunted by the effects of his marathon journey, complied without further ado. For once the King of the Bluffers had been bluffed, because the steamer did not possess such a thing as a gun. Understandably, he was furious. The boot had been on the other foot all the time. At point-blank range, he could easily have mown down all the policemen in their cutter with the machine gun. As it was, Hills had not even drawn his revolver. Later, in custody on board the *Amra*, Luckner was heard to mutter, "We did not come all this way to be captured by an unarmed boat." On the contrary, that was exactly what they had done.

Meanwhile, back on Mopelia, the American prisoners were all alone, except for an army of big rats (such as inhabit many lonely tropical islands) which stole the fallen coconuts with surprising agility before the sailors could gather them. And the Germans? They had gone!

Leutnant Kling, who had been left in charge on the island, had occupied himself by listening to the wireless apparatus every day, scouring the wavelengths trying to pick up any Allied messages broadcast from Honolulu, Papeete, Tahiti or Pago Pago which might have had a bearing on their situation. Luckner had only been gone for ten days when the set crackled and pipped into life. It was an announcement that a search was to be mounted for the overdue *A.B. Johnson*. It appeared that the authorities were as yet unaware that the *R.C. Slade* and the *Manila* were even late, let alone at the bottom of the Pacific. Kling was alarmed. When the news erupted about the other two ships, a red-hot hue and cry would be set up. The time had come for them to leave Mopelia, and quickly. Kling inspected the other motor boat, but she was far from seaworthy. Luckner had taken the best one. They were trapped.

On 5 September salvation arrived. A little fore-and-aft rigged schooner, the 120-ton *Lutece*, came silently over the horizon from Papeete. Kling did not hesitate. He rowed out to meet her, climbed aboard and took her at gun-point. There had been no sign of Luckner for a fortnight and it was likely he had met with misfortune, which indeed was the case. He had already decided to go for glory by taking the first schooner that appeared, sail her round the Horn and home to Kiel. But the tiny *Lutece* could not take the Germans and Americans, plus her crew and three passengers, and enough food to sustain them, on a voyage of 16,000 miles.

The answer was simple. Only the Germans would go. And so, leaving the Americans and the little schooner's crew and passengers on Mopelia with some supplies and the crippled motor boat, Kling set sail for Cape Horn, home and the congratulations of the Kaiser.

It was soon apparent that the *Lutece* was shipping a good deal of water and Kling decided to put into the remote Easter Island, which sits on the Tahiti–Valparaiso sealane and is Chilean territory. Little seems to have been recorded of what happened next, except that she ran aground there. Whether the *Lutece* was still habitable, or whether they made some kind of shelter ashore, or were afforded hospitality, enforced or otherwise, by people already there we do not know. But we do know that they spent several months on Easter Island. *The Times* correspondent cabled from Valparaiso on 4 March, 1918: "A Chilean schooner arrived at Talcahuano yesterday from Easter Island bringing 58 members, officers and men, of the crew of the German raider *Seeadler*. The men state that they were wrecked at Easter Island when in the schooner *Fortuna*." *The Times* editor added a footnote, "There has hitherto been no intimation of the fate of the *Lutece*, nor of the raider having seized a vessel named *Fortuna*. There are 14 ships of that name in Lloyd's Register, two of which are known to be war losses."

(Note: By that stage of the war up-to-date editions of Lloyd's Register were far from 'reliable', intentionally, in top-secret co-operation with the Naval Censors).

According to most contemporary accounts, Kling and his men were taken to Chile and interned for the rest of the war. This would seem to be in keeping with what one might logically assume. However, *The Times* Valparaiso correspondent cabled again, on 11 March, 1918.

"The Chilean authorities confiscated the arms of the crew of the *Seeadler* on their arrival in this country. I am advised by a trustworthy source that the crew of the raider will be treated as shipwrecked sailors and not interned."

Meanwhile, on Mopelia, the Americans had not been idle. As soon as the *Lutece* departed they set about assessing their resources. Their food supply, mainly consisting of sugar, butter, tinned milk, molasses, weevil-infested flour and whatever coconuts they could steal from the rats, would not last for ever. And the Germans had not been foolish enough to leave behind the *Seeadler*'s wireless. As far as the castaways were aware, of course, both Luckner and Kling were still sailing the ocean. Captain Smith, master of the *A.B. Johnson*, inspected the boat they had been left by the Germans. Both Luckner and Kling had considered it to be unsound, and Smith could only agree with them. Nevertheless, he carried out some makeshift repairs which he hoped would be good enough, with some luck, to make the journey to Pago Pago in American Samoa. With crossed fingers and three men he set sail. It took ten days to make the 1,000-mile trip. They stepped ashore on American soil on 6 October, 1917.

The average person may feel that the story of SMS *Seeadler* should end at this point. With Smith reaching American Samoa, it took but little time to rescue the people on Mopelia. Kling and his men were in Chile, and Luckner was in prison in New Zealand. And the pirate ship, the Sea Eagle herself, was dead, spreadeagled on the coral reef, indeed like a giant mangled bird. But that would be to assume that Captain Count Felix Von Luckner was an average man. He was nothing of the kind, and never had been. He was not 'dead' when *Seeadler* was wrecked. And he was not 'dead' now. Not by a long chalk.

They had taken him and Leutnant Kircheiss to a prison camp on Motuihi Island, which sits in the Hauraki Gulf to the north of Auckland. There they found several other Germans who had been taken from Western Samoa when New Zealand seized it at the outbreak of war, and also a company of cadets from a German freighter interned at Pago Pago. Luckner's four blue-jackets were caged with other 'hard cases' on Somes Island, in Wellington Harbour, at the other end of North Island. It had been considered improper to incarcerate officers with such characters, and therefore Luckner and Kircheiss found themselves in the more homely environment of Motuihi. The New Zealand authorities had played a wrong card again.

Luckner did not plan to hang around in New Zealand for long. As far as he was concerned, he was a raider captain, and there was more raiding to be done. The surprising thing was how easy it was for him to escape from Motuihi. The camp commander, Lieutenant-Colonel Harcourt Turner, who had clearly been born in another age, was agreeable to some engineers among the prisoners overhauling his speedy motor-launch, the *Pearl*. They were even allowed to take it on 'test runs' around the harbour! By falsely claiming the boat's needs for parts, mostly by simply adding items to the requisition list after Turner had signed it, they assembled a tidy secret stock-pile of 'spares'. With access to the workshops, they managed to make a dummy machine-gun, compasses and a sextant out of half of an old steering-wheel. The prison library contained atlases from which some rough charts could be made. Above all, the commander even allowed his guards to cease carrying their rifles and patrol armed only with canes and whistles! His own sword was left in the orderly room. Luckner's men stole it.

At last all was ready for the break. The two German engineers, who by now were the regular 'drivers' of the *Pearl*, had the job of bringing the camp staff on and off the island, and simply did not return the boat to her usual moorings after one such run. Instead, they took her to a quiet spot further round the island where Luckner and the others were waiting. The alarm went up instantly and Turner tried to telephone Auckland. But Luckner was far too smart to have overlooked such a thing. He had cut the line.

The *Pearl*, now with Luckner, Kircheiss, one of the *Seeadler*'s bluejackets who had been sent up from Somes Island to act as the captain's batman, a few of the cadets and an ex-planter from Samoa named Albrecht on board, streaked up Hauraki Gulf towards Cape Colville and the open Pacific. Just around the point was the tiny Mercury Island. It was a perfect place to hide and watch the sea-traffic, in and out of Auckland, and wait for a schooner to steal. It was 14 December, 1917. Half a world away, in the blustery South Atlantic, *Wolf* was about to sink the *Maréchal Davout*, which was to provide Nerger with his Christmas dinner.

For two days, the German escapees lay in ambush on Mercury Island, but no ships came by. And then, two came along together; little coastal vessels laden with cargoes of sawn *rimu* timber, tripping northward up to the coast for Auckland. They were the *Rangi*, Captain Francis, and the *Moa*, Captain William Bourke, about five miles astern of her. For all the bungling mistakes made by his erstwhile captors, Luckner was about to commit a fatal error of his own. He put to sea in the motor-boat, with the New Zealand flag at her stern cracking in the stiff wind, and sped towards the ninety ton *Moa*. Captain Bourke saw the *Pearl* approaching, and hove-to. Luckner, accompanied by an escort (presumably armed with the dummy machine-gun), climbed aboard and announced to Bourke that he, his crew of four plus a boy, and his ship were all now prisoners of war to Germany. The skipper looked at the motor-boat riding alongside, and saw that she now wore the German Ensign.

Taking the *Pearl* in tow, the *Moa* then turned about and headed north-north-east towards the Kermadecs, once a favourite hide-out of a certain Karl Augustus Nerger. That was where Luckner made his mistake. All of this had taken place within the sight of Captain Francis, on board the *Rangi*. Francis and Bourke had, in all probability, sailed in each other's company many times before. Maybe they were even looking forward to drinking beer together in a comfortable Auckland bar. Anyhow, the watching Francis had become very suspicious. He had observed the motor-boat speeding towards the schooner; seen the latter take her in tow and then both proceed on a course away from the mainland. It was certainly strange behaviour. Francis ran the *Rangi* into the nearest harbour, the tiny Port Charles on the Cormandel Peninsula, and informed the postmaster of his fears. After an hour or so, the government cable steamer, *Iris*, was seen coming round Cape Colville. Francis grabbed a boat, and went out to confer with her skipper. As it happened, she had been hastily fitted with two six-pounder guns in case she should run into Luckner. The chase was on.

Back in Auckland, the population seethed with anger at the news of the escape. The fate of the artless and trusting Lieutenant-Colonel Turner came as no surprise. He was fired.

Luckner knew from his knowledge of Pacific charts that New Zealand had installed provision dumps containing biscuit and medicines for castaways on Curtis and Macauley Islands in the Kermadec Group. (It is strange that Nerger does not seem to have known of them). The plan was to raid the dump on the bleak and remote Curtis Island, leave Bourke and his crew with the other store on Macauley Island to await rescue, vanish with the captured *Moa*, and sail her home in triumph to Kiel. The *Pearl* having been swamped and sunk in the heavy weather they had encountered on the five day voyage up from New

Zealand, taking the wireless down with her into the ultra-darkness of the 30,000 foot deep Kermadec Trench, the *Moa*'s little dinghy was having to be used to transfer the provisions from the store at Curtis Island. It was on its second trip to the beach when a smear of smoke appeared on the horizon. It was the *Iris*.

For once, the New Zealanders had managed to out-think Luckner. They had guessed correctly where to find him. The Germans frantically hoisted every inch of canvas onto the *Moa*'s masts and tried to run. If only Luckner could have kept a fair distance ahead of his pursuer until nightfall, he might have been able to give her the slip in darkness. But the steamer steadily overhauled him, and after an hour and a half, she was only a couple of miles astern. A shot across his bows was enough to tell Luckner that it was pointless to continue. He surrendered.

By this time the New Zealanders had learned their lesson. There were to be no more joy-rides in government-owned boats for the Germans. The cadets, Luckner's batman and the ex-planter from Samoa were locked up in Mount Eden jail, Auckland, and Luckner and Kircheiss were taken to an island prison in Lyttelton Harbour, near Christchurch, South Island. The intrepid captain of *Seeadler* was planning to escape yet again when the war ended ten months later.

All his life a sailor, Count Felix took a round-the-world cruise on his luxury yacht, the *Vaterland*, in the late 1920's. In New Zealand he was given a VIP's welcome, and in San Francisco, he was re-united with his old friend Kircheiss, who was also undertaking a world voyage in the *Hamburg*.

Bibliography

Alexander, Roy, *The Cruise of the Raider* **Wolf**, Angus & Robertson, Sydney, 1939.

Auten, Harold, *Q-boat Adventures*, Herbert Jenkins Ltd, London, 1919.

Blackburn, C.J., *How the Manx Fleet helped in the Great War*, Louis G. Meyer Ltd, 1920.

Bromby, Robin, *German Raiders of the South Seas*, Doubleday, Sydney/Auckland, 1985.

Brownrigg, Rear-Admiral Sir D, *Indiscretions of the Naval Censor*, Cassell, 1920.

Campbell, Rear-Admiral Gordon, *My Mystery Ships*, Hodder & Stoughton, 1928.

Carr, Frank G.G., *Sailing Barges*, Conway Maritime Press, 1931.

Chatterton, E. Keble, *The Sea-Raiders*, Hurst & Blackett, London, 1931.

Chatterton, E. Keble, *Q-ships and their Story*, Conway Maritime Press, 1932.

Coles, Alan, *Slaughter at Sea*, Robert Hale, 1986.

Dittmar, F.J. & Colledge J.J., *British Warships 1914–19*, Ian Allan, 1972.

Giffard, Edward, *Deeds of Naval Daring*, John Murray, 1910.

Grant, Robert, *U-boats Destroyed*, Putnam & Co., London, 1964.

Hoehling, A.A., *The Great War at Sea*, Transworld Publishers (Corgi), 1965.

Hurd, Archibald, *The Merchant Navy, Vols I, II and III*, John Murray, London, 1924.

Hoyt, Edwin P., Jnr., *The Elusive Seagull*, Leslie Frewin, London, 1970.

Massie, Robert, *Dreadnought*, Jonathan Cape, 1992.

Ritchie, Carson I.A., *Q-ships*, Terence Dalton, 1985.

Schmalenbach, Paul, *German Raiders*, Patrick Stephens, 1977.
The Times Review.
The History of the First World War Series, Liddell Hart.
Time-Life, *The Windjammers*.
Usborne, C.V., *Smoke on the Horizon*, Hodder & Stoughton, 1933.
Walter, John, *The Kaiser's Pirates*, Arms & Armour Press, 1994.
Winton, John, *The Victoria Cross at Sea*, Michael Joseph, 1978.

Index

272